Philosophical Dimensions of the Constitution

Philosophical Dimensions of the Constitution

edited by
Diana T. Meyers
and Kenneth Kipnis

Consulting Editor: Emily R. Gill

An AMINTAPHIL Volume

Routledge
Taylor & Francis Group
LONDON AND NEW YORK

First published 1988 by Westview Press, Inc.

Published 2019 by Routledge
52 Vanderbilt Avenue, New York, NY 10017
2 Park Square, Milton Park, Abingdon, Oxon OX14 4RN

Routledge is an imprint of the Taylor & Francis Group, an informa business

Library of Congress Cataloging in Publication Data
Philosophical dimensions of the Constitution.
"An AMINTAPHIL volume."
Includes index.
1. United States—Constitutional law—Philosophy.
I. Meyers, Diana T. II. Kipnis, Kenneth.
KF4550.P48 1988 342.73'02'01 88-141

ISBN 13: 978-0-367-28283-7 (hbk)
ISBN 13: 978-0-367-29829-6 (pbk)

Contents

Preface vii

Introduction: The Philosophical Foundations of the U.S. Constitution, *Richard T. De George* 1

Part One
The Ideals of the Framers

Introduction to Part One, *Kenneth Kipnis* 17

1 Virtue, the Public Good, and Publius, *Emily R. Gill* 19

2 The Purposes of the Constitution, *Lester J. Mazor* 40

Part Two
Democracy and the Constitution

Introduction to Part Two, *Diana T. Meyers* 57

3 Constitutional Revision, *Cornelius F. Murphy, Jr.* 60

4 Constitutional Limits on Majoritarian Democracy, *William Nelson* 75

Part Three
Interpreting the Constitution

Introduction to Part Three, *Kenneth Kipnis* 93

5 Between Clause-bound Literalism and Value Imposition: A Positivist, Noninterpretivist Theory of Judicial Review, *H. Hamner Hill* 96

6 Toward a Public Values Philosophy of the Constitution, *Stephen M. Griffin* 119

7 Constitutional Integrity and Compromise, *Kenneth Henley* 134

Part Four
Current Issues in Constitutional Law

Introduction to Part Four, *Diana T. Meyers* 155

8 Access, Enablement, and the First Amendment, *Virginia Held* 158

9 Respect for Individuals Versus Respect for Groups: Public Aid for Confessional Schools in the United States and Canada, *Michael Mc Donald* 180

10 The Right to Privacy and Personal Autonomy, *Carl Wellman* 196

11 Procedural Due Process, *Michael D. Bayles* 206

12 The Exclusionary Rule as Constitutional Renewal: U.S. Integrity and Canadian Repute, *Christopher B. Gray* 222

About the Contributors 245

Index 249

Preface

In the closing decades of the eighteenth century, the newly independent colonies along the mid-Atlantic coast of North America commenced an unprecedented public debate concerning the principles of civil government. Carried along by popular books, newspapers, and pamphlets, controversy swept through the towns and villages of the region. What is the nature of the human animal? How are people shaped by different forms of government? What goods can be gained through political association? In what ways can a polity fail? How can the dangers of failure be minimized? And, above all, given our understanding of what we are, of what is good for us, and of what is possible for us, what is the best form of political association? Here was an historic opportunity to summon accumulated wisdom to the task of crafting a new government. The ancient concerns of political philosophy, as old as Plato and Aristotle, had become at this moment the most pressing of practical issues.

The debate culminated in 1787 with the Philadelphia convention where the United States Constitution was drafted and adopted. After ratification in 1789, the Constitution became a canonical text delineating the fundamental principles of our political association. What had been a public debate born of revolutionary fervor was about to become a tradition of constitutional government and constitutional interpretation.

About two centuries later, close to where the framers did their venerated work, a group of philosophers, law professors, and political theorists gathered at the Law School of the University of Pennsylvania in Philadelphia under the sponsorship of AMINTAPHIL. Their purpose was to reexamine the philosophical underpinnings of the Constitution. Most of the papers collected in this volume were among the more than forty papers that were presented at that conference. Their concerns range over such topics as the framers' ideals, the nature of democracy, constitutional interpretation, and current issues in constitutional law. Taken together, they represent a variety of contemporary perspectives on the persistent philosophical questions raised by the Constitution.

We would like to thank the University of Hawaii Foundation, the Career Development Program at Montclair State College, the Research Foundation of the University of Connecticut, and the American Council of Learned Societies for supporting our work on this volume.

Diana T. Meyers
Kenneth Kipnis

Introduction: The Philosophical Foundations of the U.S. Constitution

RICHARD T. DE GEORGE

Individuals are born into constituted nations and grow up under the prevailing system of government, which they tend to accept as normal and legitimate. Unless they find their conditions intolerable, most people are unlikely to consider revolution or radical change and are not inclined to exchange known ills for as yet unknown demons possibly lying in wait under a new type of government. The American colonists broke with England only reluctantly. And after the revolutionary war they only reluctantly formed a union. Both the act of waging a revolution and that of forming a union were motivated by living under conditions that were perceived as intolerable. Clearly most Americans today do not find our system intolerable or feel any urgent need to break with our past or to adopt a new Constitution.

The Constitution that was finally ratified and under which the United States of America was formed is a much-praised document. The fact that it is a working document two hundred years after its ratification is without historical precedent. Its success is often attributed to the brilliance of the Founding Fathers, and one might speculate how a small backward country could produce such men when many today doubt that the United States, even at its present stage of advanced development, could find as large a number of citizens to represent it as ably. An alternative interpretation credits the brilliance of the Founding Fathers less than the ingenuity of the American people who have managed to work so successfully within the confines of a document conceived two hundred years ago.

In both views, a crucial element in the Constitution's success is that, unlike the Declaration of Independence (which is also highly praised), the Constitution is a spare political document and in no sense a philosophical one. Although there has been much discussion about the philosophical position presented in the Declaration of Independence, it is doubtful that many people today would subscribe to its doctrines of natural rights and their self-evidence. That document is safely historical, and we do not need to invoke it, subscribe to its statements for practical purposes, or interpret it in law. The same is not true of the Constitution. Had it articulated a doctrine of natural rights, had it invoked a doctrine of self-evidence, or had it been built explicitly on the philosophical beliefs current at the time, it is doubtful it could have survived any better than those philosophies. This is not to say that the Constitution had or has no philosophical foundations. But it is to emphasize that its validity does not rest on the validity of its historical philosophical foundations.

Hence the question of what the Constitution's philosophical foundations are is a question to be answered not only historically but also in light of contemporary beliefs. Because the Constitution is not a philosophical document, its original philosophical foundations do not constitute a millstone around our necks. Even if the U.S. citizens no longer adhere to the original set of principles and values held by the authors of the Constitution, we are not forced to consign the document built on them to the museum of antiquities.

The Founding Fathers were articulate, reasonably well-educated men with some knowledge of religion, philosophy, law, and letters. They were familiar with the writings of Locke and Hume, Rousseau and Montesquieu. They also had experience with the colonial constitutions, several of which served as models for parts of the Federal Constitution. The genius of the Founding Fathers lay in constructing a document flexible enough to be interpreted and reinterpreted—a document whose provisions could be stretched to fit changing times and circumstances. The doctrine of states' rights has receded in importance. The role of the Supreme Court has been developed through practice, as have the functions of the president. When one considers that the Constitution could not be adopted without the initial ten amendments—the Bill of Rights—it is remarkable that in the intervening two hundred years only sixteen additional amendments have been added, of which one was simply the cancellation of another. That appears less remarkable when one remembers that Great Britain has no written constitution and has managed well for a considerable length of time without one.

The Constitution is a political document, and as with most such documents, it is the child of compromise. Unlike the Declaration of Independence, it states no moral principles. Until amended in 1865 it allowed slavery, and until 1868 it counted slaves as only three-fifths of other persons for purposes of determining the apportionment of representatives and direct taxes among the states. Although it lists various rights, it never mentions a doctrine of natural rights. The first ten amendments to the Constitution reflect the concerns of the people and the original states at the time of ratification. The rights listed are *ad hoc* and are not systematically derived from some set of principles. Those who initially ratified the Constitution did not believe that the rights mentioned in the Bill of Rights were a complete and exhaustive list of natural, human, or civil rights, and there is no reason for us to believe so, either.

The Constitution has traceable philosophical roots. Yet whatever philosophical beliefs and presuppositions those who wrote and adopted the Constitution may have had, contemporary Americans are not bound by those beliefs and presuppositions, even though they are bound by the Constitution. Although the beliefs of the Founding Fathers are of historical importance, of contemporary importance are the beliefs and presuppositions of those who live under and interpret the Constitution today. If this is so, the genius of the Founding Fathers was in not incorporating specific philosophical views or particular moral principles into the Constitution, and in developing instead structures and practices within which the nation could develop.

To claim that the philosophical foundations of the Constitution are to be found in the present is to acknowledge that these foundations change over time. Yet this is not to embrace an arbitrary relativism. An analogy with the Ten Commandments may illustrate the point. The foundations of the Ten Commandments as received from God by Moses were clearly religious. The whole event and the authority of that document were religious. For a long time religion has been considered the only foundation for morality in general. Yet as religion and belief in God have come under attack, people have sought other foundations for morality. Although some have thrown off all moral norms, others have attempted to philosophically ground norms against killing, stealing, lying, adultery. For those who do not believe in God, the commandment to honor God cannot be grounded, but many of the other commandments can be, and most are still considered valid moral injunctions. We debate how to interpret them and how they are grounded, but there is large social consensus on their general validity.

In a comparable way, the Constitution had certain philosophical foundations when it was adopted. But to the extent that those were not built explicitly into the document, it is possible to ground the document in contemporary values and beliefs. When any portion of the document becomes incompatible with contemporary values and beliefs, then the document, if it is to be preserved, must be amended. We can view the Thirteenth, Fourteenth, and Fifteenth amendments as doing just that. They brought the Constitution into line with the moral and philosophical beliefs of the people who had reached a consensus—or imposed one—through the Civil War. The consensus reached, however tenuous at that time, is one that has solid support in our present age.

To claim that the philosophical foundations of the Constitution are to be found in the present does not imply that there is a set of contemporary philosophical views and values that uniquely underpins the Constitution. Just as the injunction against stealing or against killing other human beings can be defended, justified, or grounded in many ways and from many philosophical points of view, so it is possible to ground the Constitution in many ways and from many philosophical points of view. Of course, not every philosophical position is compatible with the document. Clearly, one that denies the importance of individual freedom or of rights would be incompatible with it. And if such a position were widely held, the Constitution would have to be either dramatically amended or replaced.

Many of the current discussions about suggested revisions to the Constitution are discussions about the contemporary values and beliefs of the American people. Revisions would be attempts to articulate changed values and beliefs via constitutional amendment.

Although the American people can live without explicitly raising or settling the question of the philosophical foundations of the Constitution, discussing its philosophical foundations is not a useless endeavor. The task may be, and is in this volume, pursued in several ways. One can attempt to articulate the basic values and philosophical beliefs that are embedded in the document as we presently understand and accept it. Once articulated, these values and beliefs can be used to test the document for consistency and to investigate changes that may be appropriate in the light of the articulated values and beliefs. Alternatively, one can attempt to articulate and justify particular values—such as equality and justice—to which U.S. society is committed and seek through amendments to bring the Constitution in line with them.

Various approaches can be used to ferret out the assumed values and moral presuppositions of the Constitution. In order to clarify these values and presuppositions, some first examine the processes, including the relation of the federal government, the states, and the people, as well as the principle of the division of powers embedded in and explicitly stated by the Constitution. They then examine the process of judicial review and use Supreme Court decisions as a touchstone of the current values assumed by the justices, and through them, by the people. A negative use of this procedure consists in analyzing those cases that are refused by the Supreme Court; these cases would be an indication in at least some instances of issues the Court feels are settled and sufficiently clear, requiring no new interpretation, and hence reflecting what it considers accepted and constitutionally acceptable practices. Others examine the shifts in the balance of powers among the legislative, executive, and judicial branches of government over time, and then attempt to articulate the values and principles implied or presupposed by the situation at any given time. Still others look for the significant changes in the foundations of the Constitution in studying its amendments, examining both those that have succeeded and those that have failed. Each approach has its strengths and weaknesses, and discussion of the foundations of the Constitution rightly involves all of these as well as other approaches illustrated by the contributions to this volume, even though their focus is not directly on the philosophical foundations of the document.

The reasons for making explicit the philosophical foundations of the Constitution are also multiple. Some do so in order to argue for possible amendment, claiming that the values or principles embedded in the Constitution are not sufficiently or clearly applied in certain areas, and they should be. Those who argue for constitutional guarantees of welfare rights, or of equal rights for women, or of equal pay for comparable work use this strategy. However, this is not the only reason for pursuing this task. A deeper appreciation of what the nation stands for as a whole as reflected in its fundamental legal document can only be achieved if the moral values and principles with which the document is compatible and incompatible are understood. Articulating the philosophical foundations of the Constitution also provides some of those subject to it with a rationale for accepting the document and adhering to its provisions. If, as I have been claiming, the Constitution can be philosophically grounded in various ways and from various philosophical points of view, then the fact of philosophical pluralism present in our society need not lead to the conclusion that we cannot agree. Rather, agreement on means to solve our disagreements becomes all the more important, and articulation of the basis for agreement on the process that the Constitution provides becomes all the more useful.

Thus the philosophical foundations of the Constitution deserve discussion and scrutiny not because consideration of them will lead to a new Constitution—whatever the merits of proposals for a new constitutional convention—and not because as a people we tend no longer to hold the same philosophical views as the Founding Fathers—although this is true. Rather, the philosophical foundations deserve scrutiny because by articulating and discussing the issues, we as a nation may make more headway in facing and perhaps solving some of our pressing problems.

In one way or another many of the papers in this volume constitute part of the search for articulating the philosophical foundations of the Constitution. The task is not one that can be accomplished easily and quickly by any scholar or group of scholars.

In the space remaining, I shall briefly illustrate an approach to articulating the Constitution's philosophical foundations by focusing on issues that raise foundational questions. The first is the foundation of federalism (and with it the questions of states' rights, sovereignty, representative democracy) and the balance of powers. The second is the issue of equality. The third is the relation of free enterprise and personal welfare. The fourth is the notion of the common good or general welfare and its relation to individual liberty and individual rights.

THE FOUNDATION OF FEDERALISM AND THE BALANCE OF POWERS

The notion of federalism was a keystone of the founders' document, and that keystone was articulated and defended in *The Federalist* papers. Federalism was possible, and ultimately successful—despite the Civil War—for a cluster of reasons that are historically unique. The colonies, in spite of their differences, were all roughly at about the same stage of development. They were all recently freed from British rule; they all shared a common language. These, as well as other factors, made federalism possible in a way that has not been feasible in countries where there are linguistic and cultural divisions among the federated units. In Switzerland the cantons are in many ways more important than the federal government; this is not true in the United States. In Yugoslavia the several states remain in tenuous union and struggle constantly amid mutual animosity and jealousy. Hopes for a politically united Europe, a United States of Europe, have diminished among those who harbored such dreams when the Common Market was founded.

The relation of the states and the federal government has changed over the course of the history of the United States, especially with the passage of the Fourteenth Amendment. Nonetheless we can articulate and defend a contemporary principle that undergirds the Constitution's federalism and balance of powers today. Both of these are in effect instances of the general principle of subsidiarity, which states that larger or higher level groups should undertake tasks only when lower level groups are unable to accomplish them. Thus the individual is considered competent to run his or her own life and to unite with others to accomplish their joint aims. Government is not to intrude into their affairs or to do for them what they are capable of doing for themselves. Local governments regulate local affairs and help facilitate communal action. States take over those tasks that require uniformity throughout the state or tasks that local governments are unable to accomplish. The federal government in its turn allows the states to run their own internal affairs, taking over only those tasks that once again must be handled collectively on the national level and that the states are unable to successfully complete themselves.

The doctrine of subsidiarity has as its moral justification respect for the autonomy of the individual. In the U.S. context of the states versus the federal government, the states operate closer to the grass roots of the nation and interact more directly with the people. At the same time, the federal government is precluded from intrusion into the private lives of the people, into their everyday affairs, and into the direct conduct of their business. The principle of federalism thus interpreted fits into the kind of socioeconomic views held by most U.S. citizens and stands as a barrier to any type of nationalism or socialism that takes away individual initiative, that centralizes the economy, that attempts as a matter of right to set prices and wages, or that tries to allocate capital and resources.

The relative independence of the states makes for diversity and allows for experimentation that can lead to precedents for other states and the federal government as well.

We have no national police force with universal jurisdiction. Instead we have local and state police that, together with national law enforcement agencies, have only limited and special jurisdiction. We have local and state courts. Education remains in the hands of the state, with local boards retaining a good deal of power. The absence of federal control and the diffusion of power through the state and lower governmental units continue to serve as important checks on the power of the federal government and on its ability to intrude into the lives of the people. The distrust of central authority can be seen in several amendments. The Tenth reserves to the states or the people any powers not delegated to the federal government or prohibited to the states; the Seventeenth provides for popular election of senators; and the Twenty-second limits any president to two terms.

The checks and balances within the federal government spring in part from and can be justified by a similar reluctance on the part of the American people to give unlimited power to any central authority. The division of powers has never been without problems, and the shift in power from one branch of government to another is part of our developing history. It is irrelevant, however, to ask what the Founding Fathers wished the division or the balance to be. For whatever they wished, they could not have foreseen present circumstances and needs. The appropriate question is what U.S. citizens presently wish the division and balance to be.

Respect for individual autonomy and a distrust of central authority are hallmarks of the American heritage and are fundamental to the Constitution today.

EQUALITY

Although the Constitution aims at establishing justice it does not specifically or explicitly aim at equality. Equality was not a value uniformly accepted by the authors of the Constitution. Yet undergirding and supporting the Constitution and its current interpretation is a basic commitment to equality, a commitment that is closely related to our contemporary interpretation of justice. This notion of equality—and therefore this notion of justice—is not the same as those that informed the views of the Founding Fathers. For them, slaves and women did not deserve the same rights as free men, and for many of the founders, nonlandholders did not deserve the same rights as landholders. There was equality before the law in the sense that all were under the law. Yet inequality was not antithetical to the thinking of many of those who drafted and approved the Constitution. Here is a clear instance in which the views of the Founding Fathers do not constitute the views of the vast majority of U.S. citizens who live by the Constitution today.

Nonetheless, important though it is, the contemporary notion of equality that underpins the Constitution is not completely clear. We have extended the notion to include all people, regardless of race or sex. A constitutional amendment guarantees the former. The proposed 1972 Equal Rights Amendment, providing "equality of rights under the law shall not be denied or abridged by the United States or any state on account of sex" was not ratified by the required three-fourths of the states, even though it came very close to such ratification. Yet one can argue that it failed not because of a principled exclusion of equality for women but for a variety of other reasons.

John Rawls's influential theory of justice articulated the importance of equality to justice. His view has not been universally accepted, but its reception has demonstrated the wide acceptance that equality has, at least among a very large portion of U.S. (some would say liberal) intellectuals.

What appears clear through the amendments thus far adopted is that the American people are committed to equality before the law and to equality of opportunity. The Fourteenth Amendment has been central in the defense of civil rights; the Fifteenth Amendment introduced black suffrage; the Nineteenth Amendment gave women the right to vote; the Twenty-fourth Amendment abolished poll taxes; the Twenty-sixth Amendment extended suffrage to all those citizens eighteen years or older. In 1861 a proposed amendment signed by President James Buchanan, which would have precluded any future amendments abolishing or interfering with slavery, was not ratified.

Nonetheless, exactly what equality of opportunity consists of is still debated, despite consensus on the principle. This is especially true in questions of equal opportunity for groups previously discriminated against, who, through no fault of their own, arguably start out at a disadvantage. We are still struggling with the problem of how to provide equal opportunity to blacks and women while not discriminating against white males.

What the Constitution does not provide for is equality of outcome. A presupposition of the Constitution is that the freedom of individuals is a sufficient justification for the government not to interfere directly with individuals in their pursuit of their own good. Some flourish more than others. Some, of course, start out with more in the way of natural talents, energy, wealth, position, useful social contacts, and the like. Although some people argue that these advantages make for inequality of opportunity as well as inequality of outcome, and hence for injustice, this view is not presupposed by the Constitution. The Sixteenth Amendment, granting Congress the power to lay and collect taxes on income, provides a mechanism for redistribution of wealth, but the amendment is neutral with respect to whether such taxes are to be progressive. That amendment, like the original Constitution itself, proclaims no principle of justice or equity and leaves the question of what constitutes just taxation to be dealt with by Congress, which can reflect the changing national consensus on the relation of justice and equality.

FREE ENTERPRISE AND PERSONAL WELFARE

The Preamble to the Constitution lists among the aims of the Constitution the securing of the blessings of liberty to ourselves and our posterity. The liberty that lay at the base of the Constitution was not only political but also economic.

The Constitution formed an implicit compact between government and business, and the link to free enterprise was present from the start. That link has continued up to the present, but not without change. For this reason, once again, it is appropriate to interpret the philosophical foundations of the Constitution not in terms of what the Founding Fathers believed but in terms of what we believe—where "we" refers to the great majority of U.S. citizens.

The U.S. commitment to free enterprise has been colored by the history of capitalist development in the United States. If capitalism means nongovernment intervention in business, we no longer defend capitalism. Rather the Constitution has provided for a working relation of the political, social, and economic spheres. Free enterprise has within it seeds that could develop to the detriment of the individual. Classical and laissez-faire capitalism do not worry about the individual welfare of those who are not able to compete or take part in the economy. Classical capitalism has no role for government. U.S. free enterprise has a significant role for government. Its first task is to keep the rules of the game fair. Here justice enters once more. A business transaction is fair when there is equal access to appropriate information on both sides, when the transaction is freely entered into on both sides, and when each side enters to achieve its own good. Competition is central to free enterprise, and keeping competition fair is a central function of government. The federal government enters the scene when transactions cross state lines. As commerce has developed and national markets for many goods and services have appeared, the role of government in keeping competition fair has increased accordingly.

A second area in which government enters is in regulating the periodic cycles characteristic of free enterprise. The point of fiscal and monetary policies is precisely to tame these cycles and keep them within tolerable limits. In so doing the government enters the market place in a variety of ways. The United States Constitution does not guarantee full employment, yet one of the aims of the federal government has been to reduce unemployment to what it deems an "acceptable" level. Exactly what level is acceptable is a controversial issue, and one that some argue is a matter of justice. There is no overwhelming sentiment yet for guaranteed full employment, even though there are many voices endorsing such as a national policy, and even though the right to employment is one of the human rights listed in the U.N. Universal Declaration of Human Rights—a document that the United States has not signed, despite its often stated commitment to human rights.

A third area of government intervention consists in its supplying a safety net for those who cannot compete or who fail dramatically in the economic realm. The state and federal governments have come to recognize the right to life of all citizens not only as the negative right endorsed by the Founding Fathers, but as a positive right involving the right to at least subsistence at a level compatible with the development of the rest of society. The Constitution did not foresee or provide for a welfare state. Yet providing for individual welfare has become a central issue, argued from a notion of justice.

The development of positive economic rights is not entirely of recent vintage; it received its impetus in the period following the Great Depression and in the legislation of the New Deal in the 1930s. That tradition has so permeated U.S. society, it is now endorsed by all major political figures and both political parties. Once again, the principles undergirding this development are principles that the Founding Fathers did not endorse. But the philosophical foundations of the Constitution are properly to be sought in today's values and principles rather than in those of the eighteenth century.

Although the Constitution fails to guarantee the right to welfare, the absence of this and other economic rights from the Constitution is not necessarily a flaw, as some claim. Any such critique of the Constitution relies on the hidden and dubious premise that the Constitution should explicitly state all accepted human rights, perhaps because of the even more dubious assumption that only if so stated can (or will) the people of the United States enjoy such rights. Yet it is possible for the human (including economic) rights of citizens to be recognized and implemented without these rights being stated in the Constitution. The appropriate question is whether the right to welfare is recognized and adequately implemented in the United States, not whether it is stated in the Constitution. If it is not recognized and implemented, and its recognition and implementation are not precluded by the Constitution, then we can seek appropriate means to implement it. Amending the Constitution is one means, but not the only means available.

For instance, the U.S. Constitution does not mention the right to education. It leaves education to the individual states. If the states so desire, they can include the right to education in their constitutions. Whether they do, education is both required and made available at public expense in all fifty states. Similarly, welfare is provided by state governments even though welfare is not mentioned as a right in the Constitution.

In like manner, Congress can pass legislation recognizing and implementing rights not mentioned in the Constitution. Thus the right to employment was proposed explicitly in the original Humphrey-Hawkins Act. Although it was not written into law, it could have been without going the route of a constitutional amendment. The U.S. government could formally commit itself to a number of human rights not mentioned in the Constitution by, for instance, signing such documents as the U.N. Universal Declaration of Human Rights. The Senate could at any time ratify the International Covenant on Economic, Social and Cultural Rights of 1966, which supersedes the U.N. Universal Declaration of Human Rights and has the legal force of a treaty for its signatories. By signing such treaties we can recognize rights not listed in the Constitution.

Still another way of recognizing and implementing rights not mentioned explicitly in the Constitution is for the Supreme Court to introduce them through its decisions, as the Court has done with the right to privacy, a right nowhere mentioned in the Constitution and yet a right used by the Court in a number of decisions including *Roe v. Wade*.

Because it would be easier to commit the nation to economic rights in other ways besides adopting a new amendment to the Constitution, what seems to be lacking is either the will or the perceived need to explicitly commit the nation on the federal level to recognize an explicit set of economic rights. Economic rights per se are not recognized, even though the economic needs of people are generally acknowledged and the legitimacy of welfare programs is widely recognized and well-established.

What is true of welfare is true of other rights as well. There is no constitutional right to medical care. That is compatible with U.S. citizens receiving what they consider to be adequate medical care. This is not to say that all U.S. citizens receive adequate medical care. It is to say that the constitutional guarantee of rights is not the only way to secure rights.

If the public becomes sufficiently convinced that welfare and other rights are human rights that can only be guaranteed if included in the Constitution, there are mechanisms for amendments by which this can be done. The spareness of the Constitution has thus far been one of its virtues. The people have been wise to tinker with it as little as they have, seeking remedies for social, political, and economic ills elsewhere.

THE GENERAL WELFARE AND INDIVIDUAL LIBERTY AND INDIVIDUAL RIGHTS

The emphasis in U.S. society on individual liberty and individual rights has a source in the Constitution. The First through Tenth Amendments and the Fourteenth Amendment can be read as guarantees of individual liberty and rights. At the time of the Founding Fathers guaranteeing individual liberty and rights was seen as compatible with the promotion of the general welfare. However, the link between the two has become fragmented in the present day, raising the issue of the priority of these possibly competing principles.

The emphasis on individual rights and liberties has reached such a peak that arguments for the common good or general welfare have a somewhat archaic ring to them. Yet there is good reason to believe that the general welfare cannot be ignored and that individual rights and liberties cannot be protected unless the general welfare is also protected.

Although I have argued that the beliefs of the Founding Fathers are somewhat irrelevant, here is one place where we have much to gain by reconsidering what they believed and rethinking our present emphasis on individual rights and liberties to the possible serious detriment of the general welfare. General welfare consists not only in common defense, as the Founding Fathers clearly saw and explicitly noted in the Preamble, but in the enjoyment of public goods such as clean air, earth, and water; parks and wilderness areas; and in roads, museums, public buildings, and institutions.

The general welfare or common good is not the sum of the good of individuals, nor some final end that all people have in common. Each individual has private interests; some of these interests overlap with those of others. What all implicitly desire are the conditions necessary for pursuing their interests, and these conditions are general or common conditions.

The common good is the good of specific human beings considered together. Individualism ignores the togetherness of human beings. Concentrating on particular individuals, it ignores their interrelations, the common society in which they operate, and the common conditions necessary for them each to pursue their own good. Individualism ignores human solidarity. Unless the common good means the good of human beings considered *together,* it is meaningless.

Concern for the common good links us to our children and their children and their children's children. The Constitution allows us to be profligate, to live beyond our collective means, and to pass burdens of debt onto future generations in a way that does not coincide well with intergenerational justice. Whether an amendment is needed to define more clearly the relation of the general welfare and individual rights and liberty is still an undecided issue.

PHILOSOPHICAL FOUNDATIONS

In searching for the philosophical foundations of the Constitution, I have argued that we should search for the principles in the present and not in the past. A possible stumbling block to this approach may be that the United States today is a clearly pluralistic society—much more pluralistic than the society in which and for which the Constitution was drafted and adopted. Yet, this situation is completely compatible with my claim that the Constitution is not a document of principles but a political and therefore a compromise document.

In a pluralistic society such as the United States, there is no basis for believing that there is or must be only one reason why its citizens accept its institutions. There are many. Some may accept the system because they accept the tradition of authority that it represents. Others may do so because they hold some notion of contract theory. Still others may give utilitarian reasons why it is better to accept the system rather than overthrow it or attempt to find another to replace it. Many people may simply accept it from inertia.

What is necessary for contemporary acceptance of the Constitution is not acceptance of a set of natural laws, natural rights, or some supposed set of principles held by the Founding Fathers. To assume that there was one such set of principles at the time the Constitution was adopted is to assume too much. There were many reasons why the people and the states adopted the Constitution, just as there are many reasons why it is currently accepted. What is necessary is not agreement by all on the principles that today undergird the Constitution, if by that we mean explicit acceptance of either a distinct and ordered set of values, or of a self-evident philosophical system, or of a specific set of ethical principles. Agreement to abide by the Constitution suffices.

As a political document the Constitution can be embraced, upheld, and defended by people with a variety of different philosophical approaches—by atheists or religious believers, by utilitarians, deontologists, philosophical pragmatists. If the document could only be accepted by those who held the philosophical views of the Founding Fathers, it would have been condemned from the start and would have long ago been replaced.

We can agree on the values of liberty, equality, subsidiarity, respect for human rights, general and personal welfare, without agreeing on the means by which we defend and interpret these values. The issue of defense is closely related to different approaches to philosophical issues of ethical justification. Yet both deontologists and utilitarians can agree on the importance of the values implicit in the Constitution. The issue of interpretation of these values and the application of them in concrete political policies set the stage for the debates and discussions, arguments and fights that make up the political scene and process. Rarely does a given position clearly triumph over another, and rarely do we find right and truth clearly on one side. This is characteristic of the political process and completely compatible with it. The Constitution provides the structure and procedures by which we work out our differences. The system has as a basis a built-in respect for a variety of views and the defense of people's right to express, defend, and argue for their views. The way progress is made is not by some genius or group of geniuses deciding what the new rules should be but through public and open debate.

The original fear of the concentration of power in individual figures, or in particular branches of the federal government, or in the federal government itself remains. The diffusion of power—political, social, and economic—forms part of the whole fabric of the United States.

Although U.S. citizens need not hold a given philosophy and can live with a pluralistic approach to values and principles, as I have noted, not every philosophy and not every set of beliefs is compatible with the Constitution.

The genius of the Constitution is that it has demonstrated its ability to grow and change with the times. It is a document that matches the basic values of U.S. citizens as they have changed over time. The people's acceptance of it is pragmatic, and it is in terms of pragmatic considerations that they will be persuaded to change the Constitution, if it is to be changed. In a number of details it might be improved. But if we have learned anything from its long history, it is that the Constitution should not contain basic principles or explicit philosophical beliefs. As dear as these are to the hearts of most philosophers, the Constitution has been a better document without them.

PART ONE

The Ideals of the Framers

Introduction to Part One

KENNETH KIPNIS

Whatever else it is, the U.S. Constitution is an historical document, penned by men who occupied places within particular social settings and discrete intellectual traditions. The political arrangements that it describes reflect the historical values that were embraced by the framers, that were endorsed by the traditions within which they worked, and that were consciously incorporated into the document itself. Attention to these values can assist us in understanding the issues that shape current debate about constitutional doctrine.

We are used to thinking that the U.S. Constitution presupposes a community of autonomous, rights-bearing individuals, each pursuing some distinctive personal conception of the good life. The Constitution, we are told, sets out the basis for a system of social institutions within which citizens can live together with stability and mutual respect, notwithstanding their pursuit of private interests. In these matters the framers were following an emerging liberal tradition in the intellectual footsteps of Locke, who had seen the state as an instrument for protecting individual rights, and of Montesquieu, who had seen that separation of governmental powers—the system of checks and balances—could best secure individual freedom. The framers did not expect U.S. citizens to sacrifice themselves in the cause of the public good or to display unprecedented levels of civic virtue. But had they forgotten these ideals entirely?

Taking up the questions whether and to what extent the framers took into account conceptions of the public good and civic virtue, Emily Gill, in "Virtue, the Public Good, and Publius," argues that they may well have been influenced by two alternatives to Lockean individualism: the classical republican tradition, which stresses the demands of virtuous citizenship, and the tradition of Scottish moral philosophy, which holds that a natural moral sense can engender an overriding concern for the public good. Focusing on *The Federalist* papers by Madison, Hamilton, and Jay (writing under their pseudonym Publius), Gill argues that threads from these earlier traditions in political philosophy are to be found interwoven in their argument. Though the concepts of virtue and the public interest may not play the same roles in *The Federalist* papers as they did in these antecedent philosophical traditions, the framers may well have sought "to recreate these ideals under the pressure of new or modern contingencies."

Gill concludes by suggesting how, for Publius, there is both an appreciation of the way in which institutional arrangements can play a role in fostering a devotion to the public good—an idea shared with the civic republicans—and an appreciation of the role the natural sentiments can play in securing social stability and allegiance to government—an idea at the core of Scottish moral philosophy. Both the structure of social institutions and the natural sentiments of their citizens can "foster actions for the common good and the virtuous dispositions that inclines to them."

While Gill looks to *The Federalist* papers and to the traditions in the political philosophy that led up to them, Lester Mazor seeks to discern the purposes of the Constitution in the document itself—in its Preamble in particular—and in the response it makes to the historical circumstances of its creation. In "The Purposes of the Constitution," Mazor reconsiders the historical ideals of national unity, defense, order, justice, liberty, and welfare. With the benefit of two hundred years of hindsight, he subjects each of these values to his contemporary critique. With respect to national unity, "altogether too much blood" has been shed in the pursuit of that ideal. With respect to national defense, the Constitution's identification of it with military power now endangers the entire world. Order is, at best, a mixed good. Justice should be superceded by a social solidarity that validates difference; the ideal of liberty superceded by an ideal of liberation. With respect to welfare, we should set aside the economics of need in favor of a new economics of desire. Mazor concludes by reflecting on the framers' ambivalence about the ideal of democracy and the contemporary need for renewed participatory scrutiny of our public purposes.

ONE
Virtue, the Public Good, and Publius

EMILY R. GILL

It seems almost a truism among commentators on the history of the United States Constitution that its framers ignored the possible existence of a public good in favor of the pursuit of private interests. This view may be found among both admirers (Goldwin, Diamond) and detractors (Barber, Hofstadter) of these intentions or of their results. The new government

> absolutely depended on a studied obliviousness to public purposes and public interests as defined by traditional republican formulas. To insist on discovering public goods was only to generate faction and occlude those private interests that alone, pitted against each other, promised the semblance of consensus. In short, the system turned necessity into a virtue and placed public purposelessness at the very core of its value structure (Barber, p. 52).

Alternatively, the idea of "the 'General Welfare' provided no objective standard of judgment for America, no way of distinguishing private interests from the public good that could be derived from an authority beyond the claims of the self" (Diggins, p. 75). Moreover, "Ultimately, the idea of virtue had no determinative content, . . . no moral vision that inspired the individual to identify with values higher than his own interests." Thus idealistic rhetoric achieved "little more than negative freedom. Freedom from political power and public authority, freedom for man to pursue his own end, individual freedom—in a word, liberalism" (Diggins, p. 31).

Additionally, commentators focus upon the framers' reliance upon the self-interested passions, ostensibly in contrast to the tactics of earlier republicans. "Why has government been instituted at all? Because the

The author is grateful to Roger Smith and Dennis Goldford for constructive criticisms that have substantially improved this chapter.

passions of men will not conform to the dictates of reason and justice without constraint" (*The Federalist Papers* in No. 15, p. 110). "The framers," notes John Diggins, had to explain the Constitution in ways that would convince the people to accept the power and controls that would be exercised not only by them but *over* them" (p. 77). "Liberal man wanted self-government, not necessarily the ideals of virtue that would enable him to govern the self" (Diggins, p. 14). In this view, the human will is determined by passions, irrational desires, or restless cravings that are beyond the individual's control. The individual cannot decide *not* to be governed by self-interest. One *can* be convinced to distrust both government and other citizens, and one can freely consent "to the devices of a well-ordered constitution" to protect oneself from them (Diggins, p. 83). But reason cannot alone "find the way back to virtue" (Diggins, p. 85). In the Constitution, then, "It is not only alienated power that must be controlled but alienated man who must be restrained, and this called for a theory of authority that required the people to consent to restrictions on their liberty to act as a democratic majority" (Diggins, p. 84). Thus the self-interested passions must be enlisted in the absence of reason, for only thus will the minimal public good of order for the pursuit of private ends be attained.

Recent scholarship on the framing of the Constitution has explored the possible impact of two alternatives to the Lockean liberal, to some minds possessive individualist, interpretation. Both alternatives suggest that the framers did recognize the need for devotion to a definable common interest if the new government were to reflect successfully their intentions. One of these is the civic humanist or classical republican tradition, which stresses the primacy of politics, the demands of virtuous citizenship, the subordination of private interest to the public good, and the ever-present threat of corruption and moral deterioration. The other is the tradition of Scottish moral philosophy, according to which a natural moral sense engenders ideals of sympathy and virtue that can submerge self-regarding desires for private gratification in a concern for the public good. One focus of this debate has been the ideas expressed in *The Federalist.* This document, as is well known, is composed of essays originally published in newspapers by three men who hoped to convince the reading public to support ratification of the Constitution. Collectively known as Publius, the authors Hamilton, Madison, and Jay set forth arguments calculated to influence their readers. In suggesting that the framers' purpose in *The Federalist* was primarily to justify a structure that would inhibit the passions of alienated individuals rather than to pursue any substantive conception of a common good, critics of the civic republican and Scottish moral traditions discount or minimize any sincere attachment by the framers to a common good. I believe, however, that parallels between these two traditions and the ideas of the framers can be sustained. And therefore, the case for the framers' recognition of the importance of devotion to a definable common interest may also be made.

Critics of parallels between the civic republican and Scottish moral traditions and the arguments of the framers make two major points. Both concern the relationship between the pursuit of the public good and the role of the self-interested passions in this pursuit. These critics differ, however, in the grounding of their criticisms. First, in the case of the classical republic tradition, Diggins suggests that the framers rejected citizen participation in politics as an expression of "man's higher nature" (Diggins, p. 63) as well as politics itself an inherently redemptive activity (Diggins, p. 67). The individual's need for restraints on his or her passions precludes the kind of citizen participation thought central to both the attainment and practice of virtue in the classical republican tradition.

Thomas Pangle, on the other hand, questions the presence of a classical republican component in Publius on the opposite basis. If in the classical tradition self-government is a vehicle for the practice and promotion of the moral virtues, those who ought to rule should possess either the most virtue or the greatest potential or concern for it. The best republic tends to be an aristocracy. But for Publius, "virtue ceases to bestow on its possessors a primary or indisputable title to rule. Individuals outstanding in their moral and political qualities gain authority only derivatively, by winning the favor of the populace—a feat they accomplish by demonstrating their efficacy in promoting popular liberties and prosperity" (Pangle, p. 594). For Diggins, Publius departs from classical republicanism on aristocratic or oligarchic grounds; for Pangle, Publius deviates on "rather radical" egalitarian ones (Pangle, p. 594). For both, the framers either cannot or will not allow for the emergence of a regime that truly promotes virtue or the common good.

Second, in the case of the Scottish moral tradition, Diggins argues that the moral bonds among citizens are too weak to inculcate virtue and to overcome self-interest. Although this tradition emphasized the social nature of human beings and the moral bonds between them, they also "regarded authority as a matter of habitual deference rather than voluntary obedience" (Diggins, p. 33; also pp. 53–54). If the framers wanted to convince people of the value of voluntary obedience to a just government as measured by an independent or external moral criterion, the views of those like Hume were ill suited to their purposes. Pangle notes that for Hume, the primary social virtues like justice are not only valuable mainly for their usefulness, but are also artificial, "constructions of habit informed by reason reflecting on the chaotic natural conditions of human society" (Pangle, p. 591). Thus, Publius and Hume together are aliens to classical republican thought and to its elevation of virtue as an end. "For the *Federalist,* virtue, when or insofar as it emerges in public life, represents for the most part an important *instrument* for fame, security, liberty, and self-government" (Pangle, p. 593, emphasis added). Whereas Diggins discounts Hume's influence on the framers because Hume's views minimize the rational and self-conscious components of virtuous human action, Pangle links Hume and Publius for what he perceives as their similarity in this regard. Both imply that deference is incompatible with the reason and virtue that alone can promote a substantive common good.

These critics are suggesting, first, that Publius is uninterested in the public good except as the sum of private interests or in virtue except as an instrument for the realization of these interests. Second, even if Publius were devoted to the realization of a substantive public good, he could not attain it because of his reliance on the self-interested passions. In this chapter I propose to do three things. First, in examining facets of the civic republican tradition, I shall argue that the attainment of virtue requires neither equal democratic participation in the modern sense, nor the nonpolitical pursuit of philosophic rationality in the classical sense. Virtue and the attainment of a common good rest on the presence of a few and a many who are interdependent. Moreover, even in civic republicanism the self-interested passions play a role in inculcating devotion to the public good. Second, similarly in *The Federalist,* the change from the tradition of mixed government to the reality of merely functional differentiation exhibits both a reliance on popular opinion and also the felt need for a natural aristocracy if virtue is to be maintained. And similarly, the self-interested passions are enlisted in the attempt to promote the public good. Finally, in examining some parallels between Hume's account of the natural sentiments and their use by Publius, I shall argue that although the operation of the natural sentiments among citizens may not overcome self-interest, they play a useful role in the arguments of Publius. They may supplement rational and voluntary obedience even in the best of governmental systems by converting prudential obligation into sentimental or nonprudential allegiance, and by encouraging praiseworthy and virtuous behavior by those who are the recipients of esteem and praise. Overall, I would argue that although virtue or the public interest may not have had the same meanings for Publius as for the original exponents of classical or philosophic rationality, Publius has not abandoned their importance as ideas to be pursued. The system of government Publius defends, far from betokening a retreat from the ideal of virtue or the public interest, may in fact demonstrate a desire to recreate these ideals under the pressure of new or modern contingencies. If this is true, we ought not to attribute the ills of today's interest-group pluralism to the intentions or predictions of the framers, but to historical developments and to our own actions thereafter.

INDEPENDENCE VERSUS INTERDEPENDENCE: THE CONDITIONS OF VIRTUE

Within the civic republican tradition appear two themes that are intertwined and often in tension with one another: independence and interdependence, both essential to the pursuit of the common good. According to Pocock, the development of culture and commerce introduces specialization and compromises the virtue of the citizen in the classical sense. "Only the citizen as amateur, propertied, independent, and willing to perform in his own person all functions essential to the polis, could be said to practice virtue or live in a city where justice was truly distributed" (Pocock 1975, p. 499). The phenomenon of specialization, in fact, introduces a contradiction. On the one hand, "Only specialization, commerce, and culture set men free enough to attend to the goods of others as well as their own" (Pocock 1975, p. 499). On the other hand, as the individual became more and more dependent upon the specialized functions of others, "He parted with an essential component of the self in proportion as he became progressively refined. The personality was impoverished even as it was enriched" (Pocock 1975, p. 502). From the perspective of civic republicanism, the absence of independence or self-sufficiency introduces corruption, which "is the replacement by private relationships of those public relationships among citizens by which the republic should be governed" (Pocock 1975, p. 93).

In the English, neo-Harringtonian interpretation prevalent in the late seventeenth century, property and virtue are linked by the idea that property allows parliamentary representatives to be independent, free of the temptations of patronage and subsequent dependence upon the court from which the representatives received their property. Corruption springs "from the economic dependence of members of the legislative upon resources controlled by the executive" (Pocock 1975, p. 408). Only the independence of inherited property allows citizens to be free from the claims of particular interests to pursue the universal or common values essential to the health of the polis and to civic virtue. The commercial individual, by contrast, is thought to discern only the particular values of particular commodities in the exchange of which he participates. Consequently, he lacks "classical rationality" (Pocock 1975, p. 464). In the eighteenth century, the passions properly play a role in the ideal of civic virtue, but are termed good or bad according to whether or not they serve the public good (Pocock 1975, p. 471). "The passions now appear as the pursuits of private and particular goods . . . virtue is the passion for pursuing the public good, with which the lesser passions may compete, but into which they may equally be transformed. And corruption is the failure, or the consequences of the failure, to effect this transformation" (Pocock 1975, p. 472).

Yet even before the rise of commerce introduces dependence and compromises virtue, the civic republican tradition also encompasses an interdependence, even in public relationships, which acts as a necessary condition of virtue. "Particular men and the particular values they pursued met in citizenship to pursue and enjoy the universal value of acting for the common good and the pursuit of all lesser goods" (Popock 1975, p. 75). Each citizen's self-sufficiency maintained not only his own virtue, but also that of others who were not "tempted . . . to injustice and corruption" by the dependence of their fellows on them. "The dereliction of one citizen, therefore, reduced the others' chances of attaining and maintaining virtue, since virtue was now politicized; it consisted in a partnership of ruling and being ruled with others who must be as morally autonomous as oneself" (Pocock 1975, p. 75). The citizen cannot practice virtue alone. Civic virtue consists in a proper balance of elements from a range of values and activities. The civic republican conception of citizenship thus involved a science of virtue. "It offered . . . a means of associating the particular virtues of men composing the political society in such a way that they would not be corrupted by their particularity but would become parts of a common pursuit of universal good" (Pocock 1975, p. 115). The civic republican constitutional tradition resolved the tension between particular and universal goods partly through mixed government or partly through a distribution of roles and functions "among the different moral types composing society" (Pocock 1975, pp. 115–116). In such a polity, "the practice of politics obliged each citizen to practice the virtue of respecting his neighbor's virtue" (Pocock 1975, p. 516). This sort of deference to "the virtues of others who in their turn defer . . . is at the root of both the Polybian concept of mixed government and the Aristotelian concept of citizenship" (Pocock 1972, p. 125).

It follows that independence or liberty in the civic humanist tradition does not carry the modern connotation of every citizen equally participating as fully as possible in decisionmaking in the same way. It also indicates a situation "in which laws, not men, are supreme and the individual receives his social benefits from impersonal public authority and not at the hands of individuals" and dictated by their particular wills (Pocock 1975, p. 227; see p. 126). Liberty is experienced both by the few and by the many, but in different ways. And deference to its experience by others is both instrumental to and constitutive of moral virtue, which also is present both in the few and in the many. According to what Pocock terms a democratic theory of prudence, this virtue is more accessible to the many than to the few, as the many are in the habit of obeying many laws and thus experience more restraints upon their passions than do the few. The many desire simply to preserve their own under the law, and thus "they are better politicized, more apt to accept public authority as legitimate, than the ambitious few" (Pocock 1975, p. 311). For the few, freedom allows for the performance of actions of excellence for the public good; by contrast, "slavery is the state of having them evaluated, permitted or prevented by particular men according to the latter's idea of what suits their interests" (Pocock 1975, p. 229). To the extent that liberty implies participation, it is for "the pursuit of excellence in moral autonomy" (Pocock 1975, p. 230), and as such it also is characteristic of the few (Pocock 1975, pp. 228–232; p. 249).

Yet even for the few, this pursuit of moral autonomy does not stem from a purely disinterested love of virtue but from passions that are self-regarding in nature. The few who seek a public role have a propensity to seek public office, the basis of which "is not wisdom or goodness or any other moral quality which renders them fit for office, not even love of the city—though they must have that too—but, quite simply, ambition and the thirst for glory" (Pocock 1975, p. 133). The liberty of the few is consummated not only in exercising their moral excellence on behalf of the public good but also in satisfying their thirst for the honor that is the basis of their public ambition (Pocock 1975, p. 249). This honor is rooted in recognition and appreciation by others. And it is this sensitivity to others' reactions that distinguishes the fulfillment of private and particular ambition from the recognition that is public glory. If the individual conducts his search for honor by acting for the public good, "his glory would consist in the recognition by his fellows of his preeminence in this activity" (Pocock 1975, pp. 133–134), and this recognition thereafter would move him to disdain lesser satisfactions. "The few exist only in the many's sight. . . . The *libertà* of the few is to have their *virtù* [relating to the imposition of form on fortune] acknowledged by the *res publica*; the *libertà* of the many is to ensure that this acknowledgment is truly public and the rule of *virtù* and *onore* [honor] a true one" (Pocock 1975, p. 253). Honor cannot exist in a vacuum; it only exists as it is accorded by others. Thus not only do the few and the many respect each other's particular virtues, the few lead *and* defer to the many who are needed to save them from corruption "so that there is a point at which deference and virtue become very nearly identical" (Pocock 1975, pp. 515–516; also pp. 485–486).

The civic republican tradition then posits perfection in neither self-sufficiency nor rationality as conditions of citizenship, and virtue encompasses both independence and interdependence. In fact, knowing which quality to promote or to emphasize in a given circumstance may be partly constitutive of virtue. I suggest that both Diggins and Pangle portray this tradition in a one-sided manner, and that this is so because both overemphasize the necessity of self-sufficiency and rationality, although in different ways.

Diggins discounts the possibility of a classical republican influence upon the framers because they rejected an egalitarian citizen participation in politics and the practice of politics as a redemptive activity. Yet even for civic republicans, mixed government begins as "a beneficent deception practiced on irrational men" (Pocock 1975, p. 299). "Mutual political dependence will compel individuals to rule for the common good whether they intend to or not, [and] such a distribution of functions . . . will make men rational; *umori* [desires] will become *virtù*"—understood as the ability to impose form and order for the public good upon the disorder of historical contingencies (Pocock 1975, p. 299). Individuals may be subject to their passions historically, but this contingency need not be definitive of their natures. The polity plays a developmental role, as it were, "assigning men functions which will require them to act in such a way that their natures are reformed and are once again what they *are*, instead of what they *have become*" (Pocock 1975, p. 300). All "participate" and play a public role, but not all play it in the same way. The few and the many must interact and defer to each other for the recognition that constitutes honor, motivates action for the public good, and maintains civic virtue.

Pangle rejects the possibility of a classical republican influence upon the framers because they are *too* egalitarian and overemphasize citizen participation regardless of the credentials that citizens might hold for promoting virtue. Yet as we have seen, this tradition separates the roles of the few and the many, assigning to each group the functions for which it is best suited. Thus it allows for the aristocracy that Pangle associates with the best republic. Pangle, however, perceives civic virtue itself as a defective ideal. The citizen aspires mainly to be "a good team member or team leader." Thus "he possesses a virtue that is radically dependent on the good fortune that places him in a decent republic; his soul is ordered by a sense of shame and honor that stems from his view of the opinions his fellow-citizens hold of him" (Pangle, p. 586). The individual of true moral virtue, to Pangle, asks not what politics can do for the city, but rather what opportunities the city provides for the practice of his or her own individual virtues (Pangle, p. 587). Like Diggins, Pangle prefers the independent self-sufficient citizen, but not because he or she can then meet others as equal participants in the political arena. Rather, Pangle wishes the citizen to be independent *of* politics, of a concern for the opinions of his or her fellow-citizens, because only then can the individual attain philosophic rationality in its true sense. Yet Pangle perhaps forgets that "a decent republic" is a necessary even if insufficient condition for the practice of moral or ethical virtue in the nonpolitical sense. Pocock implies that a recognition of this necessity is central to the civic republican tradition. "If *virtus* could only exist where citizens associated in pursuit of a *res publica*, then the *politeia* or constitution . . . became practically identified with virtue itself. If the good man could practice his virtue only within a frame of citizenship, the collapse of such a frame . . . corrupted the virtue of the powerful as well as the powerless" (Pocock 1975, p. 157).

I would suggest to both Diggins and Pangle that in the civic republican tradition, the devices of a well-ordered constitution provide an institutional framework that shapes human desires and encourages virtuous action, even as they provide an arena within which such activity may take place. Moreover, civic republicanism allows the self-interested passions to function, while nevertheless maintaining the reality of a public good apart from individual self-interest and of public virtue as the means to its attainment. I propose now to examine the aims of Publius and to demonstrate that the latter's aims are compatible with this reading of the civic republican tradition.

WE THE PEOPLE: THE FEW AND THE MANY

As we have seen, to practice virtue according to one facet of the civic republican tradition, one must be free of subjection to the will of others, free of accountability to particular interests, and free for actions beneficial to the public good. These liberties were lacking under the Articles of Confederation, according to Publius. This difficulty is most clearly stated in Madison's *Federalist* No. 10. As is well known, Madison claims that liberty gives rise to different and conflicting opinions, supported by human passions. These opinions originate in the diversity of human faculties and in the "different degrees and kinds of property" that result from these faculties. Thus "ensues a division of the society into different interests and parties" (*The Federalist Papers* in No. 10, p. 78). Property, then, is the primary source of faction and is itself an interest, as Diggins notes (pp. 61 and 81), rather than a source of liberty. Factions and the interests that inform them "corrupt" the integrity of representatives when the latter act as judges in causes in which they have a personal interest. "What are many of the most important acts of legislation but so many judicial determinations . . . concerning the rights of large bodies of citizens? And what are the different classes of legislators but advocates and parties to the causes which they determine?" (*The Federalist Papers* in No. 10, p. 79). Madison is concerned about corruption that springs from dependence on the will of others, upon accountability to particular interests. Where the neo-Harringtonians fear dependence on the executive and regard property as a means to legislative independence, Madison fears dependence upon one's constituents as an obstacle to the pursuit of the public good and looks to control the factions to which property gives rise. Madison additionally implies concern about factions that legislators themselves may create by rallying constituents around their own interests.

Although Madison here implicitly recognizes the disintegration of a corporate ideal of the general will or public good, yet the American Revolution still represented "a final attempt . . . by many Americans to realize the traditional Commonwealth ideal of a corporate society, in which the common good would be the only objective of government" (Wood, p. 54; also see pp. 59–60). Americans still accepted the theory of virtual representation, which assumes that a people, despite differences in rank and property, should be considered "a unitary homogeneous order with a fundamental common interest" (Wood, p. 174); therefore the people can be represented by independent legislators who may decide by their own consciences what is in accord with this "one definable interest" (Wood, p. 175). The difficulty with the virtual representation of the colonists in the British Parliament was precisely that a disparity rather than a harmony of interest existed between those on either side of the Atlantic. Thus the theory of virtual representation *demanded* American independence, which in turn would ensure that the requirements of a proper virtual representation would be fulfilled. "Republicanism with its emphasis on devotion to the transcendent public good logically presumed a legislature in which the various groups in the society would realize 'the necessary dependence and connection' each had with the others" (Wood, p. 179).

Current developments, however, threatened the republican ideal. The early republic did not manifest "a naturally distinguishable few and many, performing complementary roles and practicing complementary virtues" (Pocock 1975, p. 516). Yet the classical republican tradition required reciprocity in the practice of one's own virtue and respect for one's neighbor's virtue if politics were to remain uncorrupted. The desire to identify qualities of learning, wisdom, and stability of character resulted in an emphasis upon men of wealth and property in state senates as the most likely to possess these attributes (Wood, pp. 217–218). Yet this distinction between the rights of persons as individuals and the rights of property belied the republican assumption of a unity and homogeneity of interest, according to which the few and the many have an identical interest but simply contribute to it differently. In fact, the discrepancy between an emphasis upon honor and wisdom, on the one hand, and wealth and property, on the other, led some republicans to conclude that mixed government should be overridden in favor of government by and for an undifferentiated people (Wood, pp. 222–225; also see pp. 246–251). As the people became conceptualized as one undifferentiated mass, however, the unity of their interest as each part fulfills its particular role or function paradoxically becomes less convincing. The few who represent the rest do not in fact embody particular virtues that contribute to the common interest. What results is a growing distrust of government and the evolution of a new theory of interest and representation such as that characterized by Publius in *The Federalist*. This theory suggests an attempt to carry on civic republican ideals through new means.

Initial attempts to restore a mutuality of interest between representatives and the people involved making representatives more dependent upon their constituents' opinions and instructions (Wood, p. 409). However, "The republican emphasis on talent and merit in place of connections and favor now seemed perverted, becoming identified simply with the ability to garner votes. . . . Republicanism was supposed to unleash men's ambitions to serve the state. But what was praiseworthy ambition and what was spurious?" (Wood, p. 398). The people in essence seemed to distrust themselves, or at least each other's ability to distinguish wisdom and virtue from their opposites in those who sought the public trust. Yet the more accountable representatives became to specific individuals and interests, ostensibly as a remedy for this difficulty, the greater the suspicion on the part of given individuals or groups that representatives might be accountable to the *wrong* individuals or interests. Moreover, what seemed to be a universal desire for riches, luxury, and the pursuit of private interest over the public good (Wood, pp. 414–425) led many to conclude that corruption had supplanted virtue and that only mechanical devices and institutional contrivances would fill the gap (Wood, pp. 428–429). "The Federalists hoped to create an entirely new and original sort of republican government—a republic which did not require a virtuous people for its sustenance" (Wood, p. 475).

Yet Madison still believed "that the public good, the real welfare of the great body of the people, is the supreme object to be pursued; and that no form of government whatever has any other value than as it may be fitted for the attainment of this object" (*The Federalist Papers* in No. 45, p. 289). Moreover, the public good was "a goal that should be positively promoted. He did not expect the new federal government to be neutralized into inactivity by the pressure of numerous conflicting interests. Nor did he conceive of politics as simply a consensus of the various groups that made up the society" (Wood, p. 505). If, in the civic republican tradition, virtue lies in the interaction of individuals in pursuit of a definable common interest, "The aim of every political constitution is, or ought to be, first to obtain for rulers men who possess most wisdom to discern, and most virtue to pursue, the common good of the society; and in the next place, to take the most effectual precautions for keeping them virtuous whilst they continue to hold their public trust" (*The Federalist Papers* in No. 57, p. 350).

Thus Madison proposes his well-known scheme of representation. In a large republic, the chances are decreased that one or a few selfish interests will prevail throughout. Moreover, the ratio of constituents to their representatives will necessarily be higher. Aspiring candidates will find it more difficult to practice deceit and "the vicious arts" when their appeals must be to larger numbers. "The suffrages of the people being more free, will be more likely to center on men who possess the most attractive merit and the most diffusive and established characters" (*The Federalist* No. 10, pp. 82–83). Hamilton notes that the representative who seeks the people's favor "and who is dependent on the suffrages of his fellow-citizens for the continuance of his public honors" will certainly consult their inclinations and "allow them their proper degree of influence upon his conduct" (*The Federalist Papers* in No. 35, p. 216). Madison amplifies this theme by suggesting that the representative's awareness of the honor, esteem, and confidence that election betokens "is some pledge for grateful and benevolent returns" to the electors (*The Federalist Papers* in No. 57, p. 352). Besides, "His pride and vanity attach him to a form of government which favors his pretensions and gives him a share in its honors and distinctions" (*The Federalist Papers* in 57, p. 352). Thus the representative is unlikely to attempt to subvert the people's authority when he is dependent upon their favor for advancement.

Publius is making two separate but interrelated points. First, government under the new Constitution ought to identify and restore a natural aristocracy whose foremost aptitude and interest would be the pursuit of the common good. "In short, through the artificial contrivance of the Constitution overlying an expanded society, the Federalists meant to restore and to prolong the traditional kind of elitist influence in politics that social developments . . . were undermining" (Wood, p. 513; also see p. 517). If the people came to distrust their governments, it was because they questioned their representatives' ability to recognize and pursue the common good. In this context, I believe Garry Wills is correct to impute to Madison the implication that a major purpose of election is to choose "impartial adjudicators of the varying interests" (Wills, p. 224). Madison allows for the presence of many factions neither to avoid precipitous decisions, as some conservatives have argued, nor to provide a free market for the competition of ideas, as liberal pluralists have asserted. "If a multiplicity and interplay of interests is encouraged, it is to *block them all;* so that, above their self-defeating squabble, the true interest of the entire body of the people may shine clear by contrast, for pursuit by virtuous men" (Wills, p. 205). In Wills's interpretation, the need for impartial adjudication in the public interest is understood both by the people and by their representatives. "The strength of a republic was . . . public virtue. If men do not want that quality represented, first and foremost, in their national councils, then they have ceased to be republicans and that form of government must fail" (Wills, p. 224).

Second, as Wills suggests, Publius retains a confidence in the people in spite of the perceived need for a natural aristocracy (Wood, p. 518). The people's views may require refinement, but not by "the chains of despotism." The "degree of depravity" in human beings requires some circumspection and distrust, but simultaneously there exist "other qualities in human nature that justify a certain portion of esteem and confidence. Republican government presupposes the existence of these qualities in a higher degree than any other form" (*The Federalist Papers* in No. 55, p. 346). Again, "The supposition of universal venality in human nature is little less an error in political reasoning than the supposition of universal rectitude. . . . there is a portion of virtue and honor among mankind, which may be a reasonable foundation of confidence. And experience justifies the theory" (*The Federalist Papers* in No. 76, p. 458).

In civic republican terms, then, the Constitution not only should ensure roles for both the few and the many, but also should operate so that the few do not merely "*represent* interest instead of judging it" (Wills, p. 214). What the Federalists accordingly developed was a theory of multiple representation, in which the people were considered to be represented, albeit differently, in each branch of government.

> The people's representatives taken as individuals formed a plurality of functionally differentiated groups, and to that extent might still be looked upon as a natural aristocracy; the plurality of functions which they exercised ensured the existence between and among them of a system of checks and balances, so that it could be said they were prevented from becoming

> corrupt, or corrupting the people, by any one's acquiring so much power as to bring the rest into dependence (Pocock 1975, p. 521).

Pocock adds, "It could be argued both that all government was the people's and that the people had withdrawn from government altogether" (Pocock 1975, p. 521; also pp. 523–524). The intertwining themes of independence and interdependence again recur. In carrying out its own function, each branch practices its own "virtue" and respects that of the others to avoid the taint of a corrupting dependence. Yet the interdependence of branches means that none may by itself define the common good. Moreover, the few and the many are interdependent. The people are sovereign, yet they are dependent upon the few they elect to define and pursue the common interest through a representative scheme that will maximize this possibility. The few are dependent upon the many for their elevation and recognition, and they become attached to the success of the government that honors and distinguishes them, which in turn ought to reinforce their devotion to public virtue or the common interest. As we have seen, the "thirst for honor" is in civic republicanism the basis for public ambition. Recognition and honor for the few keeps their aims high and toward the public good; recognition and honor accorded by the many is a means of participation by this group. Federalist theory likewise recognizes the role of self-interested passions and constructs a government that rules "partly by direct authority, partly by appeal to those passions, and partly by conversion of those passions into perception of a common interest" (Pocock 1975, p. 525). If the *politeia* or Constitution is "practically identical with virtue itself" (Pocock 1975, p. 157), this is because it is a framework or way of life that, in the eyes of its architects, encourages action for the public good on the part of both the governors and the governed.

It might trouble some that the concept of the common good or public interest appears in *The Federalist* to be purely formal, rather than substantive, in nature. Virtue and wisdom also retain this formalistic quality, referring to the ability to perceive the long-run interests of the polity as a whole. Yet even in civic republicanism, the substance of the universal common interest or of the virtue required for its attainment is no more determinate than in the writings of Publius. I believe that critics like Diggins, and by implication Pangle, are in error to assume that if concepts like these do not carry a substantive content, the field is thereby abandoned to those who would define the common interest simply as the interests of the winners in the political competition for influence and advantage. For both civic republicans and Publius, a well-ordered constitution may utilize the self-interested passions to make individuals rational and to direct their actions toward the public good. What matters to both, however, is that citizens believe that a common good transcending individual self-interest *does* exist in any given situation, and that they seek to discover it through their own actions and/or those of the representatives they select. What *is* right action or in the common interest is relative to circumstances. But if moral virtue refers to "an established disposition for free and deliberate conduct of the right sort" (Kosman, p. 103), Publius, like the civic republicans, is attempting to create the conditions for its realization.

LEADERSHIP AND THE OPERATION OF DEFERENCE

If to recent commentators the aims of civic republicanism are more elevated than those of Publius, the aims of the Scottish moralists are less so, and in fact are too low to be compatible with Publius's intentions. Diggins asserts, for example, that although Scottish philosophers such as Hume emphasize the social nature of human beings and the moral bonds between them, Hume has

> no concern for man's rightful relation to authority—order is not a result of rational, voluntary obedience but merely habitual deference and submission; no esteem for government as a just institution—most regimes originate in conquest and usurpation; and no interest in classical politics—the subversion of "virtue" by patronage and bribery is merely the paranoia of the "corruption mongers" (Diggins, pp. 53–54).

On the other hand, as we have seen in the civic republican tradition, "Leadership and deference were both active virtues; virtue, in a more abstract and formal sense, was a relationship between two modes of civic activity" (Pocock 1975, pp. 485–486). In this section, I shall concentrate on deference, which to Pocock was "not a hierarchical but a republican characteristic" (p. 515). In this context, the relationship between the few and the many "took shape best in a society of relative freedom, mobility, and outspokenness . . . aristocracy, although a function of property as well as personality, was a natural rather than an institutional phenomenon, which worked best when it was not entrenched but left to the recognition of the many" (Pocock 1975, p. 395): that is, left to the operation of deference.

Certainly Hume would seem in many ways an odd choice of thinkers to associate with the framers, notwithstanding some parallels between Hume's and Publius's views on representation (Wills, *passim*). Pocock associates Hume with the Court ideology, as opposed to the Country or Whig ideology animating many Americans of the revolutionary generation. To Court advocates, government was neither founded upon nor needed discipline by principles of virtue, "but might without suffering harm appeal to the passions and interests of men. It saw personal morality as private rather than public . . . which did not require to be expressed in acts of civic morality or statesmanlike virtue" (Pocock, p. 487). Hume accepts the necessity of a strong central executive that could influence the legislature, since he sees "government as a filtering device which induced them [men] to transform their short-term perceptions of their private interests into long-term understanding of the general identity of interests—and in that sense, of the public good" (Pocock 1975, p. 495). The public good, then, is not something that transcends private interests and requires sacrifice, but instead implies the sum total of private interests as they might emerge from bargaining and compromise. In any case, it is these aspects of Hume that cause Pangle to link him with Publius in seeing virtue as merely instrumental in disciplining the passions, and that cause Diggins to reject him as support for any system emphasizing rational and voluntary obedience. How then might Hume's ideas fit in with those of Publius?

In Hume's view, the stability of any society is based upon the natural sentiments, which in turn arise from the human propensity to sympathize with others. "The same disposition . . . makes us enter deeply into each other's sentiments, and causes like passions and inclinations to run, as it were, by contagion, through the whole club or knot of companions" (Hume, "Of National Characters," 1903, pp. 207–208; also see 1978, Book II, Part ii, Section 11, p. 318, and II, iii, 1, pp. 575–576). We sympathize with one another's vices, however, as readily as with each other's virtues. Moreover, our sympathy is strongest toward those who seem most like us; we prefer ourselves and our own interests above others and our relations and friends to strangers. Thus, as is well known, Hume's remedy for the partiality of human affections lies in convention, including the stability of property, its transference by consent, and the performance of promises, all culminating in civil government. "The remedy, then, is not derived from nature, but from *artifice;* or more properly speaking, nature provides a remedy in the judgment and understanding, for what is irregular and incommodious in the affections" (Hume 1978, III, ii, 2, p. 489). It is artifice and convention, not regard for the public interest, benevolence, or reason, that give rise to the sense of justice and to the observance of the rules of justice.

Natural inclination, however, still plays a part in social stability. With respect to the rules of justice, we feel satisfaction or uneasiness when their observance or nonobservance touches our own interests but also when our own interests are uninvolved. We see the behavior of others as supportive of or prejudicial to stability. The sense of justice is founded upon self-interest but also upon morality "when this interest is once observ'd to be common to all mankind, and men receive a pleasure from the view of such actions as tend to the peace of society, and an uneasiness from such as are contrary to it" (Hume 1978, III, ii, 6, p. 533; also see pp. 527–533, and III, ii, 2, pp. 499–500). Although morality is based upon artifice, rather than a perception of natural moral beauty in actions, and relies upon a framework of convention, the existence of natural sentiments is still necessary to support the artificial virtues and to allow them to become operative. "Had men not a natural sentiment of approbation and blame, it cou'd never be excited by politicians" (Hume 1978, III, iii, 1, p. 579). Again, "The utmost politicians can perform, is, to extend the natural sentiments beyond their original bounds;

but still nature must furnish the materials, and give us some notion of moral distinctions" (Hume 1978, III, ii, 2, p. 500; also see 1902, Section V, Part I, p. 214).

In view of Hume's opinion of the natural sentiments, it is hardly surprising that he relies upon popular opinion and habit as the ultimate source of obedience to government (Hume, "Of the First Principles of Government," 1903, pp. 29–31). Governments normally are not based upon consent but upon usurpation or force. In fact, "Were one to choose a period of time when the people's consent was the least regarded in public transactions, it would be precisely on the establishment of a new government," when public order may be unstable and the constitution unsettled (Hume, "Of the Original Contract," 1903, p. 461; see pp. 461–466). Most individuals would never claim that either their rulers' authority or their own obligation is based upon consent; if asked, they "wou'd be inclin'd to think very strangely of you; and wou'd certainly reply, that the affair depended not on their consent, but that they were born to such an obedience" (Hume 1978, III, ii, 8, p. 548; see pp. 539–549).

Hume's point is that however a government originates, "Habit soon consolidates what other principles of human nature had imperfectly founded," so that individuals once accustomed to obedience continue to acquiesce (Hume, "Of the Origin of Government," 1903, p. 37; see pp. 35–39). Hume thus implies that what begins as an artificial virtue—necessary acquiescence to government as a scheme that promotes overall social stability—evolves into what is almost a natural virtue, into spontaneous natural sentiments resulting in deference to the institutions and leaders of the community. The individual's opinion of what is in his or her interest, based upon prudence, is replaced by an opinion of what is right, based upon natural sentiments nurtured by habit. The sense of obligation resolves into a feeling of allegiance. If we return to Publius, I think we shall find that he, like Hume, relies upon the natural sentiments to accomplish what neither voluntary intentions nor prudential calculation can do alone.

Throughout, Publius remarks upon the human partiality to that which accords with one's immediate interests and aims. It is "that strong predilection in favor of local objects" that misleads the leaders of state governments and renders it difficult for them to cooperate and/or act in the national interest (*The Federalist Papers* in No. 15, p. 112; also see No. 17, pp. 119–120). And the people within each state, Hamilton implies, have developed a customary and habitual loyalty to their governments because of these governments' continuing activity on their behalf. This activity "contributes more than any other circumstance to impressing upon the minds of the people affection, esteem, and reverence towards the government." The benefits deriving from the national government, however, are less apparent, "less apt to come home to the feelings of the people; and, in proportion, less likely to inspire an habitual sense of obligation and an active sentiment of attachment" (*The Federalist Papers* in No. 17, p. 120).

This sentiment of habitual obligation and attachment, however, may over time develop toward the new national government. What is necessary is that the operations of the national government penetrate to the "common occurrences" of citizens' political lives and extend to what have traditionally been thought "matters of internal concern." The greater this penetration and extension by the national government,

> the more it is familiarized to their sight and to their feelings, the further it enters into those objects which touch the most sensible cords and put in motion the most active springs of the human heart, the greater will be the probability that it will conciliate the respect and attachment of the community. Man is very much a creature of habit. A thing that rarely strikes his senses will generally have but a transient influence upon his mind. A government continually at a distance and out of sight can hardly be expected to interest the sensations of the people (*The Federalist Papers* in No. 27, p. 176).

Publius also warns against too frequent recurrence by government to the people through constitutional conventions or other devices of direct democracy. As Madison suggests, "Frequent appeals would, in great measure, deprive the government of that veneration which time bestows on everything, and without which perhaps the wisest and freest governments would not possess the requisite stability. If it be true that all governments rest on opinion," enlightened reason will not suffice to guarantee correct decisions, and "the most rational government will not find it a superfluous advantage to have the prejudices of the community on its side" (*The Federalist Papers* in No. 49, pp. 314–15). Habit, then, will serve to attach the moral sentiment of the citizens to the new government, and where possible, this sense of allegiance should be left undisturbed.

Thus Publius does rely upon the natural sentiments to consolidate the loyalty of citizens to their community. But does this allegiance amount to very much? Richard Sinopoli answers, "Publius' model citizen is not the active citizen we associate with civic humanist ideals. . . . Love of the republic and a corresponding willingness to be a good citizen is not attributed, except very indirectly, to any moral qualities of the state but simply to the fact that it will grow old" (pp. 29–30). For Diggins, we saw that the natural sentiments are too weak to overcome self-interest or to promote virtue. For Pangle, the natural sentiments provide a means of attachment, but to institutions justified by convention rather than by their suitability for promoting what is good for human beings by nature. Sinopoli is implying that what the natural sentiments promote is citizenship of a very weak quality, in which virtue is simply constituted by obedience. Can we admit to a Humean influence upon Publius without simultaneously conceding that the latter's expectations of citizenship are minimal? I believe that we can, and for two reasons.

First, Hume's description of the conventions that support the existing distribution of property and power is just that—a description, not a normative account of the only possible justification. On power, Hume cautions, "My intention here is not to exclude the consent of the people from being one just foundation of government. Where it has place, it is surely the best and most sacred of any. I only contend, that it has very seldom had place in any degree" (Hume, "Of the Original Contract," 1903, p. 460). Thus the persistence of other than ideal arrangements must be explained, and Hume does so in his discussion of the artificial virtues and of conventional justice.

Deference to convention can work two ways. To many Americans prior to 1776, the docility, obedience, submissiveness, and passivity of the people in the face of tyranny were explained by customery deference, which "'gradually reconciles us to objects even of dread and detestation'" (Wood, p. 38). Similarly, to the anti-Federalists in the 1780s, the authority of name and fortune was difficult for the people to resist because of their habit of deference, even when popular liberties were threatened as a result (Wood, pp. 489–490). The Federalists, however, held that authority possessed by those with neither the ability nor the desire to discover and promote the common interest was the root of the difficulty. "'That exact order, and due subordination, that is essentially necessary in all well-appointed governments, and which constitutes the real happiness and well-being of society' had been deranged by 'men of no genious or abilitics' who had tried to run 'the machine of government'" (Wood, p. 507). Construct a scheme that maximizes the prominence of those who can and will define and pursue the common interest, and deference becomes an aid to governmental stability.

Thus it is not surprising that Publius would rely upon the natural sentiments to consolidate the loyalty of citizens, when so many were already questioning the rational grounds for a government that could never seem justified on these grounds to everyone. Voluntary consent and rational obedience are "the best and most sacred" foundation of government, but the natural sentiments provide a necessary supplement when these foundations are weak. Deference in itself is neither positive nor negative; it may be either. Its true value, as Publius realizes, is not as a sufficient measure of citizenship but as a necessary support to a governmental scheme that may be justified by other means. "The real alternative to a society containing strong conventions enforced by public opinion is not a Millian bohemia, but a Hobbesian state of nature. . . . convention is a condition of liberty and not . . . one of its enemies" (Gray, p. 100).

Second, the "active sentiment of attachment" to one's government *is* active, in Hume's view, in that it promotes virtuous behavior by those who hold public trust. In the civic republican tradition, the desire for honor encourages action for the public good on the part of the few who play the most public roles in the community. Hume goes further, suggesting that a love of praise for virtuous action is almost inseparable from a love of virtuous action for its own sake (Hume, "Of the Dignity or Meanness of Human Nature," 1903, pp. 87–88). Moreover, "The praises of others never give us much pleasure, unless they concur with our own opinion, and extol us for those qualities, in which we chiefly excel" (Hume 1978, II, i, 11, p. 322; see pp. 316–324). Thus we respond to praise by trying to deserve it. "When a man is prepossessed with a high notion of his rank and character in the creation, he will naturally endeavor to act up to it, and will scorn to do a base or vicious action which might sink him below that figure which he makes in his own imagination" (Hume, "Of the Dignity or Meanness of Human Nature," 1903, p. 83; also see Wills, pp. 29–33 and pp. 190–192). The natural sentiments of loyalty and approbation that attach citizens to their government, then, promote and reinforce the intentions of magistrates to act honorably. Such actions will call forth still greater loyalty and approbation from the citizens, setting in motion a self-reinforcing dynamic. Thus the natural sentiments not only play an essential role in converting prudential obligation into sentimental allegiance, they also figure actively in a theory of citizenship that intends to promote public virtue.

CONCLUSION

In this chapter I have attempted to show that although the ideals of virtue and the public good may not have had for Publius the determinative content or transcendent quality that some commentators would wish, these ideals did not constitute empty rhetoric on his part. With regard to civic republicanism, I have argued that the interdependence of individuals is as central to public virtue as is self-sufficiency, and that the self-interested passions play a role in inculcating devotion to the public good within an institutional framework. Moreover, the theory of representation as it evolved in the framers' thought aimed at restoring the interdependence between few and many that civic republicanism portrays as necessary to the definition and promotion of the common interest. Thus reinterpreted, the aims of civic republicanism and of Publius are compatible, rather than at odds. With respect to Scottish moral philosophy, I have argued that in Hume's case, the natural sentiments play a crucial role in social stability and allegiance to government, and that this same reliance on the moral sentiments is reflected in the arguments of Publius. I am not denying, as Diggins or Pangle might imagine, the influence of Locke or Calvinism upon the framers; I merely assert that civic republicanism and the Scottish moral tradition, and thus the importance of devotion to a common good, should not be written off with arguments by recent critics. Pocock states, "It is not the historian's business to go about with a pair of scales, weighing the importance of one 'factor' against another; the problem is to study the relations between them" (Pocock 1981, p. 54). This same caveat applies to the political philosopher.

I shall conclude with an observation that may serve to link the two traditions in question both with Publius and with each other. It has been noted that a moral virtue is not only an established disposition for the right sort of free and deliberate conduct but also a disposition toward the right sort of feeling. As two modes of human conduct, acting and feeling are interconnected. We ordinarily assume that the proper action in a given situation flows from the proper feeling or disposition. Yet in another interpretation of Aristotle, "one becomes virtuous by impersonating a virtuous person, and in that impersonation, through the process of habituation, becomes the virtuous person one impersonates" (Kosman, p. 112; see pp. 103–115). One may choose the proper actions in a given situation without the proper disposition, but these actions may give rise to the "right" feelings, prompting in turn subsequent actions that do flow from a proper disposition. "Acts are chosen, virtues and feelings follow in their wake, though in logically different ways" (Kosman, p. 112). The civic republicans rely on mutual political dependence within the institutions of a well-ordered constitution to prompt action for the common good and the subsequent disposition that describes moral or civic virtue. Hume also relies initially on self-interest as a basis for obligation, but habitual obedience nurtures natural sentiments, or a disposition, if you will, of affection and allegiance. And Publius, in turn, utilizes both a framework of institutions *and* the ties instilled by habit to foster actions for the common good and the virtuous disposition that inclines to them.

REFERENCES

Barber, Benjamin R. 1986. "The Compromised Republic: Public Purposelessness in America." In *The Moral Foundations of the American Republic,* 3d ed., edited by Robert H. Horwitz. Charlottesville: Univ. Press of Virginia.

Diamond, Martin. 1986. "Ethics and Politics: the American Way." In *The Moral Foundations of the American Republic,* 3d ed., edited by Robert H. Horwitz. Charlottesville: Univ. Press of Virginia.

Diggins, John Patrick. 1984. *The Lost Soul of American Politics: Virtue, Self-interest, and the Foundations of Liberalism.* New York: Basic Books.

The Federalist Papers. 1961. Clinton Rossiter, ed. New York: New American Library.

Goldwin, Robert A. 1986. "Of Men and Angels: A Search for Morality in the Constitution." In *The Moral Foundations of the American Republic,* 3d ed., edited by Robert H. Horwitz. Charlottesville: Univ. Press of Virginia.

Gray, John. 1984. *Hayek on Liberty.* Oxford: Basil Blackwell.

Hofstadter, Richard. 1986. "The Founding Fathers: An Age of Realism." In *The Moral Foundations of the American Republic,* 3d ed., edited by Robert H. Horwitz. Charlottesville: Univ. Press of Virginia.

Hume, David. 1902. "An Enquiry Concerning the Principles of Morals." In *Enquiries Concerning the Human Understanding and Concerning the Principles of Morals,* 2d ed., edited by L. A. Selby-Bigge. Oxford: Clarendon Press.

———. 1903. *Essays Moral, Political and Literary.* London: William Clowes & Sons, Ltd.

———. 1978. *A Treatise of Human Nature,* ed. by L. A. Selby-Bigge; 2d ed., ed. by P. H. Niddich. Oxford: Clarendon Press.

Kosman, L. A. 1980. "Being Properly Affected: Virtues and Feelings in Aristotle's Ethics." In *Essays on Aristotle's Ethics,* edited by Amelie Oksenberg Rorty. Berkeley: Univ. of California Press.

Pangle, Thomas L. 1986. "The *Federalist Papers'* Vision of Civic Health and the Tradition out of Which that Vision Emerges." *Western Political Quarterly* 39:577–602.

Pocock, J.G.A. 1972. "Virtue and Commerce in the Eighteenth Century." *Journal of Interdisciplinary History* 3:119–134.

———. 1975. *The Machiavellian Moment.* Princeton: Princeton Univ. Press.

———. 1981. "The Machiavellian Moment Revisited: A Study in History and Ideology." *Journal of Modern History* 53:49–72.

Sinopoli, Richard. 1985. "The Founders' Liberalism and the Problem of Civic Virtue." Paper delivered at the Annual Meeting of the American Political Science Association, New Orleans, Louisiana, 1985.

Wills, Garry. 1982. *Explaining America: The Federalist.* New York: Penguin.

Wood, Gordon S. 1969. *The Creation of the American Republic: 1776–1787.* Chapel Hill: Univ. of North Carolina Press.

TWO

The Purposes of the Constitution

LESTER J. MAZOR

> WE THE PEOPLE of the United States, in order to form a more perfect Union, establish Justice, insure domestic Tranquility, provide for the common defense, promote the general Welfare and secure the Blessings of Liberty to Ourselves and our Posterity, do ordain and establish this CONSTITUTION for the United States of America.
>
> —*U.S. Constitution, Preamble*

> The fabric of the American empire ought to rest on the solid basis of THE CONSENT OF THE PEOPLE.
>
> —*Hamilton,* The Federalist, *No. 22*

The purposes of the Constitution of the United States of America are stated explicitly in its Preamble, implicitly in its particular provisions, and can also be derived from an analysis of the response it represented to the circumstances of its creation. The Constitution is situated on the cusp between the eighteenth and nineteenth centuries, not only in a chronological sense, but also in terms of what those two centuries have come to mean in the history of ideas and institutions, of political attitudes and social revolutions. The alterations and amendments, interpretations and applications, idolizations and attacks during the past two centuries have amplified the Constitution's meaning without significantly shifting its location from the place where it was born—the borderland of two centuries, one as classical as Mozart, the other as revolutionary and romantic as a steam engine. It has been called "a constitution for the ages," a document whose genius lies in the flexibility built into it, in its broad language and vague clauses, which has allowed it to serve the needs of a people whose way of life is beyond the furtherest imaginings of those who drafted it. But if the men who met in secret in Philadelphia and those who have given public meaning to the constitutional text ever since are to be saluted for a wisdom and foresight sufficient to establish a government that might long endure, it is for us who live in a quite different juncture of two centuries, whose world has both shrunken and expanded a millionfold, to search out our own needs—and if we dare, our desires—in order to fashion them into purposes and to measure this venerable Constitution accordingly.

UNION

Is it to be supposed that one national government will suit so extensive a country, embracing so many climates, and containing inhabitants, so very different in manners, habits, and customs?

—*George Mason, at the Virginia convention on ratification*

To form a more perfect union was a controverted aim in a society not yet molded into a nation, far from indivisible, a land where fierce local loyalties had been forged in struggle with the soil, in conflict with the indigenous peoples and in battle with the armies of a distant sovereign. In Europe in the eighteenth century national unity was coming to be favored more and more over feudal particularlity; the advantage of power seemed to reside in whomever had the greatest number of inhabitants, and wars were fought as much to acquire population as territory. But in America fear of excessive centralization was widespread. The smaller states did not trust the larger ones. Two, perhaps even three, distinct regions already could be discerned, made up of groups of states with enough resources to have formed separate countries, each with differing social institutions and economic interests. Within the individual states there were also areas that doubted each other. The hinterland chafed under the rule of the seacoast. To the people of western Massachusetts, for example, Boston was a remote, distant, and often hostile capital. More than once they threatened secession. Yet on the whole there was an overpowering thrust toward nationalism. There were some who dreamed of an empire spanning a continent, though there were also those who feared that so extensive a nation would necessarily exceed the limits of the capacities of republican and representative government. Nationalism was full of the momentum it had been given by the example of unified and prosperous countries like England and France, soon to be emulated by the Germans and even the Italians.

The federal solution to these competing pressures has been hailed as a brilliant compromise, one that has provided the strength and scope, the resources and market of a vast nation while tolerating local differentiation, encouraging variety, and permitting social experimentation in the laboratories of the individual states. The qualms of the anti-Federalists seemed to have been assuaged by the limitations upon the powers of the central government, by the structure of the federal parliament, by the system of elections to both the legislative and the executive branches, and finally by the Bill of Rights. Hamilton and those of like mind could rest content in the knowledge that the national market, which the Constitution guaranteed more than anything else, once developed, ultimately would sweep away every obstacle in its path.

From the perspective of the bridge between the end of the twentieth and the beginning of the twenty-first century, the goal of nationhood takes on a rather different coloration. Altogether too much blood has been spilt in the name of nationalism, for one thing. So many peoples have chased and continue to chase this particular chimera as to make a mockery of the very notion of the sovereign nation-state. For our purposes, the goal of national unity may appear simultaneously too grand an ambition and too puny. The cost in a deadening uniformity, in the reduction of cultural diversity, in the denial of opportunity for direct participation, in the separation of act from consequence, in the toll required to maintain a continental empire and control a hinterland that extends to the antipodes, has become insufferably high. At the same time, the most elementary claims to the benefits of sovereign nationhood seem incapable of being fulfilled, and anything less than a globally coordinated political arrangement seems insufficient. No longer can any nation purport to guarantee its citizens protection within its borders, safety from foreign intrusion. Acid rain, radiation clouds, thermal change in the atmosphere cannot be barred at the national frontier. A nuclear winter cannot be met by any national heating plan. We are left only with the illusions of roofing over the nation, of escaping under the earth or to another planet, of paralyzing the enemy (if only this enemy could be found—and named), with which to attempt to sustain the belief in the capacity of the national state to provide a region of safety for its people.

Nor is even a continental nation large enough in scale to suit the demands of economic enterprises for markets and materials. At the very moment when they seek to intrude themselves into every corner of the earth, corporate operations become abstract enough that a tiny island suffices as the headquarters for a thousand gigantic firms. How much more will the planet shrink under the changes in communication and transportation already visible in film and fantasy? How much will our sense of human scale and of the need for global solidarity be altered by the first experiences of contact with extraterrestrial intelligences, an event that lies within a time horizon no more distant than that which the framers of the Constitution beheld in contemplating their handiwork? It is not only that nationalism has become a deadly anachronism, but that the territorial principle itself upon which it rests has become obsolete. The multilayered, polycentric relations of the coming era are developing among people for whom there can be neither tariff nor passport, neither center nor periphery, neither nation nor state, neither metropolis nor village, in the senses to which we have become all too accustomed.

DEFENSE

If we mean to be a commercial people, it must form a part of our policy to be able one day to defend that commerce.

—*Hamilton,* The Federalist, *No. 34*

The Constitution gave Congress the power to declare war, to raise armies, to maintain a navy. It designated the president as commander in chief and forbade the states, whose militias were presumed to continue in existence, from embarking on any military adventures of their own. Though 1789 generally was felt to be a moment of profound peace, the British were still to be feared, though some, and particularly those with expansionist aims, had the Spanish, French, and perhaps even other European countries in mind. It would be 1835 before someone would suggest that two great continental powers, the United States and Russia, were destined to oppose each other, and even then it required an extraordinary presience to draw such a conclusion. The Indian tribes, as the Constitution called them, were a more immediate danger. They had already showed themselves stubbornly unwilling to surrender their native lands, and in the years to come they would turn out to be equally "unreasonable" in their insistence on the observance of the treaties made with them, refusing to acknowledge changes in circumstance and technological condition. It would be necessary to defend the Union not only from its mother country and her rivals, but also to protect its long frontier from attack by the Indians, and ultimately to subdue them completely.

Nothing was clearer to those who argued for the adoption of the Constitution than that the military powers it contained must be entirely without limit. It would be pointless to engage in hostilities without the capacity to sustain them to whatever point the occasion and the will of the opponent required. Though procedural restrictions were placed on the invocation of the military powers, it must have been assumed that even these would be ignored under conditions of extreme necessity. After all, on such grounds the war of independence itself had been fought. It was with that experience in mind that the need for an unlimited military power and the unlimited taxing power that could sustain it was conceived.

In an age of expansion there has always been something euphemistic about the notion of defense, but it was not until the holocaust with which World War II ended that the Orwellian step was taken that renamed the minister of war in the president's cabinet the secretary of defense. The tongue often balks at the expression, preferring to say "the Pentagon," with all the mythological connotations that image implies. Quakers and pacifists of other persuasions there have always been in the land. On occasion, their sons have refused to go to war, or to accept military office, and some even have declined the position of secretary of war, if not of commander in chief. But a widespread and fundamental rejection of the use of military force had to await the day when its futility had become transparent, when even the bishops would be willing to make plows of their swords. Though there are those whose beliefs would accept—if not welcome—Armageddon, the rest of the world may wish that the country that first risked setting the atmosphere on fire might seek to be the leader in the renunciation of all armaments, rather than in their manufacture and distribution. The moment already has been reached when the only credible defense is the extinction of the kind of military power that the Constitution has unleashed. The militias that the Constitution eventually subordinated are far less dangerous—and perhaps more useful, judging from recent encounters. But in any case, warfare can no longer be acceptable, if it ever really was, to the ordinary person as a purpose for which a society or government is organized. It may require the universalization of the principle of conscientious refusal to set us upon a course that offers survival as a viable option.

ORDER

The insurrections in Massachusetts admonished all the states of the danger to which they were exposed.

—*Madison, at the Constitutional Convention, June 19, 1787*

One of the main reasons for opposing the existence of the kind of standing armies that the Constitution permits was the awareness that armies may be justified on the grounds of external danger yet be used primarily to control the domestic population. In a government with an element of popular participation it may be especially necessary to cloak the one objective in the other. The framers, nevertheless, were not unwilling to admit that one of the grand objectives of the Constitution was the suppression of internal rebellion. Daniel Shays and his ilk were much on the mind of the delegates who gathered in Philadelphia, and their own successful uprising against the British can never have been far from view. The sources of rebellion closest at hand were debtors and slaves, but others might be anticipated. The Constitution made specific provision to protect both creditors and slaveholders, but it also granted explicit power to quell domestic disturbances. Before the end of the nineteenth century it would prove capable of permitting the use of the army of the national government against strikers and dissidents, sometimes over the opposition of the political authority within a particular state. The Constitution would enable the government to suppress the mob, whether it took the form of outraged miners, disaffected steelworkers, distressed railway men, or an "army" of veterans on the steps of the capitol. Securing property in its two chief forms of land and slaves, as it was in 1787, was a primary objective of the constitution. The increase of wealth would be inevitable if commerce was facilitated and the useful arts encouraged. Despite its tenuous position in a more ancient version of Christian theology, both religion and secular philosophy had long ago come to terms with wealth, especially when it could be called property. Life, and liberty itself, by now had also come to be called property. Granted the inevitable inequalities that the Constitution surely contemplated, it would only be wise to provide adequately for a power of suppression.

In an age when not only the forms of property but also those of slavery have become so much more subtle and elaborate, in which the techniques of surveillance and control have been extended and refined beyond measure, in which the strategies and tactics of opposition and dissidence also have been developed and embellished accordingly, is it possible to contemplate a society grounding itself not in a commitment to suppression of domestic conflict but in the fostering and nurturing of the opposition arising within it? Can a community be formed around the principle of continuous revolution, or is it paradoxical to go so far as to risk self-destruction already in the moment of foundation? Even to articulate such a Heracletian view within our Parmenidean culture is difficult, as Jefferson discovered. Yet the political and social history of the United States suggests that the capacity of a society to tolerate contradiction is greater than one might have imagined at any given point. The kind of criticism of official persons and actions that some of the founders thought necessary to condemn as criminally seditious came to be accepted as the very meaning of freedom of the press. The strike and the boycott have been absorbed into the realm of legitimate forms of protest. The sit-in and civil disobedience increasingly are coming to be recognized as falling within the scope of peaceful assembly and presentation of grievances. Perhaps the social psyche, like the particular self, is capable of being much more complex, diverse, even ambiguous and ambivalent than once was thought, and perhaps it is even more adaptable and resilient when it is. If so, the way is open for the building of a social framework that is less a hierarchy than a network, in which, as in the mind itself, there need be no ruling authority, no censorious center, no determinate sovereign.

JUSTICE

> The spirit of trade produces in the mind of a man a certain sense of exact justice, opposite, on the one hand, to robbery, and on the other, to those moral virtues which forbid our always adhering rigidly to the rules of private interest. . . .
>
> —*Montesquieu,* Spirit of the Laws
> *Book 2, Section 2*

Over and above the foreign and domestic perils for which military force might be required, those who wrote the Preamble to the Constitution placed the sacred value of justice. The Constitution would serve to establish it, whatever it might be. Indeed, few social ideals have attracted so large and diverse a following. The claims that have been made in its name, the movements that have voiced their demands in its vocabulary, the theories that have sought to explain its nature, span a broad range of human desires and detractions. Yet, within the political culture shared by men of property in 1787, the establishment of justice meant more than anything else the protection of rights. Natural rights, inalienable rights grounded in natural law, and above all, the rights to life, liberty, and property were at the core of the conception of justice. The possessive individualism that underlay this view of justice sought safety and comfort in the erection of barricades, the building of walls of separation, the construction of homes that might be treated as castles, the creation of zones of privacy. From this politics of exclusion would issue an ever-growing list of entitlements. But justice as rights kills with its Midas touch, renders lifeless what it tries to fix so neatly within its glass-covered cabinet of specimens of human wants and desires. Those who are denied rights in such a system suffer accordingly. But those who have them suffer the irony that in the end they are alone with the possessions, are as miserable as Crusoe.

The Founding Fathers were not unaware of the classical formulation according to which justice consists in giving everyone his due. The concept of just deserts, however, notoriously is cursed with a Kantian emptiness, or, at the other pole, is burdened with specificity grounded in a system of distinctions based on caste or class, on belief or color, on age or gender, on talent or ability. Thus could the Constitution establish justice without abolishing slavery, without offering women dominion over their own bodies, without guaranteeing subsistence to the propertyless, without granting the young protection from abusive parents, without providing assistance to the infirm and the disabled. Little wonder that contemporary movements seem less inclined than their predecessors to inscribe the name of justice upon their banners. The odium of injustice remains strong, the sense of injustice has not been stilled, the cry for justice continues to be heard. But the limitations of equal justice under law have become apparent enough—insufficiency of pleas for justice that entreat those with power to treat more fairly those without it, and the relativity of the claim of justice to the prevailing social arrangements—that nothing short of a notion of justice encompassing the whole of society could be persuasive. Even the broadest and most liberal ideas of social justice, which find justification for privilege in supposed benefit to the mass, or to the downtrodden, or to the least of all of us, do so on the presupposition that there are those born with ability and those born without it, as if ability were not itself derivative of social arrangements. It is easy enough to see this at a distance, to see that to the plantation owners slavery was just, so much so that they could erect an elaborate system of legal regulation around it, to see that the establishment of justice still permits people to sleep under bridges, to forage through garbage cans, to be refused a chance to work or to learn. It is harder to remember that equal justice under law endorsed the placing of citizens in concentration camps, accepted the hanging of people for their public statements, approved the shooting of people demonstrating for their livelihoods, and harder yet to see that justice is used to legitimate the punishment of those who resist paying taxes used to produce chemical weapons or who give sanctuary to people fleeing from a devastation made with the bloody hand of the nation.

In place of justice then, one seeks an ideal of social solidarity, an attitude of integration and interdependence that validates difference rather than seeks to control it, to obliterate it, or even to compensate for it. The image of justice should be not that of blindness and the scales of calculation, but the image of the garden and the eye that sees its intricate ecology and seeks neither to make a lawn nor a desert. What is required is solidarity of such an order that it is not satisfied by the restricted and cramped version of freedom that the Constitution knows as liberty. For in the constitutional idiom, justice and liberty are closely bound together, providing the underpinning as well as the limits to each other.

LIBERTY

> The necessity of preserving men in the possession of what honest industry has already acquired, and also of preserving their liberty and strength, whereby they may acquire what they further want, obliges men to enter into society with one another.
>
> —*Locke,* A Letter Concerning Toleration

For many years, liberty has seemed the most noble of the Constitution's purposes—an objective whose attractions invited the oppressed masses of Europe—a goal worthy of the sacrifices of local autonomy, of lives given in battle, of the fruits of one's labor, which the Constitution demands. Without law, there can be no liberty, so the framers understood. Philosophers sought to reconcile the conflicting claims of liberty and order, of liberty and equality. Courts attempted to locate the boundaries of liberty, to find the point where one person's liberty ends and the liberty of the other begins, to determine when that clear and present danger exists that justifies the denial of liberty, to define away those assertions of freedom unworthy of liberty's name. It is these efforts of more than two centuries that have given the dimensions of liberty, which make it possible to say just what kind of a concept of freedom liberty is, and to see more clearly how it is related to justice and to the other purposes of the Constitution.

For despite the attempt to collapse the concept of freedom into that of liberty, its history, its usage in ordinary language, and its place in political and legal theory indicate that liberty is a rather particular brand of freedom. Its ancestry lies in part in the English law of property, in which a liberty was a special exemption from an obligation otherwise obtaining with respect to a given land tenure. Its broader connotations are connected to the efforts of towns and their burghers to reduce their feudal duties and become more autonomous. It was such hard-won privileges that the Magna Carta promised to preserve, and these became the basis for the demands for political and civil liberty in the struggles of the seventeenth century that were more fully generalized only in the nineteenth century. It was not unusual then when Locke described liberty as a form of property and Mill feared its fate at the hand of the emerging masses. The language of liberty is that of acquisition, possession, exclusive control, territorial defense, individual assertion. The price of liberty is eternal adversariness, the willingness to do battle against the other for the recognition of one's entitlements.

Liberty seeks to prescribe an area within which intervention is forbidden, where no questions may be asked. In itself it offers little support for cooperation, connection, interaction. Alone, it tolerates the hermit almost as easily as it salutes the trader in the marketplace, where liberty is most obviously the pursuit of gain, serving the common weal only insofar as the invisible hand deigns to guide it. No doubt the forefathers of the framers had crossed the ocean in quest of religious liberty, but that did not include freedom for the services of worship led by people like Anne Hutchinson, not to mention the followers of Mohammed. Liberty from English rule had been the object of a hard-fought war, but the blessings of independence were not especially intended to benefit the slave and the servant, much less the Native American. The concept of liberty is closely allied with that of interest. In its mature form liberty is the right to pursue one's interests, it is that part of individual interests that ought not to be restricted even by the principle of justice, which requires that all social arrangements look toward the improvement of the lot of the weakest member of society. The dimensions in which personal liberty grew in the latter part of the nineteenth century in the United States were granted constitutional validation in judicial decisions in the middle of the twentieth; liberty of belief and disbelief, of political debate and private communication, of collective action and communal association are that recent. More controversial liberties such as artistic expression and gay rights still waver in debate. But the main course of the twentieth century has seen a nation grown fat and proud acquire all the fears appropriate to its station among the powers of the earth, and as it has, so has liberty gradually lost favor among a people committed to endless preparation for war, living in a state of siege, under constant threat of dissention, subversion, espionage, sabotage, and terrorism.

Liberty, encompassing both the rights of property and restrictions on the powers of government officials, once was seen as the very embodiment of security. Now the one is balanced against the other, and more often than not it is liberty that is found wanting. Liberty, we are told, is a luxury that cannot be afforded when one is looking down the barrel of a gun, when someone has been kidnapped, when terrorists are on the move. The preservation of liberty may be the ground for which all government is instituted, yet for the sake of its preservation, it too must be sacrificed. So searches of the person become routine rather than something requiring a special kind of justification. They are only made inconspicuously electronic. The dread of labeling every person with a universal number, first raised when the social security system was instituted, becomes a reality when every child is required to have one. The internal passport that had long been the symbol of the controlling hand of bureaucratic government in other lands is adopted in the name of protecting against competition for scarce employment by illegal immigrants. And inquiry shows that there are no limits to the restrictions on liberty that the populace is willing to embrace in the face of the claim that someone is carrying a nuclear bomb or a poison capable of polluting an entire water supply, or is the carrier of a contagious and deadly disease. The best defense is a good offense, a preemptive strike. Shoot first and a court can explore the motivations later. Better yet, detain all those who are suspect or emplace implants so that their every movement can be taced.

The issue here is less the decreasing fulfillment of the promises of liberty under the eye of the Panopticon; it is more the inadequacy of the ideal itself, the reasons why to both the peoples seeking freedom for themselves throughout the world and for the dissenting movements within the United States liberty has ceased to be a watchword. Not that there is any lack of people eager to flee torture, persecution, oppression, and exploitation for the main chance; not that liberty's torch no longer attracts, though it especially welcomes those members of the privileged classes or those allied with them fleeing from a social revolution. But in recent terms the word *liberation* voices the freedom sought by those seeking to escape from neocolonial domination, as well as by those attempting to overcome the colonization of the body and of the soul within the United States. What began as a civil rights movement shifted from a crusade for the fuller liberty of the emancipated slaves, from a campaign for equal justice for the Negro, to a movement for the liberation of Afro-Americans, and thus ultimately for liberation from the tyranny of the color line itself. So, too, have women turned from the more limited objectives of political and economic liberty to the broader goals of personal and social liberation, thereby marking out whole new ways of living in free solidarity, forming a different consciousness, and building coalitions among those seeking the expansion of freedom. Liberation is neither to be received as a blessing nor treasured as a possession. It is not waiting to be reified but engaged in as an open process. If liberty is a prize that the sons wrest from the father, liberation leads to a place beyond gender role, hierarchy, and domination. Liberty understands nature as something to be tamed, controlled, used, exploited. Liberation looks to find its ecological niche—to tread lightly upon the environment, of which it is, of course, a part—but also seeks to avoid rising too far into the ether of abstraction—instead, to touch the earth. Where liberty is bounded by the system of rules necessary and proper to a common social life, liberation is open to risk and change and living as a work of art. Yet it is embarrassing to attempt to offer even this much of a characterization of the notion of liberation. Liberty may be too tired and old an idea to be much harmed by definition; liberation is still in its infancy and bristles at being confined and hobbled by the act of naming.

WELFARE

The public good, the real welfare of the great body of the people, is the supreme object to be pursued.

—*Madison,* The Federalist, *No. 45*

Of all the Constitution's purposes, the promotion of the general welfare might be thought to be the most elastic and benign, the most generous and sociable. Indeed, in the history of the interpretation of the Constitution it has sometimes been asserted that, unlike the other purposes stated in the Preamble, this one finds no particular implementation in the provisions of the document, but is at most an expression of its overall intent. As early as the controversy over the National Road and as late as the debate over the New Deal it was argued that neither the taxing power nor the Commerce Clause was so broad as to allow the federal government to engage in vast projects or assume a general superintendence of the economy in order to ensure the well-being of the people as a whole. But the utilitarian perspective with which the general welfare clause is pregnant has found increasing favor. The area of dispute has become instead the question of how much and what kind of intervention should be made by the national government. In the debates about the military budget and welfare spending, in the concern over the national debt, in the argument over regulation and deregulation, this controvesy continues.

The utilitarian view has its detractors, of course. Within the constitutional perspective, this takes the form of those who give priority to the protection of liberty. Majority rule versus minority rights has been a common formulation. But most of the protection given to minorities has been devoted to corporate capital, and because there are devices in the constitutional system that are conducive to majority rule, there is something to be suspected in this formulation. The utilitarian notion of the general welfare also has been criticized by the adherents of ancient ideals of virtue. Yet without recurring to the tradition of rights nor attempting to resurrect the polis, one might question the notion of the general welfare from another direction. Implicit in it is not only the subsumption of the particular by the general but also of desire by need. Both in its classical liberal and in its socialist variety, the pursuit of welfare is situated within the comfortable assumption that the world is governed by scarcity. At the same time, the notion of progress that they share conceives the world as a container of resources whose potential at any given moment can be fixed and measured, the costs and benefits of any course of action calculated and weighed. The wishes of remote generations yet unborn are sharply discounted in this process. And the value of a single unit of utility seems to elude the kind of definition that the system demands.

Those who seem to fear that state intervention in the name of a beneficial social policy might be grounded in utilitarian argument have proclaimed their preference for the harder coin of uncontaminated wealth as a measure of virtue. Some people of this mind may yet come to hold the interpretation of the Constitution in their grasp. Unintentionally, perhaps, they endorse the skeptic's view that might makes right and that justice is just a name for the will of the stronger.

Promise for the future lies not in the false security of views long declared bankrupt, but in a different kind of economy. To extract ourselves from the morass of a bottomless and consumptive materialism we may turn instead to an economy of desire: not "to each according to his needs" but "to all in resonance to the imagination." Of course, it may be claimed that to adopt such a credo is to risk the rule of the sadistic and the paranoid, and especially the megalomaniac. Or is this to say that to seek to live according to the suggestions of desire, of imagination and fantasy, calls for a subtlety and complexity, a sophistication that not only the U.S. Constitution and the United States, but the whole crude civilization to which they belong has not yet shown itself capable of achieving? It is the dream that has tempted and terrified the West ever since Columbus, or should one better say, since Marco Polo. To embrace it, to enter into it, to embark upon it would be to feel the full energy of its creative power, that is, to begin to let go of that civilizational neurosis to which we cling, on which the Constitution is founded.

DEMOCRACY AND BEYOND

The evils we experience flow from the excess of democracy.

—Elbridge Gerry, at the Constitutional Convention, May 31, 1787

Molding a people into a nation, endowing it with a military force, providing the means for suppressing rebellion, maintaining the distribution of wealth and privilege, protecting the possessors of property, and producing a level of material consumption sufficient for the prosperity of the few and the cooptation of the rest—these purposes of the Constitution paraphrased from its Preamble tell a part of the story. But the purposes of the Constitution are cast into sharper relief when one considers what they do not include. Democracy, for example. The framers were divided on the merits of the democratic ideal, for the most part dubious of it if not entirely opposed, and in any case convinced that it could not be practiced on the national scale that they sought to create with the Constitution. For them, the more limited goal of winning the consent of the governed would be enough.

Even after it was enunciated as an American value in the early nineteenth century, democracy has remained always in tension with the liberal republicanism of the Constitution. Not that the Constitution explicitly prohibits democratic forms of self-government insofar as they may be created within the states. Or does the constitutional provision guaranteeing the states a republican form of government provide the opening through which the federal government could intercede to prevent a state from abandoning representative forms in favor of direct participation? No one really can say, of course, for no state ever has come close to becoming so democratic, though for a moment at the end of the 1960s some people dreamed of trying to take over Vermont with that in mind. So far as the national government is concerned, the representative structure of the Congress, the long senatorial terms, the presidential veto, the power of judicial review in a court well insulated from the people by age and tradition—all this and more has served to restrain and control the democratic impulse, all the while invoking the name of democracy to increase the legitimacy of the regime. At the apex of this hierarchy now sits the constitutional monarch, wearing the mantle of the pseudodemocracy. Direct participation in the decisions affecting one's life, meanwhile, has come to be viewed as something so peculiar that it must be given yet another name, in order to differentiate it from that diluted ritual that passes for democracy in the political vocabulary served up in the schools and purveyed in the media.

Participatory democracy is only one of many values that might be included within the imagination of a contemporary restatement of general aims. To extend the list would be to call forth a process quite different from that that took place long ago in Philadelphia: not proceedings held in secret, by a select group of delegates, leading to the writing down on paper of a set of rules to be interpreted by courts and enforced by an executive armed with military force, but, rather, the open, open-ended and inclusive process of giving birth to images and metaphors that can be embraced across cultural borders, nurtured as the basis upon which an ecologically situated solidarity can grow. What better contribution to such a process can we make than to strive to bring an end to the worship of the Constitution of the United States of America as an idol, to scrutinize its purposes as closely as we can, to call into question its sufficiency for the century we are entering, to struggle to imagine a set of purposes worthy of our pledge, and to make that effort the measure of our actions?

SELECTED BIBLIOGRAPHY

Bookchin, Murray. 1982. *The Ecology of Freedom*. Palo Alto: Chesire Books.

Epstein, David F. 1984. *The Political Theory of The Federalist*. Chicago: Univ. of Chicago Press.

Goldwin, Robert A., and William A. Schambra, eds. 1982. *How Capitalistic Is the Constitution?* Washington: American Enterprise Institute for Public Policy Research.

Hoffman, Ronald, and Peter J. Albert, eds. 1981. *Sovereign States in an Age of Uncertainty.* Charlottesville: Univ. Press of Virginia.

Horwitz, Robert H., ed. 1979. *The Moral Foundations of the American Republic.* Charlottesville: Univ. of Virginia Press, 2d. ed.

Lynd, Staughton. 1967. *Class Conflict, Slavery, and the United States Constitution.* Indianapolis: Bobbs-Merrill.

Padover, Saul K. 1962. *To Secure These Blessings.* New York: Washington Square Press.

Szatmary, David P. 1980. *Shay's Rebellion.* Amherst: Univ. of Massachusetts Press.

PART TWO

Democracy and the Constitution

Introduction to Part Two

DIANA T. MEYERS

The history of the pursuit of democratic ideals is a long and venerable one. Ancient Athens practiced democratic government, but during the Middle Ages and the Renaissance, rule by hereditary aristocrats eclipsed democracy. It was not until the seventeenth century that democratic political theory began to gain ascendance. Moreover, it was not until the creation of the United States after the revolutionary war against England that democratic institutions found a permanent home and subsequently began to spread to other nations. Though many countries do not have democratic governments today, political leaders—the most despotic, as well as the most humane—typically enunciate democracy as an ideal. Yet, the nature of this ideal continues to provoke controversy.

People who agree that democracy is the best system of government often disagree sharply about what makes democracy good. Some hold that people fulfill their highest capacities as human beings through active participation in a political community and that this fulfillment is intrinsically good. Some hold that the value of democracy derives from a set of basic rights that can only be respected through democratic institutions. Still others see the instrumental value of democracy in terms of a broader view of justice, such as John Rawls's principles of justice or utilitarian maximization of preference satisfaction. Either they believe that democracy increases the probability of just legislation, or, more pessimistically, they believe that democracy reduces the probability of tyrannical legislation.

Not surprisingly, advocates of democracy also disagree about what institutions should be established and what principles these institutions should observe. The term *democracy* brings to mind government by the people, government accountability to the people, individual liberty, and equality. But each of the latter concepts is open to diverse interpretations. Does government by the people require that adult citizens enact legislation in popular assemblies or only that citizens elect representatives to do this work on their behalf? Is a government accountable to the people if it provides regular opportunities for the electorate to "throw the scoundrels out of office" or only if it obtains the consent of every adult citizen? Are the members of a society free when they obey laws over which they have some control or only when a constitutional document specifies a range of conduct that is protected from government interference? Are people equal before the law if each of their ballots counts equally or only if each has the same power to influence the outcome of the election? These are among the core questions that democrats debate, and the answers to these questions define a spectrum of democratic positions ranging from elitist to populist conceptions.

An elitist view of democracy regards society as divided between, on the one hand, a small group of concerned and suitably educated citizens who take an active part in public affairs and, on the other hand, the electorate as a whole, which tends to be apathetic in regard to public issues and to defer to leadership. According to this theory, the function of elections is neither to ensure that constituencies will be represented as they want nor to secure justice. It is to oblige elites to compete for power. As political parties must court at least a plurality of the electorate in order to win elections, they stake out positions well away from radical and reactionary extremes. In this way, injustice is thought to be minimized. Though this type of democratic theory is fully compatible with implementation of a wide variety of personal and civil rights, it is not a theory that sees any point in programs designed to enhance the power of the people, such as limitations on personal contributions to election campaigns or access to the media for unorthodox viewpoints. For elitist democratic theory views the people with some suspicion.

Whereas elitist democrats always defend a system of representation, populists may (but need not) favor direct democratic enactment of legislation. Populists who are sympathetic to the ideal of rule by consensus, as opposed to majority rule, find such direct democratic mechanisms as town assemblies particularly attractive; populists who see rule by consensus as impractical often support greater use of referendums. But whichever method of setting public policy is preferred, populism supports maximizing citizen participation in politics. Whether the people are seen as a repository of collective wisdom regarding the social weal or merely as independent individuals entitled to affiliate themselves with interest groups in order to promote their self-interest, widespread engagement in public life is to be fostered. Precisely because populists are committed to maximum political participation, they may be skeptical of constitutional rights that are shielded from simple majoritarian control. These rights may be condemned as antidemocratic. Yet, populists emphasize material as well as procedural equality, since inequality impedes political participation.

The chapters in this part focus on specific dimensions of these problems. Both of the positions presented in these chapters can be located toward the populist end of the elitist-populist spectrum. Both advocate drawing the wider public into the political sphere. However, both raise questions about the consequences of doing so. Cornelius Murphy asks whether our society should place much greater faith in the people and hold regular constitutional conventions. William Nelson addresses the question whether a commitment to popular sovereignty is compatible with enshrining a set of rights in a constitution that exempts them from the ordinary political process.

In "Constitutional Revision," Murphy contends that, unlike other political thinkers of their age, the framers of the Constitution acted on the assumption that the people possessed a sovereign constituent power. "We the people of the United States . . . ," the Constitution begins. The people would confer legitimacy on the Constitution proposed by the Philadelphia convention by ratifying it. Still, it was understood that the people would retain the right to change the basic law. Of all the rights of which people cannot divest their posterity, the most important was that of determining their political destiny. Yet, today, fears of confrontation and chaos have generated strong opposition to the convening of a second constitutional convention. And echoes of an ancient and undemocratic theory of political authority that holds that society can only survive through obeisance to a fundamental law that is interpreted by the wise have redoubled this opposition. Murphy maintains that the practice of periodic constitutional conventions should be embraced in order to grant the people their rightful opportunity to cultivate a capacity for self-government through deliberation on the conditions of social life.

Nelson, in "Constitutional Limits on Majoritarian Democracy," points out that a number of legal and political theorists have recently expressed their concern about the apparent conflict between the Bill of Rights and the provisions for democracy in the U.S. Constitution. Some of these commentators have proceeded to offer a democratic interpretation of the Bill of Rights. They have claimed, in particular, that democracy implies freedom of speech and equality before the law. Nelson finds these arguments unconvincing. In their place, he proposes an instrumentalist justification of both democracy and constitutional rights based on a contractarian conception of morality. Assuming that we have good reason to establish a procedure for enacting legislation, Nelson argues that a system of representative democracy constrained by a Bill of Rights is best. According to Nelson, democracy and rights are not competing values. Together, they provide the best answer to the question of how legislative decisions should be made. Nelson develops his thesis with reference to the rights to free speech and equal protection.

THREE

Constitutional Revision

CORNELIUS F. MURPHY, JR.

In recent years, there have been various efforts to compel the Congress of the United States to call a convention for proposing amendments to the Constitution. Although hundreds of petitions have been submitted by states, no conventions have been called because proper applications from the required two-thirds of the states have not been received. Nevertheless, the possibility of sufficient applications being made on certain subjects, such as a balanced budget amendment, cannot be discounted. The prospect raises deep concern among constitutional scholars. They fear that neither the Congress nor the proposing state legislatures are empowered to define and enforce limits upon the range of issues that delegates to such a convention would be free to consider.

Such a convention could set its own agenda. As the range of issues escalates, the dangers of confrontation over sensitive policies could cause substantial public discord. A runaway convention could subject the entire constitutional system to plenary revision. Such a prospect is viewed as a potential calamity.[1]

Whether a convention called at the behest of the states can be limited is a question of constitutional law for which there is no definitive answer.[2] The controversy, however, also raises questions of political theory that have generally been ignored. The dangers implicit in a plenary convention cannot be discounted. Yet they do not address the question whether the people of the United States are entitled to examine the Constitution of 1787 and determine whether they wish to reaffirm or modify the basic law under which they must live for the foreseeable future. The possibility of a second constitutional convention raises difficult problems of political judgment. It also engages theoretical concerns of ultimate political authority.

I shall explore these questions by explaining how the drafting and ratification of the Federal Constitution was the act of a sovereign people who, in establishing their government, did not relinquish their ultimate authority to revise their fundamental law. I shall also address some of the major theoretical arguments against constitutional revision.

THE GENERAL RIGHT OF REVISION

In the European tradition reflections upon the nature of sovereignty were bound up with the problem of how to constitute a new government. Political philosophers were able to imagine the contractual foundations of organized life and the consensual aspects of government. Some could identify the people as the legitimate possessors of sovereign political authority. Yet they had no idea of the people as a constituent power. U.S. political theory and practice are, in this respect, distinctive. The Constitutional Convention, which convened in Philadelphia in the summer of 1787, was the means by which the people exercised their sovereign power:

> The Constitutional convention in theory embodied the sovereignty of the people. The people chose it for a specific purpose, not to govern, but to set up institutions of government. The convention, acting as the sovereign people, proceeded to draft a constitution and a declaration of rights. Certain "natural" or "inalienable" rights of the citizen were thus laid down at the same time as the powers of government. It was the constitution that created the powers of government, defined their scope, gave them legality, and balanced them one against another. The constitution was written and comprised in a single document. The constitution and accompanying declaration, drafted by the convention, must, in the developed theory, be ratified by the people. The convention thereupon disbanded and disappeared, lest its members have a vested interest in the offices they created. The constituent power went into abeyance, leaving the work of government to the authorities now constituted. The people, having exercised sovereignty, now came under government. Having made law, they came under law. They put themselves voluntarily under restraint. At the same time, they put restraint upon government. All government was limited government; all public authority must keep within the bounds of the constitution and of the declared rights. There were two levels of law, a higher law or constitution that only the people could make or amend, through constitutional conventions or bodies similarly empowered; and a statutory law, to be made and unmade, within the assigned limits, by legislators to whom the constitution gave this function.[3]

The drafting and ratification of the U.S. Constitution was the act of a community, rather than the expression of separate individuals seeking to escape a state of nature. There was not an identity of people and government. The people consented to be governed, but they did not make an absolute transfer of their power of self-governance. The powers of political institutions were defined and limited. The people were principals, the branches of government, agents.

The framers feared that the legislature might abuse its authority. The potentials for abuse were to be checked by the vigilance of an independent judiciary. According to Hamilton, if courts declare legislation void because contrary to the Constitution, they would not be asserting a dominion over the legislature. The judges would be acting on behalf of the people whose will is superior to both.

Hamilton's defense of judicial review in *The Federalist* No. 78 is a familiar part of constitutional literature. What is less well known is that in the same essay Hamilton recognizes that the people retain an ultimate authority to revise the Constitution. In rejecting the claim that legislation reflecting the desires of a majority is in accord with the people's will, he wrote

> . . . Though I trust that the friends of the proposed constitution will never concur with its enemies in questioning that *fundamental principle of republican government, which admits the right of the people to alter or abolish the established Constitution whenever they find it inconsistent with their happiness,* yet it is not to be inferred on this principle, that the representatives of the people, whenever a momentary inclination happens to lay hold of a majority of their constituents, incompatible with the provisions in the existing Constitution, would on that account be justifiable in a violation of those provisions; or that the courts would be under a greater obligation to connive at infractions of this shape than when they had proceeded wholly from the cabals of the representative body. *Until the people have, by some solemn and authoritative act, annulled or changed the established form,* it is binding upon themselves collectively, as well as individually; and no presumption or even knowledge of their sentiments can warrant their representatives in a departure from it, prior to such act.[4]

Hamilton recognized the right of the people to revise the Constitution when it is no longer consistent with their happiness. For Jefferson, the question was whether the dead may bind the living. A generation may bind itself as long as a majority of its citizens remain alive, but when a new majority takes its place, it holds all the rights and powers of its predecessors. The new generation can change the laws and institutions to suit themselves. The earth belongs in usufruct to the living, and the most important right of which citizens cannot divest their posterity is that of determining its own political destiny. The power of self-government should remain forever with the whole people.[5]

Jefferson's idea of the perpetual character of the people's right of self-governance was challenged by the argument that the legislative authority can never revert to the people as long as the government lasts. Noah Webster contended that all the authority of the state was necessarily vested in elected representatives; the right of election was the only constitutive act that the people could, with propriety, exercise.[6] The debate over the power of the people to change their constitution was aggravated by the alarm created by the French Revolution and its proclamation of the Rights of Man.

In 1789, on the anniversary of the English Revolution of 1688, Dr. Richard Price delivered a sermon in London in which he asserted that three rights were derived from the Glorious Revolution: the right of the people to choose their own government, to remove rulers for misconduct, and to form a government for themselves. The sermon provoked a rejoinder from Edmund Burke. Burke argued that the people of England had disclaimed such rights because, by parliamentary declaration to William and Mary, they had made submission of themselves, their heirs and posterity, to the end of time.[7] Burke's views, which were expressed in his *Reflections on the French Revolution,* were attacked by Thomas Paine.

In "The Rights of Man," Paine, like Jefferson, insisted that every generation must be free to act for itself. "The presumption of governing beyond the grave," Paine observed, "was the most ridiculous and insolent of all tyrannies."[8] As the power to bind a future generation is not a human right, it could not be the right of Parliament. Burke believed that a constitution cannot be made by a deliberative act but that it grows organically, in the history of a nation. But, for Paine, such an understanding obscured the sources of sovereignty. Governments must arise either *out of* or *over* the people. The constitution of a country is not the act of its government, but of the people who constitute a government. And, in matters of constitutional concern, every age must be free to determine its form of government.

The principle that the people retain the power of constitutional sovereignty was an integral part of the political experience of the New World. But there were serious differences over when and how the power was to be exercised. Madison objected to Jefferson's proposal for the calling of future conventions to correct breaches of an existing constitution. Madison thought it unwise to make provision for recurrence to the people as a means of keeping the departments of government within their constitutional limits. Such a procedure would deprive government of the veneration that is a condition of its stability. Frequent references of constitutional questions to the whole of society, even if done at fixed periods, would endanger tranquility, provoke factions, and set the various branches of government against each other. Passion, rather than reason, would sit in judgment.[9]

Madison insisted that civil society could not subsist without tacit or implied consent to established government. He was not, however, opposed *in principle* to constitutional revision. Nor did he give the established Constitution idolatrous reverence. What he resisted was the use of conventions to enforce the Constitution or subject it to constant change. Madison recognized that the document was subject to principled alterations, upon "great and extraordinary occasions," to meet the demands for conditions that would encourage growth and self-respect. Indeed, without such sensitivity to the needs of successive generations the existing Constitution becomes itself an "act of force and not of right."[10]

In the minds of the Founding Fathers the possibility of constitutional revision was not to be restricted to catastrophic occasions of potential rebellion. Those who exercise authority within the constitutional system may perform admirably, but the proper execution of their trust was not the primary reason for assuming the possibility of fundamental change. The understanding of the framers was that the proposed Constitution would gain its legitimacy from the sovereignty of the people and that the people retained the right to change their basic law, at some future time, if it was their desire. This is clear from a perusal of *The Federalist*, the writings of Jefferson, and "The Rights of Man" of Thomas Paine. Even Madison accepted the principle of constitutional revision although he would substantially limit its occasions.

Under British rule, the colonists lacked a public realm in which they could affirm a supreme and exclusive political authority. The revolution, in bringing freedom to the American people, provided them with an opportunity to exercise the power of self-government. The right of the people was not limited to the election of representatives to established offices. As subjects became rulers they established a government and created a new political society.

The Constitution of 1787 was a great achievement, but if it were immutable, its permanence would deprive the people of their right of participation in establishing the conditions of a life in common. For Jefferson, the Republic would be endangered if the Constitution was understood as reflecting the authority of the people without giving them positive future opportunities to express those principles of self-government.

The convening of a second constitutional convention during this bicentennial period would create the opportunity for the people to participate in public life in the manner envisioned by the Founding Fathers. Yet resistance to the idea of a plenary convention is intense. As we have noted, resistance is based upon fears of confrontation and chaos.[11] It is also based upon certain attitudes toward the nature of public life that have their roots in ancient political thought.

JUDICIAL REVIEW UNDER THE SOVEREIGNTY OF THE PEOPLE

For the Greeks, man was understood to be a creature belonging to two orders of existence. Like other animals, he was subject to the mere necessity of living together for purposes of survival. As a citizen, he led a second life, a *bios politikos*. In the polis, individuals came together as equals to deliberate and act in a world common to all. But the ancient philosophers realized that the rule of the many, *polyarkhia*, brings confusion. When each is entitled to participate in public affairs the outcome is uncertain and unpredictable. Chaos could be avoided and stability secured if, in the public realm, action was replaced by thought.

For Plato, the uncertainties and perplexities of political life could be resolved by treating them as though they were solvable problems of cognition. A philosopher-king would possess an image of how human affairs should be arranged. Living among men, he would possess standards of right and justice that could be invoked to measure and rule the multiplicity of human acts. The principles discovered by the philosopher-king would possess an objective certainty similar to the guidance that the idea of the bench or table gives to the carpenter.[12]

The analogy of fabrication requires a division between making and doing. It was a useful justification for established political authority. Those who know should rule and command; all others should obey and carry out the original plan of government. The idea of a possible human community is thought of as a fundamental law that, while subject to interpretation by the wise, need only be obeyed by the multitude in order for the good polis to be realized. The division between those who know and those who obey leads to the banishment of the citizen from the public realm. For it implicitly denies the capacity of the ordinary person to intelligently contribute to the resolution of common problems.

This consequence was reinforced by the experience of authority in the life of ancient Rome. Through the displacement of action by thought, the foundations of the body politic were given a permanence and protection from the discord that occurs when a multiplicity of persons seek to resolve public issues. The statesmen who found the *politeia* on ideas have begun something of lasting importance that must be preserved. The foundations are sacred. Once established, they bind the future. In the ongoing life of society those who possess authority augment the foundations received from their ancestors. According to Cicero, power resides in the people, but authority resides in the Senate.[13] The will of the people is subject to mistakes and needs correction by a council of Elders who possess the wisdom to understand the ongoing traditions. Those who exercise authority do not have power. But they need not command, as they are reminding the public of the deeds of the past and binding them to their origins. These traditional ideas on the formation and preservation of the polis are of great importance to the problem of constitutional change. There is a striking similarity between these ancient ideas and contemporary opinion on the permanence of the Constitution.

The prevailing view is that the original document is immune from revision except through the action of those qualified to interpret the Constitution in a manner consistent with the intentions of the Founding Fathers. Some interpretative authority is assumed by the Congress and the president, but it is the Supreme Court that is assumed to be the institutional embodiment of an enduring Constitution. It is also taken for granted that any attempt by the people of the present generation to reexamine the basic law would result in that chaos that arises whenever a multitude acts within the public arena. The public must be excluded from the constitutional domain. If they should exercise a sovereign authority the personal liberties enshrined in the Bill of Rights could be placed in jeopardy. A general convention to review the Constitution could endanger all that had been accomplished from the beginning.

The Supreme Court has attained a position in the U.S. polis similar to that of the ancient Roman Senate. Through the power of judicial review, the Court has become the source of ultimate constitutional authority. Although its decisions are subject to change by specific amendment, any general review of the Constitution by a body purporting to reflect a higher authority would imperil the Court's role as the guardian of liberty and fundamental law. This, in brief, is the essence of the most compelling arguments against public interference with the constitutional system. Its value depends upon the position of an independent judiciary within a democratic republic.

In *The Federalist* No. 78, Hamilton described the judiciary as an intermediary institution responsible for protecting the people from the transgressions of their representatives. Acting on behalf of the people, the courts would uphold their will as embodied in the Constitution.[14] This justification, while of continuing importance, is no longer persuasive. We know much more about the discretionary power of judges than did our ancestors. We understand that in complex constitutional litigation judgment must be made amid competing values, and the choices are not predetermined by text or precedent. Even the most conscientious interpretation is more the personal act of the judge than the discovery of a common will. Nevertheless, an independent judiciary is indispensable to the protection of personal liberty; it ensures the overall harmony of a federal system of constitutional government.

The high purposes served by judicial review require submission to the interpretations of the Constitution that result from the exercise of that power. Obedience is required even though the power is exercised by a branch of government that is insulated from the normal processes of political accountability. Under the pressure of events, the legislative and the executive branches, as well as state governments, reinterpret the powers granted them by the Constitution. There must be an authoritative body that can resolve doubts over the various renditions, and the judiciary must protect constitutional liberties and remind the people of their commitments to human rights.[15] To understand the limits of this authority, however, it is important to draw a crucial distinction: *Judicial review is indispensable, but the results of its exercise are not immutable.*

The Supreme Court may sit as a continuous constitutional convention, but neither logic, nor political theory, confers permanence upon its deliberations. If the process of judicial review and interpretation were subject to *constant* review, the value of the Court to the nation would be compromised. At some point, however, judicial revision must be reconciled with the principles of democratic self-government. Constitutional interpretation by the judiciary results in a significant revision of the original document. If the judicially developed Constitution was *never* ratified by the people, the claim that the justices serve as guardians of their will would lose its legitimacy. The Constitution would then be a higher law imposed upon the people rather than an expression of their own aspirations.

If the Constitution developed through adjudication were forever immune from review and revision, the courts would occupy a position in the U.S. polity that would be incompatible with the principles of sovereignty upon which the Republic was founded. The people of the United States have not given up to the judiciary their supreme political power. Nor is the Supreme Court the equivalent of either Hobbes's *Leviathan* or Locke's sovereign legislature. Such was not the theory of republican government that inspired the Constitution. The founders never assumed that the Constitution or the Court had authority to bind future generations. Hamilton justified judicial review, but he made it clear that the people retain an ultimate authority to determine what shall be the basic law under which they shall live. Reenactment of the Constitution by the whole people is more compatible with the theory of democratic government than that of perpetual revision by a nonaccountable independent judiciary.

Through the opinions of the justices, the Supreme Court is engaged in a continuous colloquy with the people over the nature and purposes of our law. The justices explain their interpretations and try to persuade the people to accept them.[16] Public acquiescence in the decisions of the Court is based upon various motives, from habitual accommodation to *de facto* power, to a vague reverence for the rule of law. If the institution of judicial review is to be compatible with democracy, the response of citizens to the interpretation of their law must, at some point in U.S. history, shift from sheer acceptance to actual assent. If there is to be a positive allegiance to a *lex supra legis*, the society as a whole should have an opportunity to affirm that attachment.

It may be objected that this reasoning does not sufficiently take into account the deeper purposes of judicial review. A primary objective of U.S. constitutional tradition is to secure personal rights against the power of the community as well as that of the state. If the community, through a constitutional convention, were empowered to review judicial interpretations of the Bill of Rights, these paramount purposes of constitutional law would be compromised.

This argument is similar to the earlier contention that the public should be disqualified from participating in political affairs. Because they lack knowledge of the ideas that should guide the development of fundamental law, chaos would ensue if they meddled in affairs that are better left to the judgment of the wise. The present form of the argument reflects convictions concerning the inherent dignity of the individual person and the belief that his or her entitlements are antecedent to the Constitution. These rights, as embodied in the Bill of Rights, are under the protection of the courts and should be forever immune from collective evaluation. The sovereignty of the people may be recognized, but with the proviso that each individual retains an autonomy that is to be perpetually protected from public scrutiny.

Such an argument is morally attractive but it has several serious flaws. In the first place, it has no basis in historical experience. The drafting and ratification of the Constitution of 1787 were the acts of a concrete political community. It was not the implementation of an antecedent moral agreement preserving individual rights.[17] The Bill of Rights was adopted to protect individual rights from the encroachments of legislative majorities and other abuses of governmental power, but it did not eliminate the reserved sovereign power of the people that is at the foundation of the American Republic.

Constitutionalism involves the right to govern. It is an entitlement of the whole society. It does not reside in individuals considered in isolation. This does not mean that ultimate authority resides in a sociological mass or, in Hobbes's parlance, a "disunited multitude." Constitutional revision, if it were to occur, would be the act of a people as a political society. It would be a public act rather than an expression of mass opinion.

A constitutional convention is a deliberative assembly: a place where elected delegates gather to discuss and reflect upon matters of fundamental importance to the whole society. At such a gathering persons would come to manifest their abilities as citizens to participate in the power of self-governance. They would debate and reason together over matters at issue, always acting with the knowledge that whatever the convention should decide is subject to further debate and ratification or rejection by the people.

Such deliberations would take place within the framework of basic political ideals that precede, transcend, and guide all constitutional developments. The principles of liberty, equality, dignity, and procedural fairness would inhere in the agenda.[18] These values act as constraints upon all. They are authoritative elements of the nation's deepest commitments and reflect the most important dimensions of U.S. conscience and tradition. Of course, some constitutional questions are controversial. Efforts would be made to change, as well as to add to, some interpretative decisions. But such demands are unavoidable. They are part of the risks and uncertainties that are part of any public assembly. If a general-national convention were called, there would be legitimate cause for concern whether reason would prevail. But a belief that the convention would be rent with passion is a platonic extravagance. As a form of absolute opposition, it reveals a desire to exclude citizens from public life that is a persistent theme in the history of political philosophy.

THE NEED FOR CONSTITUTIONAL REVISION

In the political theories of the Founding Fathers the people were considered to be the constituent authority. The idea that ultimate political power resides in the general population was not a novel insight. It had already been recognized in the thought of Locke. What was unique was the assertion that popular sovereignty was not *permanently* transferred to the established institutions of government. Sovereignty was not fully expressed by the adoption of the document submitted to the people for ratification. The Constitution of 1787 was to last, but it was not to be of unalterable duration. The people reserved the right to revise the fundamental law when it was no longer consistent with their happiness.

These principles of democratic self-government are compromised in prevailing theory and practice. The authority to propose specific amendments to the existing document is conceded, but the principles of political authority upon which the Republic rests are implicitly denied. The chairman of the Commission on the Bicentennial of the Constitution, former Chief Justice Warren Burger, calls upon the people to view the Constitution as the embodiment of "the principles constituting us as a self-governing people dedicated to the rule of Law." Reverence for the original document is taken to be the only means by which liberty can be preserved. It is assumed that a nation of such disparate groups and interests can only be united through unreflective submission to a fundamental law over which the people have no authority.

In the minds of the commissioners, fidelity to the rule of law is equivalent to obedience to interpretations of the Supreme Court. One may concede that obedience to existing precept is essential to ordered liberty. But if any fundmental law is maintained indefinitely by established institutions, it is no longer the expression of a free people. Such a regime of imposed rules becomes an act of power rather than of justice.

Submissional authority depends upon a passive population. It is appropriate to a primitive society. In an advanced democracy, the legitimacy of the basic law depends upon the consent of those whom it governs.[19] In the eighteenth century, the consent of the governed was expressed at the beginning of our constitutional experience; in this bicentennial period we must forge a constitutional system that will be adequate to our needs in the centuries to come. A higher level of participatory assent by all citizens will be required. If our constitutional law is to ensure our future happiness, active concurrence of the governed is necessary to ensure that the Constitution embodies the values and principles for which we, as a people, are prepared to stand.

If justice is the realization of the public's aspirations through law, it can be enjoyed when social aspirations are widely shared and when all have opportunities to contribute to the affirmation of these public values.[20] A second constitutional convention would provide such an opportunity. It would make possible the exercise of *public* liberty: the freedom "to remember what we have learned, to consider where we should go."[21] Prevailing opinion, however, resists these opportunities. It understands liberty as freedom from community rather than as a realization of freedom through the creation of a common vision. As it exaggerates the division between private judgment and public order, it assumes that we cannot have a general recognition of either a common morality or a common good. Deeply suspicious of the public, it wants a fundamental law shaped by platonic guardians. This was not the system envisioned by the Founding Fathers. Nor is it a theory of government that can be reconciled with democracy.

CONCLUSION

The Constitution of 1787 established a system of government that, by the standards of the eighteenth century, was a remarkable achievement. It provided for the securing of liberty, the separation of powers, and a balanced distribution of national and local authority. Its adequacy to the needs of present or future generations is questionable. The document does not, of itself, delineate the boundaries between personal freedom and social order, nor has the Supreme Court resolved these issues in a decisive manner. Nor is the original document hospitable to human entitlements that are of contemporary importance. Because the original Bill of Rights seeks to secure civil and political liberties, it is not amenable to the development of these economic, social, and cultural entitlements that are an integral part of the Universal Declaration of Human Rights.[22]

There are also profound problems of structure. The delegates to the Philadelphia convention were preoccupied with the weaknesses of central authority. They made a great effort to persuade the states to relinquish enough of their sovereignty to make a union. The sufficiency of the reserved state power to the exigencies of subnational authority was never in doubt. No one questioned the capacity of the thirteen states to properly discharge their retained competences. Now, with fifty states spread across the vast continent and beyond, such assumptions are no longer warranted. It is time for the existing states to be combined into new regional units of government with a geographical range adequate to the proper discharge of their modern responsibilities.[23]

There are structural weaknesses at the national level of government as well. For the Founding Fathers, the separation of the executive from the legislative branch was of paramount importance. The division would allow each to prevent the other from acting arbitrarily. However, the extent to which the separation would paralyze the process of creating national policy was not anticipated. Fractionation of power makes it extremely difficult to determine who is accountable for either domestic prosperity or the management of foreign affairs.[24]

These are but a part of the fundamental problems that pervade all levels of government. When left unresolved, they block those aspirations for living well that Aristotle placed at the heart of political life. To assume that they can be corrected within the inherited constitutional structure is to ignore the magnitude of the changes that the United States has experienced in the more than two hundred years of its national existence. Nor can reform be achieved by piecemeal amendment. Problems of structure and aspirations are deeply interrelated and must be addressed in their entirety.

All of the problems of constitutional reform must be subject to careful study and research. But it is unreasonable to assume that substantial change will be instituted by those departments of government that benefit from the imperfections of the existing system. At some point, these basic concerns must be discussed and decided upon by the people as a whole. The circumstances under which that will occur cannot be known in advance. For the present, it suffices to understand that the Constitution of 1787 was the act of a sovereign people whose authority was not expended in the acceptance of that document. It remains as a continuous legacy that we, the People, are entitled to revive to ensure the survival and prosperity of the Republic.

NOTES

1. A forceful expression of this alarm may be found in the writings of Professor Charles Black. See, for example, "Amending the Constitution," 82 *Yale L. J.* 189 (1972); "The Proposed Amendment of Article V: A Threatened Disaster," 72 *Yale L. J.* 957 (1963). Similar apprehensions have been expressed by Professor Gerald Gunther. See his statement before the Committee on Ways and Means of the California State Assembly, February 15, 1979. His view and those of others are summarized in the *National Law Journal,* March 5, 1979, p. 1.

2. Compare Dellinger, "The Recurring Question of the Limited Constitutional Convention," 88 *Yale L. J.* 1623 (1979), with Van Alstyne, "The Limited Constitutional Convention, the Recurring Answer," *Duke L. J.* 985 (1979). See also, Tribe, "Comment," 97 *Harvard L. Rev.* 433 (1983). A special Constitutional Convention Study Committee of the American Bar Association concluded that Article V of the Constitution permits both limited and general conventions; see ABA Special Constitutional Convention Study Committee, *Amendment of the Constitution by the Convention Method Under Article V* (n.d.).

3. R. R. Palmer, "The People As Constituent Power," in *The Role of Ideology in the American Revolution,* J. R. Howe, Jr., ed. (New York: Holt, Rinehart, & Winston, 1970), p. 73. See also R. R. Palmer, *The Age of the Democratic Revolution,* (Princeton, N.J.: Princeton Univ. Press, 1959), p. 214. The Convention was not chosen to establish a constitution but to amend the Articles of Confederation.

4. *The Federalist* No. 78. (Italics added.)

5. A summary of Jefferson's views can be found in A. Koch, *Jefferson and Madison* (New York: Oxford Univ. Press, 1964), ch. 4. In a letter to John Cartwright, dated June 5, 1824, Jefferson affirmed the view that all just power is derived from the people and cannot be changed without their authority: "A generation may bind itself as long as its majority continues in life; when that has disappeared another majority is in its place which holds all the rights and powers their predecessors once held and may change their laws and institutions to suit themselves. Nothing then is unchangeable but the inherent and unalienable rights of man. . . ."

In a letter to Thomas Earle, written from Monticello on September 24, 1823, Jefferson referred to the convenience of being subject to the laws of predecessors on a theory of implied consent, until positively repealed by an existing majority. "But," he went on, "this does not lessen the right of that majority to repeal whenever a change of circumstances or of will calls for it. Habit alone confounds what is civil practice with natural right."

6. Noah Webster "On Government," in *A Collection of Essays and Fugitive Writings* (Delmare, N.Y.: Scholar's Facsimiles, 1977).

7. Edmund Burke, *Reflections on the Revolution in France* (London: Oxford Univ. Press, 1950).

8. Thomas Paine, "The Rights of Man," Part 1, in *Common Sense and Other Political Writings*, Nelson F. Adkins, ed. (Indianapolis, Ind.: Bobbs-Merrill, 1953).

9. Madison was opposed to *frequent* referral of constitutional questions to the whole society. The problems connected with such a process are reviewed in *The Federalist*, Nos. 49–50. There is some dispute whether Madison or Hamilton was the author of those papers. Madison's position is, however, well documented. See A. Koch, *Jefferson and Madison*, ch. 4. Madison opposed Jefferson's idea that each generation had a right to choose its own constitution and laws. Such an approach was unrealistic—particularly in light of Jefferson's belief that a generation could be computed in short intervals. With a mechanical limit for the duration of a constitutional system, there would be problems of an interregnum, and government lacking a sense of tradition would lose the respect of its citizens. Periodic revision would agitate the public mind "more frequently and violently than might be expedient."

10. See Koch, *op. cit.* for the view that Madison believed in principled revisions at some future time. Justice Goldberg, writing of the dangers of a "runaway convention," cites Madison as one who recognized the perils inherent in a second constitutional convention in Goldberg, "The Proposed Constitutional Convention," 11 *Hastings Con. L. Q.* 1 (1983). The authority is a letter from Madison to George Lee Tuberville, dated November 2, 1788, in which Madison expressed his objections to a proposal made by New York for a second general convention. Such an assembly, he believed, could not be conducted peaceably or produce results that would promote the general good. It is clear from the text, however, that Madison's basic fear was that a convention so close upon the first would have destabilizing consequences both at home and abroad. *The Papers of James Madison*, vol. 1, 330, R. A. Rutland and C. F. Hobson, eds. (Charlottesville: Univ. Press of Virginia, 1977). In 1829 Madison was prevailed upon to be a delegate to a convention to revise the Constitution of Virginia (M. Myers, *Sources of the Political Thought of James Madison* [Indianapolis, Ind.: Bobbs-Merrill, 1973], ch. 39).

11. See the authorities cited *supra*, note 1.

12. Plato, *The Republic*. H. Arendt, "What is Authority?" in *Between Past and Future* (New York: Viking Press, 1961), ch. 3; *The Human Condition* (Garden City, N.Y.: Doubleday, 1958), ch. 5. According to Hegel, the ancient ideal of individual identification with public affairs could not be achieved under the conditions of modern life. Concern for the polis is the responsibility of state representatives, especially civil servants (G.W.F. Hegel, *Philosophy of Right*, T. M. Knox, trans. [London: Oxford Univ. Press, 1952], §§ 300–310; C. Taylor, *Hegel* [New York: Cambridge Univ. Press, 1975], ch. 16). Mill accepted the extension of the franchise because no arrangement of the suffrage could be permanently successful if any class or person was excluded. He would, however, qualify the right to vote by minimal educational requirements and give additional voting power to those who had superior mental capacities (John Stuart Mill, "Considerations on Representative Government" in *Essays on Politics and Society*, J. M. Robson, ed. [Toronto: Univ. of Toronto Press, 1977], ch. 8). The views of James Fennimore Cooper should also be considered, for he was antagonistic toward Jacksonian democracy. See his *The American Democrat* (New York: Knopf, 1931).

13. Cited in H. Arendt, *Between Past and Future*, ch. 5. See also ch. 3.

14. The justification developed by the judicial branch itself begins with Chief Justice Marshall's opinion in *Marbury v. Madison* 1 Cr. 137 (1803). See the discussion in E. S. Corwin, *The Doctrine of Judicial Review* (Gloucester, Mass.: P. Smith, 1963).

15. M. J. Perry, *The Constitution, The Courts, and Human Rights* (New Haven, Conn.: Yale Univ. Press, 1982); R. Dworkin, *Taking Rights Seriously* (Cambridge, Mass.: Harvard Univ. Press, 1978).

16. E. Rostow, *The Sovereign Prerogative: The Supreme Court and The Quest for Law* (New Haven, Conn.: Yale Univ. Press, 1962).

17. The attempts to secure individual rights by reference to an antecedent hypothetical contract have become an important aspect of modern legal and political philosophy. See J. Rawls, *A Theory of Justice* (Cambridge, Mass.: Harvard Univ. Press, 1971). For a general discussion of contractarian philosophy see B. Ackerman, *Social Justice in the Liberal State* (New Haven, Conn.: Yale Univ. Press, 1981), pp. 327–348. For a discussion of the relationship between individual rights and the sovereignty of the people see L. Henkin, "Rights: American and Human," 79 *Col. L. Rev.* 405 (1979).

18. Compare Tribe, "Comment," 97 *Harvard L. Rev.* 433 (1983).

19. Compare E. Cahn, *The Sense of Injustice* (Bloomington: Univ. of Indiana Press, 1949), ch. 4. The late Professor Edmund Cahn traces the evolution of the tension between power and justice. At a primitive stage of government, authority is maintained by force. Then, what Cahn calls submissional power appears; the population is passive. At a further stage, when lawmakers possess a constitutional competence, power becomes consensual because it is exercised with the consent of the governed. A higher level, the assensual, engages the active concurrence of the governed, who have assumed a participatory role as an enlightened electorate. "At the assensual level, major decisions concerning positive law express the considered opinion of the citizenry, the values and standards for which it is willing to answer" (p. 49).

Professor Cahn meant to use the evolutionary theory to illustrate the influence of freedom of thought and opinion upon representative government. In my judgment, the assensual thesis is equally applicable to the proposition that the people, at some point in the history of the nation, are entitled to express their convictions concerning constitutional principles.

20. C. Morris, *The Justification of the Law* (Philadelphia: Univ. of Pennsylvania Press, 1971).

21. *Op. cit.*, p. 76. In the same passage Professor Morris remarks, "Adequate respect for the humanity of man will be only theoretical, however, unless and until society consists of an all inclusive public capable of maturing widely shared values and served by men capable of discovering and implementing the public's aspirations."

22. See *San Antonio Independent School Dist. v. Rodriguez*, 411 U.S. 1 (1973), as an example of no right to a public education. But see *Plyer v. Doe*, 457 U.S. 202 (1982), in which the Supreme Court, in a 5 to 4 decision, upheld the rights of children of undocumented aliens to attend public schools. On welfare rights see *Dandridge v. Williams*, 397 U.S. 471 (1970). The conflicting academic views on the constitutional status of welfare rights are illustrated by Michelman, "Welfare Rights in a Constitutional Democracy," *Washington Univ. L. Q.* 659 (1979) and Bork, "The Impossibility of Finding Welfare Rights in the Constitution," *Washington Univ. L. Q.* 695 (1979). Franklin D. Roosevelt tried, unsuccessfully, to promote an Economic Bill of Rights. In his State of the Union message of January 11, 1944, he said:

This Republic had its beginning, and grew to its present strength, under the protection of certain inalienable political rights—among them the right of free speech, free press, free worship, trial by jury, freedom from unreasonable searches and seizures. They are our rights to life and liberty.

As our Nation has grown in size and stature, however—as our industrial economy expanded—these political rights proved inadequate to assure us equality in the pursuit of happiness.

We have come to a clear realization of the fact that true individual freedom cannot exist without economic security and independence. "Necessitous men are not freemen." People who are hungry and out of a job are the stuff of which dictatorships are made.

In our day these economic truths have become accepted as self-evident. We have accepted so to speak, a Second Bill of Rights under which a new basis of security and prosperity can be established for all—regardless of station, race, or creed. Among these are:

The right to a useful and remunerative job in the industries, or shops or farms or mines of the Nation;

The right to earn enough to provide adequate food and clothing and recreation;

The right of every farmer to raise and sell his products at a return which will give him and his family a decent living;

The right of every businessman, large and small, to trade in an atmosphere of freedom from unfair competition and domination by monopolies at home or abroad;

The right of every family to a decent home;

The right to adequate medical care and the opportunity to achieve and enjoy good health;

The right to adequate protection from the economic fears of old age, sickness, accident, and unemployment;

The right to a good education.

All of these rights spell security. And after this war is won, we must be prepared to move forward, in the implementation of these rights, to new goals of human happiness and well-being.

America's own rightful place in the world depends in large part upon how fully these and similar rights have been carried into practice for our citizens. For unless there is security here at home there cannot be lasting peace in the world (90 *Cong. Rec.* 57, 78th Cong. 2d sess., January 11, 1944).

23. Conflicting views on the function of states in our constitutional system can be found in *Garcia v. San Antonio Metropolitan Transit Authority,* 105 S. Ct. 1005 (1985). See also the proposal for regional republics in Rexford Tugwell, *Draft Constitution for a United Republics of America* (Santa Barbara, Calif.: Center for the Study of Democratic Institutions, 1972). See also, L. D. Baldwin, *Reframing the Constitution* (Santa Barbara, Calif.: ABC Cleo Press, 1972).

24. Lloyd N. Cutler, "To Form a Government," 59 *For. Affairs,* 126 (1980). See also, W. Wilson, *Congressional Government* (New York: Columbia Univ. Press, 1908). These problems are also analyzed in Tugwell's draft constitution. Tugwell envisions a stronger executive as well as a more widely representative legislative branch. His proposal also includes ideas concerning regulatory authority and the place of political parties in a general theory of constitutional government.

FOUR

Constitutional Limits on Majoritarian Democracy

WILLIAM NELSON

DEMOCRACY AND LIBERTY

Why should we have any kind of government more extensive than the minimal state? One answer is that some moral requirements on individuals and states will be met only if the government has more extensive powers. A very different answer is that, in the minimal state, people are unable to attain many of their goals. In particular, in the presence of what economists call externalities, individuals, exercising their rights and respecting the rights of others, will either impose costs on others (for example, pollution) or fail to produce goods (flood control, adequate water supplies) despite a desire to avoid these costs and to have these goods. A government with more extensive powers is in a position to intervene and see that these desires are satisfied.

It is worth noting that externalities can arise in more than one way. In some cases, they arise from people's private desires concerning their own or their family's consumption: They want a reservoir because they want to drink the water, or they want to be rid of air pollution the same way they want to be rid of garbage. But people also have social and impersonal preferences. They want *others* to have jobs, more equal incomes, or access to parks and pools. They want children in their society to be raised differently, to have more opportunities, and to be better behaved. They want to preserve natural resources and endangered species. These preferences are, in various ways, preferences about the general character of one's community, about the lives that others live or can live, and about the natural and social environment. Failure to recognize preferences like these can lead us to underestimate the extent of externalities. Like my desire to avoid pollution, my desire to preserve the whooping crane and to have a better educated populace leads me to want others to behave differently. Yet these preferences are not the kind that I can satisfy in the market the way I can satisfy my taste for exotic beers.

In the minimal state, where only property rights, rights of contract, and negative personal rights are enforced, it is relatively easy for people to satisfy many of their private, personal desires. Not all of these desires can be satisfied, of course, partly because of limited time and money, and partly because of externalities. It is relatively difficult, on the other hand, to satisfy impersonal and social preferences, especially when these concern large scale, society-wide matters, such as income distribution, better opportunities for minorities, or the preservation of large tracts of wilderness. It is not impossible. People can form voluntary associations, collect money to buy up land, preach sermons (to anyone who will listen), write letters to editors, and so on. Still, in the absence of a government that is both responsive to citizen preferences and empowered to effect changes through coercive means, people will tend to concern themselves mainly with the satisfaction of private preferences. These are the preferences over which they have some control. The objects of other preferences will, so to speak, never appear on their agendas. To favor the minimal state, then, is, among other things, to favor the pursuit of private, personal goals over the pursuit of impersonal, social, and moral goals.[1]

If we believe that moral requirements will be met only in a state more extensive than the minimal state, there is reason to institute a more extensive government. If we believe that social preferences have a claim to be satisfied along with private preferences, we have another reason to want more extensive government, and we have a reason for wanting it to be democratic and responsive to citizen preferences.[2] But we need to realize that not all social and impersonal preferences are benign. Some are altruistic, but others are racist or sexist. Some of us may want every child to have a good liberal education. Others may want every child to have a good Christian education. Democrats, by broadening the agendas of individuals to include social goals open the way to bitter and divisive controversy among people who might otherwise find it easier to live and let live, never discussing religion or politics with anyone they don't already agree with. Moreover, just as private preferences aren't all satisfied in the market, social preferences aren't all satisfied in a democracy; the ones that are can be immoral.

Some people, Michael Walzer for example, seem not to regard this as a serious objection to democracy. When people have conflicting visions of society, he seems to think that these conflicts ought to be brought into the open. Controversy is good for us, and, in any case, people have a right to govern themselves quite independent of whether they will do it well (Walzer, 1981; 1980).

Others, myself included, are not prepared to go as far as Walzer here. I am as dubious about absolute or nonderivative rights to democratic government as I am about absolute property rights. And, while it is clearly sometimes desirable that the self-satisfied beneficiaries of the status quo be called upon to defend their positions and their actions, it is also important for all of us, that each be able, most of the time, to take his or her authority in a certain area for granted. The system of private rights creates a kind of division of authority and responsibility that is probably essential both to our individual development and well-being and to the efficient functioning of society. This system determines simultaneously what we can depend on using for our own purposes and what we can be held responsible for. Relative to the need for a division of authority, the demand for democratic decisionmaking is an annoying intrusion. Still, it is unclear both how serious the dangers of democratic government are and what the best response is to these dangers.

No doubt these observations are some argument for a radically limited government—the minimal state again—but these arguments are incomplete unless they acknowledge that personal and property rights constitute an assignment of decisionmaking authority to individuals and unless they also include a proviso that these individuals will use this authority to good purpose. This system needs to be judged by the same external standards imposed on the system of democratic decisionmaking (*cf.* Nelson, 1986).

A different response to the dangers of democratic government is to argue for democratic government, as I already have, but to constrain the operation of majority rule by a bill of rights understood to incorporate and so protect basic moral rights against the possibility of legislative abuse. Unfortunately, this approach seems to require either that we have a great deal of faith in judges, or that we are able to specify the relevant moral rights or principles in advance, secure in the knowledge that these are the right ones. Some may think that this is not a serious problem, but, in my view, it is. Morality is complicated. Most of the requirements of morality—at least those that are likely to be involved in controversies about legislation—are highly context dependent. They depend crucially on what else the legislature may have or not have done; they depend on changing economic circumstances; and they depend on cultural factors that can vary from time to time.[3] Indeed, my doubts about the possibility of laying down, in advance, a system of rights that represents the requirements of morality are among my reasons for objecting to the minimal state, for it, too, simply freezes a particular system of (libertarian) rights.

What is needed is a system of government that is relatively flexible and responsive to changing needs and circumstances. Democracy, of course, seems to be just such a system. It provides people with an opportunity to promote their values and satisfy their preferences, and, as I have argued elsewhere,[4] there is some reason to believe that a well-designed and properly functioning democratic government will operate without violating important moral requirements.

This argument depends on what might be called a democratic conception of morality—a form of contractualism. What morality requires, in this view, is compliance with principles that no one, given an interest in general principles for the regulation of conduct, can reasonably reject.[5] What the democratic process requires is that bills be subjected to public scrutiny and that opponents have an opportunity to register their objections. When voters and legislators exercise their authority as they should, one question they ask themselves is essentially the question of contractualist morality, namely, whether the proposals in question can be justified to each in the sense that they do not violate principles no one can reasonably reject.

CONSTITUTIONAL PROTECTIONS

The argument just given for democratic institutions is an instrumentalist argument. It does not assume a basic right of self-government, nor does the argument rest on the intrinsic values of democratic experience. The case presented here thus differs from some more "pure" democratic arguments (for example, Walzer, 1981, pp. 383–387). On the other hand, as the underlying account of morality is itself recognizably democratic, this position may not differ that much from that of theorists who regard democracy as intrinsically desirable. Indeed, I suspect that what they actually value intrinsically is never some system of democratic institutions, but something closer to a moral ideal perhaps not unlike the ideal embedded in contractualism. In any case, my argument, like any instrumentalist argument, rests on contingent assumptions, perhaps most importantly assumptions about the character and motives of voters and representatives. And, we all know, or anyway, we all believe, that the system sometimes fails. Therefore, there is at least a *prima facie* case for a constitutional bill of rights. That there is a chance of failure, however, is not enough to justify a bill of rights and judicial review, unless we believe that the democratic process, qualified by judicial review, will do at least as well over time as the democratic process alone. (The issue is complicated. Would democracy work better—be more vigorous—if we didn't have review?) At the same time, even if we were to conclude that a vigorous democracy is the best protection against immoral legislation, it would not follow that there is no need for judicially enforced constitutional limits on the power of the legislature. Some limits may be defensible not because their infringement would violate substantive moral requirements, but because violations would be in some sense undemocratic.

A similar line of argument can be found in recent works by Amy Gutmann (1983) and John Hart Ely (1980). This argument is worth examining because judicial review has been attacked as undemocratic both by writers on the left, like Walzer,[6] and also by theorists on the right like Robert Bork (1971). What I shall argue is that certain constitutional limits on the power of majorities—in particular, rights of free expression and rights of equal protection—are supported by the main values that underlie a rational commitment to democracy itself. Hence, finding the right balance between the principle of majority rule and (some) constitutional rights is not a matter of compromising between two independent and conflicting values. Instead, it is a matter of trying to construct a complex system of rights and procedures that is at least as likely as any alternative to promote individual and community values within the constaints of morality. One advantage of this view is that it provides both an argument for constitutional rights and an approach to their interpretation. Another advantage is that the alternative arguments for democracy, or for at least some constitutional rights, are not compelling.[7]

Most people would concede, of course, that the arguments for some basic constitutional requirements are not independent of the arguments for democratic procedures themselves. Constitutional guarantees of the right to vote are an example. But it is not too great a step from there to rights of free expression. The assumption is that the democratic process does not consist merely of deciding issues by voting. At least as important is that action should be taken only after a reasonably thorough discussion of its pros and cons and after interested parties have had an opportunity to make the strongest case they can for their proposals and against contrary proposals. Democracy, as conceived here, is essentially *open* government. It is government by public discussion and debate. What makes it a relatively good form of government is that it tends not to adopt policies that violate basic moral requirements, partly because voters and legislators, by and large, are moved by moral argument and are unwilling to hold to positions publicly in the face of strong, publicly expressed moral objections. But this process is only effective if people have an opportunity to become informed about the relevant facts and evaluative considerations and are then free to express their opinions.

This argument for freedom of expression as a constituent of democracy is a strong argument, but it seems to carry with it a rather narrow interpretation of what freedom of expression protects. In particular, it seems to provide a strong argument for protecting *political* speech and writing but not other forms of expression (Meiklejohn, 1960; Bork, 1971, p. 20, pp. 26–27). The argument can, however, be extended further to defend a wider conception of freedom of expression.

So far, I have characterized democracy as a system in which decisions are made by voting after extensive, public discussion of the alternatives, and, in particular, after interested parties have had an opportunity to put forward objections to proposals they do not like. So understood, democracy seems to require freedom to express political opinions. Democracy, therefore, tends to produce legislation that is rationally justifiable *to* those who have to live with it. But, given this aim, democracy requires protection for acts of expression that are not overtly "political." People learn from dramatic and literary work. They develop their sense of what is possible and what, among the possibilities, is valuable; and as their conception of what is possible and valuable changes, what can be justified to them also changes (*cf.* Putnam, 1978, pp. 83–94). Thus, if we assume that people do learn from exposure to art and literature, and if we assume that the aim of democracy is to produce legislation justifiable to persons with a developed conception of what is possible and valuable, democracy then requires protection of a robust freedom of expression. From this standpoint, virtually any form of artistic or literary work, including erotic or pornographic material, can be relevant to political decisionmaking.[8]

The same argument that I have claimed provides the best case for democratic legislative procedures is also a strong argument for including rights to free expression in the democratic constitution. What I have not argued, and do not believe, is that democratic majorities, even constrained by firm guarantees of free expression, can be relied upon not to adopt seriously immoral legislation. In particular, laws imposing disadvantages on despised or misunderstood minorities, for example, racial minorities or homosexuals, are a clear danger. People in these categories have some protection, of course, given rights to vote and rights of free expression. But in the case of small minorities, the right to vote does not go very far; and, when one is the object of widespread fear or hostility, to appeal to the conscience of the majority by speaking out publicly can be dangerous.

Faced with the danger that the legislature can do serious harm, we might be tempted to enumerate those disadvantages that no one should have to suffer and write them into a constitution as limits on what the legislature can do. But what is the right list of disadvantages? Can we reasonably list them in advance? We permit many serious restrictions on individual liberty, such as taxes, conscription, and punishments for crimes. What is permissible seems to depend on a variety of things, including the context in which it is done and the reasons for which it is done. Not every burden is an unjustifiable one, and not every refusal to grant benefits constitutes a serious deprivation. Part of the argument for democracy, indeed, is that it enables individuals to promote their own values, even though this may sometimes require imposing burdens on themselves and others. But we ought to be particularly wary when the burdens fall largely or exclusively on small, isolated or politically powerless groups. The natural constitutional restriction on the power of the legislature, then, is not some form of "substantive due process," but, rather, something like the Equal Protection Clause. Ely has made basically the same argument in *Democracy and Distrust* (1980). He also claims that this requirement, properly interpreted, is not a limitation on democracy but, like the right to vote and rights of free expression, a part of the democratic process itself.

Why should we accept this latter claim? Why shouldn't a commitment to democracy include the belief that, if majorities choose to impose special burdens on minorities (restrictions on free speech and the right to vote aside), they may do so? Ely considers this question (pp. 76–77), and his reply is that violations of the Equal Protection Clause compromise a basic democratic "opportunity to participate either in the political process . . . or in the accommodation those processes have reached . . ." (p. 77). We might reply, however, that this argument proceeds too quickly: The slip from a right to participate in decisionmaking to a right to "participate" in the results is a clear case of equivocation.

According to Ely, this objection rests on an overly simple conception of what democracy is all about. "The 'republic' [the founders] envisioned," he says, was not some " 'winner take all' system in which the government pursued the interests of a privileged few or even of only those groups that could work themselves into some majority coalition. . . ." Rather, it was ". . . one in which the representatives would govern in the interest of the whole people" (p. 79).

What it means to govern in the interest of the whole people is, of course, obscure. Leaving that aside, however, Ely's argument sounds not like an argument that an equal protection requirement is essential to the democratic process itself, but rather like an argument that this requirement is needed if government is to serve the values it ought to. In that case, it is similar to my argument for freedom of expression; and my thesis, which speaks not of "the interest of the whole" but only of legislation that can be justified to each, actually seems to make a case more strongly and clearly for a requirement of equal protection.[9]

INTERPRETATION AND APPLICATION

In sum, rights of free expression and equal protection can be defended by reference to the same contractualist conception of morality that underlies the strongest argument for representative government itself. To institute such rights, of course, is to restrict the authority of the legislature and to grant appellate courts the authority to interpret and apply these rights. How should they be interpreted? How should courts exercise their authority? The answers to these questions depend partly on the kind of argument given for the rights, that is, whether we defend constitutional rights in terms of the kind of argument presented here or in terms of an independent argument. According to this argument, constitutional rights function mainly to prevent the adoption of laws or policies that cannot be reasonably justified to those who must live under them. This is basically a negative function, important in light of the not unreasonable fear of legislative excess. Yet government has the capacity to do good as well as harm. I do not make the libertarian assumption that government has no business promoting citizens' values. Too strict an interpretation of constitutional rights can prevent the government from producing important benefits or preventing serious harms.[10]

In the discussion that follows, I will try to indicate how freedom of expression and equal protection might be interpreted in light both of the basic function I have assigned them and of the concern that they not be overly restrictive.

Freedom of Expression

In establishing freedom of expression as a right, we deny lawmakers the authority to outlaw speech, publication, and the like. We thereby create for citizens an area of protected liberty, but it is a liberty the exercise of which can itself be harmful. Acts of expression can disturb sleep, cause offence, lead to riots or lynchings, endanger troops (by revealing military plans to the enemy), or provide people bent on terrorism with the means to their end (by explaining how to construct bombs, for example). Most of us believe that acts like these should be regulated, at least to some extent, to prevent harm. In exercising their authority to review statutes regulating expression, the courts should not invalidate all such statutes. In that sense, the right of free expression should not be seen as absolute. Yet it should be seen as a right, in the sense that the legislature should be unable to regulate expression at *its* discretion. The commitment to the values of democracy requires that citizens have an opportunity to make their own judgments about what is true or false, reasonable or unreasonable, against the background of a free and open interchange of ideas. We should not trust lawmakers to make these judgments for us, both because they are not necessarily elected for their expertise and because they are partisans of their own views.

It would be convenient if we could provide, as a guide to the process of judicial review, a clear, general account of the type of expression that can or cannot be regulated—if we could say that, within this area, at least, the right *is* absolute. The most interesting such proposal I know of is Scanlon's suggestion that the right of free expression should be understood to exclude any interference to protect against harms of a particular type, namely, harms that consist of someone's coming to have false beliefs or mistaken values (1972, p. 213). But Scanlon himself now regards this as too broad. He notes that it would rule out restrictions on false advertising (1979, p. 532), and it is not clear that it can be squared with legitimate restrictions on someone's egging-on a lynch mob.

A proposal similar to Scanlon's would define the right of free expression as a right of *political* expression. I have argued, however, that the interests we have in political autonomy are served by acts of expression that do not count in any ordinary sense as cases of political expression. To define protected speech explicitly as political speech is to invite courts and lawmakers to take an overly narrow view.

The problem seems to be—and, if I interpret it correctly, this is the main point of Scanlon's later paper—that, for any category of expressive act we specify as receiving protection, there will be cases in which legitimate interests in having such acts regulated will far outweigh the interests served by the acts themselves. There is no reasonable alternative to looking at those interests and to weighing and balancing them in particular cases.

What the courts must do is to focus on protecting the fundamental interest in individual and collective autonomy served by the right of free expression. In so doing, they must be sensitive to the issue of the abuse of authority—to the fact that those in power at a given time, including judges, are already convinced of their conception of social good and so will see little harm in limiting discussion of alternatives. Yet they must also be aware that there are great benefits to be gained by *some* regulation, and that some regulation does little or no damage to democratic values. They do best if, first, they take the right of free expression to apply to *all* acts of expression so that all regulation is subject to review. Second, they do best to permit regulation only when it is based on a narrowly drawn statute directed at a specific and substantial harm. Wary of the effects of precedent, they should avoid attempts to specify protected categories of expression in general terms, preserving instead the idea that all expression is presumptively protected. They should be skeptical of allegations that expression is harmful and demand strong and convincing evidence before accepting them. When convinced that the harms are sufficient and that there is no threat to political self-determination, the courts should consider permitting regulation. But, even then, they should try to avoid formulaic pronouncements in their reasons for regulation.

Rights are sometimes thought to be best protected if they are carefully formulated but then regarded as absolute.[11] I propose just the opposite. Attempts to formulate a plausibly absolute conception of free expression are likely to discredit it. The best protection for free expression lies in an approach to judicial review that makes the procedure of defending regulation arduous, preserving the presumption that all such regulation can be challenged, and offering the legislature no simple formulas, which, if invoked, would make regulation easy to justify.

Equal Protection

Like freedom of expression, rights of equal protection run a risk of disabling the legislature from adopting laws or policies that otherwise serve good purposes. Although there is a genuine danger that majoritarian legislatures will unjustifiably impose special burdens on minorities, there is no general requirement that all groups should be treated equally in all respects. Narcotics dealers, as a group, *should* be singled out for hard treatment, and it is probably desirable and certainly permissible that the wealthy be subject to taxes from which the poor are exempt. An equal protection clause that is too broad can rule out clearly desirable legislative actions. The question, again, is how the right to equal protection should be understood.

This question can be seen as having two parts. First, what features of legislation should trigger judicial review; and, second, what grounds are sufficient for invalidating legislation that is reviewed? The answers must depend on what kinds of problems we seek to avoid and on how likely these problems are to arise. The concern emphasized here is the danger of legislation restricting one's opportunities or denying one benefits when these restrictions cannot reasonably be justified.

In general, we can expect democratic governments to refrain from serious, gratuitous restrictions simply because people do not choose to impose these on themselves. Problems are likely to arise only when there is a secure majority able to frame burdensome laws or policies so that they apply only to members of a distinct minority. Their motives may vary, of course, from a relatively benign desire simply to save tax money all the way to deep racial or religious animosities.

These concerns about what makes legislation unjustifiable and how unjustifiable legislation is likely to arise suggest a disjunctive test for the propriety of judicial review. First, review is required when legislation singles out for disadvantageous treatment some group toward which there is a tradition of animosity or which, for some reason, is not well-represented in the legislature and is in a poor position to articulate its case politically. These are the groups whose interests are likely to be overlooked or even intentionally disregarded in the political process. Second, review is also proper, even in the absence of these factors, when the legislature singles out for bad treatment or exclusion from benefits a group that has suffered from bad treatment historically and for which, consequently, additional burdens might be especially difficult to bear.

The rationale for this two-part test is to focus on the kinds of burdens or exclusions that are likely to be especially serious and on the kinds of conditions that are likely to lead the legislature to impose unjustifiable burdens. A request for judicial review should be dismissed unless the legislation in question satisfies one of these conditions. Supposing it does, though, we must ask what further test the courts should apply to determine whether to invalidate such legislation. In U.S. litigation under the Equal Protection Clause, the question has been whether the principle of selection in a statute or regulation is rationally related to a legitimate purpose. It has been a question of "fit" between means and ends. Indeed, this has been viewed as the *main* question, and, as a result, the clause has been applied symmetrically both to cases in which a disadvantaged minority is burdened and to cases in which a privileged class is burdened (as in the case of affirmative action). Argument tends to focus on the exactness of the fit between means and ends and on the legitimacy or urgency of the state purpose.[12] My version of the Equal Protection Clause is asymmetrical. A statute qualifies for review only when the group burdened is already disadvantaged or is a despised or politically powerless minority. Once this condition is satisfied, however,

I think the question of fit is generally the appropriate one. To ask if the classification fits a legitimate purpose is to ask what the purpose is. In the most obvious cases of unjustifiable laws—laws excluding blacks from public swimming pools, for example—there will be no legitimate purpose that fits the classification.

From the perspective of a commitment to democracy and to the values underlying it, the focus on fit seems appropriate. It leaves judgments of substantive value to the community while requiring merely that, if a goal is deemed worth pursuing or a cost worth bearing, the benefits and burdens should be distributed appropriately. But suppose that a statute is adopted excluding blacks from public parks or requiring them to observe an early curfew. And suppose that the purpose is simply to "keep them in their place." Again, and more realistically, today, suppose that there are restrictions on homosexual conduct defended simply on the ground that it is contrary to community moral standards. Such laws, I believe, should be ruled out by an equal protection requirement despite the fact that there is a good fit between their purpose and the classifications they employ. The aim that underlies the commitment to democracy is to generate laws and regulations consistent with principles no one can reasonably reject, and so, laws that can be justified to everyone. But the gratuitous imposition of burdens—gratuitous in terms of values those burdened can conceivably come to accept—is not consistent with this ideal. The laws in question, I take it, are gratuitous in just this way. The *mere* claim that conduct is immoral, or the mere *claim* that it has bad consequences, cannot be taken as an adequate justification for imposing a burden. When immorality is a reason, it is because of the features of the conduct that make it immoral. Reference to immorality itself is neither necessary nor sufficient to justify restrictions.

Lack of fit between the purposes of a statute and classification, argued earlier, should not be sufficient to justify constitutional review. Neither is it necessary to justify overturning a statute. There is a need in some cases for a substantive evaluation of the cogency of the reasons offered for imposing burdens and of their sufficiency relative to the extent of the burdens imposed. But why is this not an improper infringement of the power of democratic majorities?

Part of the answer is that majority rule is not an end in itself. The reason we should generally trust the democratic process is that it can be presumed to respect the fundamental interests of the governed. When those to whom legal restrictions apply are an isolated and powerless minority, however, this presumption is not nearly so plausible. The presumption against the review of statutes on their substantive merits is not so reasonable when the statutes apply specifically to minorities.

Some would argue, of course, that the democratic process cannot be trusted even to protect the fundamental interests of the general populace and that the judiciary should be empowered to overturn, on substantive grounds, statutes that apply quite generally. After all, there are laws against heterosexual as well as homosexual sodomy; there have been laws against the use of contraceptives, even by married couples; and there have been laws proscribing virtually all abortions. I regard these as bad laws. Yet, with the possible exception of the latter, none of them is clearly subject to review under an equal protection clause of the kind I have described. But, whether the apparently unjustifiable law applies generally or only to a minority, how might a constitutional protection invalidating such a law be formulated? What is the basic objection to which such laws are subject?

Two lines of argument suggest themselves. On the one hand, we might argue that there are certain interests so central to our well-being, certain areas within which making our own decisions and pursuing our own preferences is so important to us, that governmental interference cannot be permitted. On the other hand, we might argue that restrictions on liberty are generally objectionable. They can be permitted only with adequate justification, and the standards for adequate justification are high.

The first line of argument is reminiscent of a constitutional right of privacy, where what is private, and therefore protected, is central, personal interests. The second is reminiscent of substantive due process. I think neither, by itself, is an adequate basis for judicial review. As stated earlier, one legitimate function of the institutions of representative democracy is to enable citizens to resolve and implement their social goals and ideals—goals and ideals that cannot be easily implemented through the institutions of the private economy. The implementation of these ideals may require limitations on liberty. This would be a problem if all infringements of liberty were equally serious, but they are not. And *some* social goals are sufficiently important to justify interference even with significant private and personal interests. The difficulty of formulating a reasonable constitutional protection of liberty and privacy, then, is similar to the problem of formulating a conception of liberty of expression. It is not clear that there is any *category* of expression that should always be immune to limitation, nor, for that matter, that expression itself is such a category. Infringements of liberty require greater justification as the interests involved become more central. But a judgment always needs to be made as to the relative urgency of the personal and public interests involved.

The problems of institutional design under discussion are problems of determining who should be entrusted with the authority to make what judgments and how the limits on authority should be specified. Once we allow that the outcome of democratic decisionmaking is subject to criticism from an independent standpoint, and once we also allow that it is an imperfect procedure, liable to error, it is certainly reasonable to consider the possibility of judicial review as a protection against unjustified interference with personal interests and prerogatives. That judges may err in their application of constitutional protections is not a sufficient objection to review. But it is a legitimate concern. My general idea has been to reduce as much as possible the authority to review legislation adopted by a representative body to cases that involve freedom of expression or violations of an equal protection requirement. It is also possible that there ought to be something akin to a constitutional right to privacy. Just what form it should take, however, I am not now prepared to say.

CONCLUSION

This brief discussion of constitutional rights is no doubt radically incomplete. What I hope it illustrates, though, is the possibility of an argument for certain central constitutional rights based on the conception of morality that underlies a rational commitment to democracy itself. To the extent that there is such an argument, it is possible to provide a unified account of the Constitution, one in which representative democracy and constitutional rights do not stem from different and conflicting concerns but, rather, serve the same ends.

The main interests we have in freedom of expression[13] are very closely connected to the interests we have in the other institutions of self-government. These are the interests we have in finding laws and policies that are mutually acceptable in light of an informed understanding of what is possible and desirable. Rights of equal protection serve the same interests, only negatively: When the normal process of representation and open discussion fails to prevent the imposition of unjustifiable burdens on some minority, those unjustly burdened can seek redress by appealing to this right.

This concern about damage to the central interests of minorities might seem, of course, to be just a special case of a more general concern about the interests of anyone. It suggests that there ought to be a general protection of liberty or a general requirement that all legislation imposing burdens be backed by cogent argument. This requirement is not necessarily unreasonable, but such a general protection needs to be evaluated both in terms of the likelihood that the legislature will err and of the likelihood that the protection will not be interpreted in an overly restrictive fashion. The argument for a special protection for minorities is thus stronger, as the likelihood of unjustifiable legislation is presumptively greater.

In the U.S. Constitution, of course, there are other rights that apparently cannot be understood in the same way. The First Amendment prohibition on the establishment of religion and protection of its free exercise are examples. To some extent, one might argue, this right is already secured by an equal protection requirement, insofar as this would rule out religious persecution or a special tax imposed on certain religious groups but not on others without adequate justification. But the First Amendment seems to go further. It seems to put issues involving the legitimacy of different religious practices or activities completely beyond the reach of democratic discussion. Instead of ruling out *unjustifiable* restrictions on the practice of religion or *unjustifiable* preferences for one religion over another, it simply rules out any such restrictions or preferences. Moreover, it seems to rule out any argument for or against any legal requirement that includes religious premises. How can this restriction and others like it be justified? One possibility is that it can be construed as a special case of a general concern—restrictions on liberty must be justified by arguments that can be expected to render the restrictions at least understandable to those restricted.[14] Even though this ideal would be too vague and general to serve as a specific constitutional protection, it may be that, within the United States, with its history of religious diversity together with its experience of the possibility of relatively peaceful coexistence among religions, it was possible to bracket religious arguments as one category that everyone agreed could not be assumed to be generally compelling.[15]

NOTES

Work on this paper was supported by an ACLS/Ford fellowship in 1986. I wish to thank the ACLS, and I also wish to thank those who commented on this paper at the November '86 AMINTAPHIL meeting, especially Bruce Landesman and Steven Lee, each of whom was kind enough to send me additional comments by mail.

1. Some defenders of the minimal state, of course, might hold that the only legitimately enforceable moral principles are those giving rise to the rights protected in the minimal state. I do not discuss this position here. The argument for the minimal state that I do mean to address is based on the danger that a more extensive state will abuse its authority. This idea figures prominently in the work of the "public choice" economists. See Buchanan, Tollison, and Tullock (1980); Brennan and Friedman (1981).
2. For a defense of the idea that laws should (or at least may) be based on impersonal or social values, see Sagoff (1986) and Postema (1987).
3. It is perhaps worth noting, if only in passing, that relatively few of the rights in the U.S. Bill of Rights look much like basic moral rights.
4. See Nelson (1980, pp. 100–118). See also, my "Evaluating the Institutions of Liberal Democracy," forthcoming.
5. This formulation is due to Scanlon (1982, p. 110ff). I now prefer it to what I said in Nelson (1980, pp. 102–107).
6. Although Walzer criticizes judicial review as undemocratic, at least when it is viewed in a certain way (1981, p. 387ff), he does think that requirements of nonrepression and nondiscrimination are demanded by democracy itself (p. 384). Here, his argument seems to be like Gutmann's but different from mine in ways I will try to illustrate (see note 9).
7. I have discussed arguments for democracy elsewhere (Nelson, 1980). For a brief survey of some additional arguments, see Gutmann (1983, pp. 37–44).
8. See Scanlon (1979, p. 543ff).
9. I view democracy as a procedure for collective decisionmaking in which members of the community or their representatives decide issues by voting. One

can, of course, *say* that democratic procedures include a requirement of equal protection or nondiscrimination, as do Gutmann (1983, p. 27) and Walzer (1981, p. 384). But, in their work, this seems to me *ad hoc.* What I try to argue is that what unifies democracy, narrowly construed, and equal protection requirements is that each is part of an institutional realization of the same underlying moral ideal.

10. Constitutional rights can stand in the way of beneficial legislation, but so can the insistence on majority rule. The latter is notoriously cumbersome and inefficient. Both are imperfect institutionalizations of a moral ideal.

11. See Frantz (1962).

12. For a far more complete account of the standard interpretation of the Equal Protection Clause, see Fiss (1976, pp. 108–117). Fiss is critical of this way of reading the clause partly because of its apparent implications for the case of affirmative action.

13. But not, by any means, the only interest. See Scanlon (1979, pp. 520–528).

14. Wertheimer (1971) has argued similarly that it is not possible to provide a generally acceptable rational justification for the claim that fetuses are human, and therefore it is not possible to justify restrictions on abortion. In subsequent (I believe unpublished) work, he has defended the constitutional argument against restrictions on this basis. This line of argument represents a further possible development of a "democratic" argument for constitutional rights.

15. This claim corresponds to an accepted historical explanation for the U.S. adoption of the ideal of religious toleration. See Ver Steeg (1964, pp. 91–92).

REFERENCES

Bork, Robert. 1971. "Neutral Principles and Some First Amendment Problems." 47 *Indiana L.J.* 1 (Fall).

Brennan, G., and D. Friedman. 1981. "A Libertarian Perspective on Welfare." In *Income Support: Conceptual and Policy Issues.* Edited by P. Brown, C. Johnson, and P. Vernier. Totowa, N.J.: Rowman and Littlefield.

Buchanan, J., R. Tollison, and G. Tullock. 1980. *Toward a Theory of the Rent Seeking Society.* College Station, Tex.: Texas A&M.

Ely, J.H. 1980. *Democracy and Distrust.* Cambridge, Mass.: Harvard Univ. Press.

Fiss, O. 1976. "Groups and the Equal Protection Clause." 5 *Philosophy and Public Affairs* 2 (Winter).

Frantz, Laurent. 1962. "The First Amendment in the Balance." 71 *Yale L.J.* 1424.

Gutmann, A. 1983. "How Liberal Is Democracy." In *Liberalism Reconsidered.* Edited by D. MacLean and C. Mills. Totowa, N.J.: Rowman and Allenheld.

Meiklejohn, A. 1960. *Political Freedom.* New York: Harper & Row.

Nelson, W. 1980. *On Justifying Democracy.* Boston: Routledge & Kegan Paul.

———. 1985. "Rights, Responsibilities and Redistribution." In *Economic Justice: Private Rights and Public Responsibilities.* Edited by Kenneth Kipnis and Diana Meyers. Totowa, N.J.: Rowman and Allenheld.

———. Forthcoming. "Evaluating the Institutions of Liberal Democracy." In *Individual Liberty and the Democratic Order.* Edited by G. Brennen and L. Lomasky. New York: Cambridge Univ. Press.

Postema, G. 1987. "Collective Evils, Harms and the Law." 97 *Ethics* 2 (January).

Putnam, H. 1978. *Meaning and the Moral Sciences.* Boston: Routledge & Kegan Paul.

Sagoff, M. 1986. "Values and Preferences." 96 *Ethics* 2 (January).
Scanlon, T. 1972. "A Theory of Freedom of Expression." 1 *Philosophy and Public Affairs* 2 (Winter).
———. 1979. "Freedom of Expression and Categories of Expression." 40 *Univ. of Pittsburgh L. Rev.*
———. 1982. "Contractualism and Utilitarianism." In *Utilitarianism and Beyond.* Edited by A.K. Sen and B. Williams. New York: Cambridge Univ. Press.
Ver Steeg, C. 1964. *The Formative Years, 1607–1763.* New York: Hill and Wang.
Walzer, M. 1980. *Radical Principles.* New York: Basic Books.
———. 1981. "Philosophy and Democracy." 9 *Political Theory* 3 (August).
Wertheimer, R. 1971. "Understanding the Abortion Argument." 1 *Philosophy and Public Affairs* 1 (Fall).

PART THREE

Interpreting the Constitution

Introduction to Part Three

KENNETH KIPNIS

Like the Bible, the plays of Shakespeare, and Plato's *Republic,* the United States Constitution stands as a canonical text at the root of an interpretive tradition. As theology construes Scripture, as literary criticism and philosophical scholarship elaborate their texts, so constitutional adjudication brings forward new perspectives on the basic principles underlying U.S. political order.

The United States Constitution assigns the task of adjudicating disputes arising under it to the Supreme Court and to such lesser courts as the Congress chooses to establish. This responsibility to settle constitutional controversies has engendered many thousands of volumes of judicial opinions and scholarly commentary, all interpreting provisions of the Constitution against the differing backgrounds of cases arising over a two hundred year period. Under this system it falls to Supreme Court justices to articulate authoritative interpretations of the 1787 text and its amendments. Needless to say, the cases are rare in which the clear language of the framers decisively settles a controversy. Indeed, where the document is unambiguous, cases are less likely to be brought in the first place. And so, in general, judges are rarely able simply to read the law off of the printed page: The text must be interpreted.

Given the necessity of interpretation, it is not surprising that higher courts routinely overturn the judgments of lower ones, that dissenting judicial opinions are common on multijudge panels such as the Supreme Court, and that the Supreme Court has, on occasion, overruled its own precedents. Nor is it particularly troubling that alternative constructions are possible, for the system can operate quickly and/or deliberately to resolve conflict when ambiguity is the focus of a dispute.

What has attracted attention and some considerable concern is a philosophically deeper question about the nature of judicial interpretation itself. Given alternative constructions of the Constitution, how is a judge properly to decide which is the correct one or the best one? Flipping a coin is ruled out, for judges must provide reasons for their choices. Making decisions on the basis of personal inclination seems the very opposite of rule-governed adjudication. What type of reasoning process is called for? What interpretive principles should govern constitutional adjudication? The articles in this section address this subject.

Using the concept of political sovereignty for clarification, H. Hamner Hill, in "Between Clause-bound Literalism and Value Imposition: A Positivist Noninterpretivist's Theory of Judicial Review," seeks to position himself between two camps. On the one side are the positivist interpretivists—like William Rehnquist and Robert Bork—who hold that because the text of the Constitution is the expression of the sovereign will of the framers, ambiguity is to be resolved by appeal to the framers' intent. On the other side are the nonpositivist noninterpretivists—like Michael Perry—who appeal to extraconstitutional values to map a natural law approach to adjudication.

Hill's theory—positivist noninterpretivism—locates sovereignty in the will of the people as opposed to the intent of the framers. What changed between *Plessy v. Ferguson* in 1896 and *Brown v. Board of Education* in 1954 was not our understanding of the framers' intent, but rather our public understanding of equality under the law. Accordingly, just as Supreme Court decisions can be overturned by the popular initiative of amendment, so constitutional interpretation can properly reflect an expressed popular consensus. Hill concludes that, though his account is truer to the practices of adjudication, there is no guarantee that the positivist noninterpretivist perspective will always engender desirable judicial decisions.

Stephen M. Griffin, in "Toward a Public Values Philosophy of the Constitution," endorses what he calls a "neorepublican" philosophy in contrast to "democratic relativism." What Griffin calls "public values"—not to be confused with purely private preferences—are those values that would be embraced by parties accepting restrictions similar to those of John Rawls's original position—restrictions that in effect rule out the appeal to personal interests.

Paralleling Rawls, Griffin argues that a well-ordered society must ensure that each citizen enjoys a basic set of constitutional rights, especially the important right of participation in political processes. He expresses concern about defects in the U.S. constitutional system, particularly those arising out of concentrations of economic and political power. Griffin conceives the judicial perspective as mirroring the restrictions of the original position. Judges are to act fairly and impartially. But the task of constitutional interpretation is not the private sphere of the judiciary. In his analysis the most important interpreter is the citizenry, to whom government is ultimately accountable. Constitutional scholarship should therefore be addressed, in part, to the general public.

While Hill and Griffin look for theoretical solutions to the problem of constitutional interpretation, Kenneth Henley in "Constitutional Integrity and Compromise," grapples with a seemingly perpetual theoretical difficulty involved in applying the document to certain cases. Henley accepts Ronald Dworkin's view that interpretations must meet the standards of fit (elements of the canonical text must be consistent with the interpretation) and justification (the interpretation must place the canonical text in the best light). But, according to Henley, the "living internal compromises" in the document rule out interpretive coherence "at some deep level of principle."

In a series of cases in the 1960s, the Supreme Court ruled that states must apportion their legislative districts on the basis of population. They interpreted the Equal Protection Clause, introduced after the Civil War, as requiring "one man, one vote." But in the United States Senate, though one state may have twenty times the population of another, both states get the same number of senators. Equal representation in the Senate (but not in the House) was the product of compromise between the large states and the small states. Though arguments can be made to resolve the apparent conflict (Henley discusses several cases in which such resolution has been called for), these moves have a shallow, *ad hoc* flavor. He concludes that coherence at a deep level of political morality may be constrained by a recalcitrant text. We should not expect the Constitution to be more than the creation of its very human framers.

FIVE

Between Clause-bound Literalism and Value Imposition: A Positivist Noninterpretivist Theory of Judicial Review

H. HAMNER HILL

Judicial review of legislative enactments, so the popular analysis has it, is fundamentally antidemocratic. Nine justices, appointed for life, have the power to tell us, *inter alia,* where our children will go to school, that organized prayer in public schools is impermissible, that the several states cannot outlaw abortion. Moreover, this extraordinary power[1] can be, and all too often is, exercised in the face of clear expressions of the will of the elected representatives of the people. The very institution of judicial review (or, more exactly, the products of that institution that invalidate legislative enactments[2]) seems to be inconsistent with democracy. "This," John Hart Ely concludes at the end of a civics sermonette, "in America, is a charge that matters. We have as a society from the beginning, and now almost instinctively, accepted the notion that a representative democracy must be our form of government."[3] Judicial review, the legacy of John Marshall and *Marbury v. Madison,* is now a deeply ingrained part of U.S. political practice. Given that the courts will engage in judicial review, the standard of review remains a matter of some debate.

Current debates about the legitimacy of judicial policymaking divide theorists into two dominant camps: the interpretivists represented by Raoul Berger, William Rehnquist, and Robert Bork, and the noninterpretivists represented by Thomas Grey, Owen Fiss, William Brennan, and Michael Perry. Most of the current debates about constitutional interpretation are misleading because they suggest that there are exactly two positions, exclusive and exhaustive, that one may adopt: the clause-bound literalism of Raoul Berger and William Rehnquist (hereafter called positivist interpretivism) and the value imposing noninterpretivism of Michael Perry and Thomas Grey (hereafter called nonpositivist, noninterpretivism).[4] My goal in this chapter is to defend a theory of judicial review that stands as an alternative to the dominant theories in current legal/philosophical debates. The theory I argue for is faithful to the central tenets of legal positivism, yet it sanctions the imposition of extraconstitutional values.

This chapter is divided into three sections. In the first two sections I show why both positivist interpretivism and nonpositivist noninterpretivism are inadequate theories of constitutional interpretation. While I address the shortcomings of these theories, I also attempt to demonstrate that each has important contributions to make toward an adequate theory of judicial review. In the third section I outline the position of the positivist noninterpretivist. Primary emphasis is placed on explicating the position (showing why it is both positivist and noninterpretivist) and on distinguishing it from positivist interpretivism. I also consider the major objection against any theory of noninterpretive review: How are the values that the Court may impose to be determined? The answer I provide to this question has a legacy traceable through Alexander Bickel back to Edmund Burke: consensus of the citizenry.

THE FAILURE OF POSITIVIST INTERPRETIVISM

Positivist interpretivists argue that when engaging in judicial review of legislative enactments, the criterion of constitutionality to be applied by the courts is the express language of the Constitution. If only judges would follow the criterion of constitutionality recommended by the positivist interpretivists, there would be no cause for popular resentment of the judiciary. A true positivist interpretivist judge would follow the suggestion of Justice Roberts in *U.S. v. Butler,* that when exercising judicial review the Court should simply "lay the article of the constitution which is invoked beside the statute which is challenged and determine whether the latter squares with the former."[5] Only if the act cannot be squared with the relevant constitutional provision should the Court strike the act.

Roberts's suggestion as to how courts should act when reviewing legislative enactments is appealing, but it simply does not work. His approach looks nice until one tries to figure out how to implement it when the constitutional provision involved is not completely clear. The Eighth Amendment protection against cruel and unusual punishment says nothing about which punishments are cruel and unusual, the due process clauses of the Fifth and Fourteenth amendments say nothing about how much process one is due, nor does the Equal Protection Clause indicate how much protection citizens are to enjoy. In short, many of the operative clauses of the Constitution simply are not amenable to interpretivist analysis. Accordingly, one faces a dilemma. Either one must abandon interpretivism or one must be willing to concede that certain constitutional provisions that appear to place some restraints on the actions of both state and federal government officials do not, in fact, have any force at all.[6] Those unwilling to surrender so powerful a tool as the Equal Protection Clause cheerfully conclude that interpretivism must be abandoned and that some form of noninterpretivism must be embraced. Such a rejection of interpretivism, however, is too quick. It fails to ask what motivates one to embrace interpretivism at all. It fails to realize that at one level at least, interpretivism seems to follow from a positivist conception of law.

There are two distinct theses that are central to contemporary legal positivism. First there is the famous separability thesis: the view that there is no noncontingent link between law and morality. The separability thesis is the most widely noted feature of legal positivism, and it is the target of most of the philosophical attacks directed at legal positivism.[7] Despite the attention that separability has drawn, it is not of great moment to this discussion. Rather, I want to focus on the other thesis central to legal positivism—what Joseph Raz calls the sources thesis[8] and what Hans Kelsen calls the doctrine of authorization.[9]

Put roughly, the sources thesis states that for a norm to be a valid law, that norm must have been issued (posited) by a particular source (the exact source being relative to a legal system). A norm, regardless of its form or its moral force, that does not issue from sources recognized as legitimate within a legal system simply is not a valid legal norm within that system. In a government of limited, delegated lawmaking authority, the importance of the sources thesis for a theory of constitutional adjudication should be clear. Only those governmental bodies charged with lawmaking functions can make law, and then only within the scope of the authority delegated. As the judiciary is not charged with lawmaking, the courts are not proper sources of law. But when the courts engage in noninterpretive review, they do make law. Striking an act as unconstitutional is no less an act of lawmaking than is the original promulgation of the act. Thus the sources thesis appears to cut against noninterpretive review. It is, I believe, the sources thesis that underlies the philosophical allure of positivist interpretivism, and it is the sources thesis that ultimately leads me to develop a positivist noninterpretivism.

What, then, is wrong with positivist interpretivism, given the powerful brief the sources thesis appears to provide against noninterpretivism? Why even attempt to retain the sources thesis and still condone noninterpretive review? Because positivist interpretivists adopt an overly restrictive concept of sovereignty.

Following Bentham, positivist interpretivists contend that valid law must be tied directly to the will of the sovereign in a state. As Bentham puts it: "A law may be defined as an assemblage of signs declarative of volition conceived or adopted by the *sovereign* in a state, concerning the conduct to be observed in a certain *case* by a certain person or class of persons, who in the case in question are or are supposed to be subject to his power."[10] When a law is viewed with respect to its source,

> the will of which it is the expression must, as the definition intimates, be the will of the sovereign in a state. Now by a sovereign I mean a person or assemblage of persons to whose will a whole political community are (no matter on what account) supposed to be in a disposition to pay obedience. . . . A mandate [law] is either referable to the sovereign or it is not: in the latter case it is illegal, and what we have nothing to do with here.[11]

The lesson drawn from Bentham is that law is an expression of the will of the sovereign. Any expression of will other than that of the sovereign, regardless of the form of the expression, is not, indeed cannot be, law. Law is created when and only when the sovereign expresses its will. The only modification of the basic Benthamite theory of law necessary to make it applicable to a constitutional democracy is that lawmaking organs to whom the sovereign has delegated lawmaking powers may make valid laws only when acting within the scope of the authority delegated to them. Thus, only the sovereign and agents of the sovereign may make law, and, then, in the case of the agents, only when acting within the scope of delegated authority. But where is the sovereign will expressed and where is political authority delegated?

For positivist interpretivists, the constitutional text is the sole expression of the sovereign will; that text, and that text alone, is determinative of law and of legitimate delegations of lawmaking power (authority). Any piece of legislation or court action that contravenes constitutional requirements is, *eo ipso*, subject to judicial invalidation as is any delegation of lawmaking authority (on the federal level) not sanctioned by the text. The text of the Constitution, for positivist interpretivists, serves the function of Kelsen's *Grundnorm*: It underwrites the legitimacy of all other laws or delegations of lawmaking authority.[12] Given that the fundamental expression of sovereign will is contained in the text of the Constitution, one may still ask of whose will is the document an expression? Put another way, who is sovereign? The positivist interpretivist answers this question in an unacceptably narrow way. The will of which the constitutional text is an expression is the will of the framers of the document.[13]

The excessive narrowness of the Benthamite concept of sovereignty, which is adopted by modern positivist interpretivists, can be seen in Bentham's few remarks concerning the institution of judicial review. Being wed to the idea of an *unlimited* sovereign, Bentham finds the institution of judicial review inconsistent with the very idea of sovereign authority. "By this unicompetence, by this negation of all limits, this also is to be understood, namely, that let the legislature do what it will, nothing that it does is to be regarded as null and void: in other words, it belongs not to any judge so to pronounce concerning it: for, to give such powers to any judge would be to give the judge . . . a power superior to that of the legislature itself."[14] Bentham's dislike for the institution of judicial review can be traced directly to his theory of unlimited sovereign power—a theory of sovereignty expressly rejected by the framers of the Constitution. Accordingly, any theory of constitutional interpretation applicable to a government of limited powers must reject the Benthamite theory of sovereign power. Despite this clear need, positivist interpretivists at least tacitly accept Bentham's concept of sovereignty. In the third section of this chapter I develop a theory of sovereignty that is markedly different from Bentham's, but one that is nonetheless consistent with Bentham's positivist theory of law.[15]

For the positivist interpretivist, having adopted both a Benthamite theory of law and a Benthamite (though not Bentham's) theory of sovereignty, determining what a particular constitutional provision requires—what the standards of legal validity under that provision are—requires looking first to the express text and then, if the text is not self-explanatory, to the intentions of the framers of the provision. To be sure, the positivist interpretivist program is an inviting one, but it cannot, as will be demonstrated shortly, succeed.

At first blush, the positivist interpretivist project is quite alluring. Using the positivist interpretivist criterion for judging legislative enactments unconstitutional, only those enactments that violate clear passages in the Constitution could legitimately be struck by the courts as unconstitutional. Judicial review, as an institution, would thus be immune from charges of government by judiciary and improper judicial policymaking. If the positivist interpretivist project were viable, only those enactments that, to borrow a Quinean aphorism, wear their unconstitutionality on their sleeves could, and would, legitimately be struck as unconstitutional. There are few, if any, legal theorists who could find fault with judicial invalidation of legislative acts running afoul of so stringent a criterion of constitutionality.[16]

Unfortunately, adopting such a criterion of unconstitutionality is unacceptable on several grounds. First, assuming, *arguendo,* that the position of the positivist interpretivist does not fall into the intentionalist fallacy, there are still good reasons for believing that the project cannot succeed. Gary Sherman states the case with admirable clarity and eloquence:

> Christopher Hogwood has a simple goal: the reinterpretation of all major Western symphonic works according to "original intention," using original instruments, original ensembles, original stylistic methods and so forth. Which is a laudable effort that, if carried out with Maestro Hogwood's usual skill, should contribute greatly to aesthetic enlightenment. However, there is one aspect of the original performance that cannot be duplicated: None of us can listen to the result with 18th or 19th-century ears or feel its effects with 18th or 19th-century hearts. The world has changed and we cannot pretend that Antonin Dvořák, Bela Bartok, Aaron Copeland, jazz and rock 'n' roll never happened. Irrespective of the purity of the presentation, we will not hear what our forebears heard.[17]

Even if one could determine the original intention of the legislators who enacted a provision, it is not clear that that intention would be of any use to a modern court attempting to apply a two hundred year-old provision of the Constitution to one of today's problems.

Even politically honest[18] positivist interpretivists seem to miss the importance of this point. William W. Crosskey, a much neglected proponent of positivist interpretivism, was fond of quoting Justice Holmes on the true nature of legal interpretation. Holmes said that when interpreting a provision: "We ask not what this man meant, but what those words would mean in the mouth of the normal speaker of English, using them in the circumstances in which they were used."[19] The Holmes approach to interpretation lends support to the positivist interpretivist just in case the speaker whose words were in need of interpretation was one of the framers of the provision. If the question raised by a party challenging some governmental action as unconstitutional were "Would this action, had it been undertaken in 1789, have been unconstitutional?" then emphasizing original intentions would be completely correct. But such is *not* the question asked. Rather, the question is whether a particular governmental action, undertaken today, in the last quarter of the twentieth century, is unconstitutional. Today's "normal speaker of English" speaks the language of the late twentieth century, not the late eighteenth. The crucial words are used in the context of today, not two hundred years ago. The approach of the positivist interpretivist is thus not so much wrong as it is wrongheaded.

Second, positivist interpretivism, taken seriously, makes hash of accepted Supreme Court practice. Regardless of the political bent of the decisions involved, interpretivism holds that most of the major decisions in constitutional law, including *Marbury v. Madison*,[20] are illegitimate because, *inter alia*, there is no clear expression in the Constitution that the Court may review the constitutionality of acts of Congress. Among the cases other than *Marbury* that end up being illegitimate on an interpretivist basis are *Lochner v. New York*,[21] *Brown v. Board of Education*,[22] *Griswold v. Connecticut*,[23] *Mapp v. Ohio*,[24] and *Roe v. Wade*.[25] The difficulty with positivist interpretivism is that it is not at all faithful to actual legal practice. Courts do not, and have not in the U.S. legal experience, behaved as the positivist interpretivists would have them behave. A theory of constitutional adjudication that bears precious little relevance to the phenomena of which it is a theory or that seriously misdescribes the phenomena to be explained is, at best, a poor theory.

Finally, positivist interpretivism leaves no role for courts to play as agents of social change. Legal scholars have, over the past thirty years, gradually, sometimes grudgingly, come to recognize the legitimacy of the claim of the American Legal Realists that courts can, do, and should act as agents of social change and social reform. The clearest example of such action by the courts is the *Brown* decision and its progeny. Other examples can be found in the areas of criminal procedure, voting rights, and freedom of expression. In the positivist interpretivist model of constitutional adjudication, there is no place for such action. Anyone committed, as I am, to defending at least some role for the courts to play as agents of social change must reject positivist interpretivism. Adequate explication of Supreme Court behavior and support of the courts as agents of social change require a theory of judicial review that allows the courts to impose extraconstitutional values.

Simply rejecting positivist interpretivism does not, however, settle the issue. One must develop a theory that allows judicial imposition of values not expressed in the Constitution. One such theory is nonpositivist noninterpretivism. In the next section I show why such a theory cannot succeed.

THE FAILURE OF NONPOSITIVIST NONINTERPRETIVISM

Nonpositivist noninterpretivism sanctions judicial imposition of extraconstitutional values. In so doing, this theory underwrites the legitimacy of *Brown* and similar decisions. The difficulty with this theory is that one needs a defense of the values one would have the courts impose when engaging in judicial review. One obvious approach to defending nonpositivist noninterpretivism lies in natural law theory. Natural law, so the argument goes, provides a legitimate source for extraconstitutional values. Michael Perry provides a sophisticated natural law defense of nonpositivist noninterpretivism in *The Constitution, the Courts, and Human Rights.*

Perry's natural law defense of nonpositivist noninterpretivism is limited to human rights cases. He contends that noninterpretive review serves a special political function that cannot be served by any other institution or practice. For Perry, "[t]he function of noninterpretive review in human rights cases, then, is the elaboration and enforcement by the Courts of values, pertaining to human rights, not constitutionalized by the framers; it is the function of deciding what rights, beyond those specified by the framers, individuals should and shall have against government."[26] Deciding what rights people should and shall have against government involves deciding what is, at heart, a *political-moral* question. What is more, if the decision is to be politically legitimate, then the decision on the matter must be correct.[27] But what, one must ask, is the criterion to use in judging the correctness of an answer to a political-moral question? For Perry, the criterion with which to judge the correctness of an answer to a political-moral question, and the ultimate source of extraconstitutional values, is "a particular conception of the American polity that seems to constitute a basic, irreducible feature of the American people's understanding of themselves. The conception can be described, for want of a better word, as religious."[28]

Perry recognizes that his answer to the question invites misunderstanding. The religious self-understanding that lies at the heart of Perry's defense of nonpositivist noninterpretive review is in no sense sectarian or theistic. Rather, it involves a commitment "to the notion of moral evolution,"[29] a commitment that recognizes that the will of the people is not the definitive answer to moral questions: The people may be (and often are) mistaken in their moral appraisal of certain questions. What is more, Perry believes that the people recognize their fallibility and are committed to a search for right (or at least better) answers to fundamental moral questions. The people have a commitment to a higher law, a law that determines the correctness of an answer to a political-moral question "independently of what a majority of the American people [believes or] comes to believe in the future."[30]

Thus, "noninterpretive review in human rights cases enables us to take seriously—indeed is a way of taking seriously—the possibility that there are right answers to political-moral problems."[31] The possibility that there are right answers, Perry argues, is one to which the American people are "religiously" committed. Assuming that Perry's views on the religious self-concept of U.S. citizens is correct, what problems follow from entrusting to the courts the task of moving popular moral beliefs in the direction of correct moral beliefs? At least two quite distinct challenges can be leveled at Perry's delegation of moral decisionmaking. The first concerns political theory (why the courts rather than the legislature?); the second concerns the epistemological worries raised by skepticism.

To the charge that the courts are institutionally less competent to make moral decisions (or to reach decisions on difficult moral questions) than are legislatures, Perry gives a predictable answer in terms of political insulation. The courts, Perry argues, being free from the will of the voters, are less likely to decide moral questions through reference to established moral conventions than are legislators. To be sure, Perry's claims seem to be susceptible of empirical confirmation. A detailed study of judicial as opposed to legislative behavior concerning decision of moral issues should allow one to determine whether courts do in fact reach correct moral decisions more often than do legislatures. Of course, this suggestion leads directly to the epistemological problems presented by skepticism.

On the epistemological level, Perry's thesis raises serious questions about how the courts can come to know one of the right answers to a moral question. An ethical skeptic or a moral relativist would simply challenge Perry's assertion that there are context-independent right answers to moral questions. The ethical skeptic argues that even if there are right answers to moral questions (if there is moral truth), those answers are beyond the scope of human knowledge. There may well be moral truth, but human beings cannot obtain it and judges certainly have no better claim to it than do electorally responsible legislators. Because judges have no better claim to moral truth than do legislators, and because judges are electorally unaccountable, entrusting to the courts the task of determining which moral standards a society shall adhere to runs the risk of a moral dictatorship by the judiciary. Hence the rejection of noninterpretive review on skeptical grounds. Perry recognizes that the skeptic presents serious difficulties for his view, and he attempts to reject the position (Perry seems unaware of just how worthy an opponent the Pyrrhonic skeptic has proven in the history of philosophy). Unfortunately, Perry simply rejects the position of the ethical (and, in passing, epistemological) skeptic without arguing against it. To be sure, Perry notes that many people reject ethical skepticism on many different grounds. Perry's response to the skeptic smacks of question begging. Unless Perry can provide a stronger refutation of moral skepticism, nonpositivist noninterpretivism seems to be indefensible on theoretical grounds.

What emerge then are strong reasons for rejecting both positivist interpretivism and nonpositivist noninterpretivism. What is needed is a middle ground position, one that accepts the strengths of the extremes of the spectrum without embracing the critical defects inherent in each. Such a position, a positivist noninterpretivism, is set forth in the next section.

POSITIVIST NONINTERPRETIVISM

The central defect in positivist interpretivism is that that theory does not sanction judicial imposition of any extraconstitutional values. Nonpositivist noninterpretivism remedies this defect, but at too high a price. The justification of judicial imposition of extraconstitutional values provided by Perry rests on unstable epistemic foundations, runs the risk of justifying a judicial moral tyranny, and pays no heed at all to the sources thesis or the principle of electorally accountable policymaking. For Perry, the moral principles that underwrite noninterpretive review exist and determine correct answers to moral questions independently of what a majority of the people believe or come to believe. What is needed, then, is a theory of judicial review that remains faithful to the sources thesis and the principle of electorally responsible policymaking while sanctioning the judicial imposition of some extraconstitutional values. Positivist noninterpretivism is just such a theory.

Central positivist noninterpretivism is the development of a coherent version of legal positivism that does not tie sovereignty exclusively to the intentions of the framers. Such a development requires major modifications of the concept of sovereignty adopted by the positivist interpretivists. The remainder of this section is divided into four subsections. The first deals with the concept of sovereignty. The second deals with the nature of the extraconstitutional values that the courts may impose under the concept of sovereignty developed in the first subsection. The third discusses the role of the courts as agents of social change under a positivist noninterpretivist theory of judicial review. Finally, the fourth subsection discusses some of the difficulties presented by the theory I advocate.

The Concept of Sovereignty

The defects noted above with positivist interpretivism can be traced directly to the overly restrictive concept of sovereignty adopted by adherents of that theory. The locus of sovereignty, for the positivist interpretivists, is the will of the framers of the Constitution. Law must be an expression of the will of the sovereign, fundamental law is expressed in the Constitution, and the will of which the Constitution is an expression is the will of the framers. Accordingly the emphasis placed on original intentions.

Positivist noninterpretivism, on the other hand, identifies the locus of sovereignty as the will of a consensus of the people (the will of the people, for short). The people are sovereign, and it is the will of the people, not the framers, that is determinative of law. At first this does not seem like a major modification, but it has far reaching implications for legal theory. Simply shifting the locus of sovereignty from the will of the framers to that of a consensus of the people allows one to see at least two critical differences between interpretivist and noninterpretivist versions of positivist constitutional theory. Two areas in which important differences are readily visible are changes in the sovereign will and the determination of the meaning of constitutional provisions.

Can the will of the sovereign, with respect to issues of fundamental law, change over time? To this question both the interpretivist and noninterpretivist positivists answer in the affirmative. Their answers differ, however, with respect to the ease with which change is possible and with respect to the mechanism of change. For the positivist interpretivist, the will of the sovereign, being linked to the will of the framers, is relatively fixed and static. The will of the sovereign on issues of fundamental law is fixed in the Constitution. Changes in fundamental law, revisions in the will of the sovereign, require amending the Constitution. If fundamental law is to be created or changed, the positivist interpretivist insists that such changes should be made in the legislature, through the amendment process, not in the courts.[32]

For the positivist noninterpretivist, on the other hand, the will of the sovereign, even with respect to questions of fundamental law, is fluid and mutable; it changes as the will of the people changes. Times and social conditions change, and law, even fundamental law, if it is to be of service to the people, must be able to change in response to changing circumstances. As Dean Harry W. Jones puts it,

> It has become a truism that law must be kept up to date, responsive to the continuing processes of social change. Present-day judges are very much aware that concepts and categories received from law's past—privity of contract, sovereign immunity, "fault" in divorce actions and many more—may not order contemporary phenomena effectively and justly. It is not that these concepts were necessarily wrong when they were handed down; we are, I think, too quick to assume that. It is simply that, whatever their original justification, they offer the wrong answers for today's problems.

> One hates, in a way, to see old friends like negligence, consideration and "state action" withering away in vitality and influence, but, to borrow a phrase from Justice Roger Traynor, "the number they have called is no longer in service."[33]

Jones's observations apply no less to questions of fundamental law than they do to questions of more mundane areas of substantive law.[34] For the positivist noninterpretivist, when the will of a consensus of the people changes with respect to a particular issue, the law on that issue has changed, and the courts should be both empowered and required to enforce the new understanding. The reason underlying such an empowerment and such a requirement should be clear: A positivist theory of law, in which sovereignty is explicated in terms of the will of a consensus of the governed, *requires* it. Law is an expression of the will of the sovereign, and sovereignty resides in the governed. As the role of courts is to enforce the laws of the sovereign, it follows that if the will of the sovereign on a particular issue conflicts with the will expressed in a particular statutory or even constitutional provision, then the courts should enforce the current will as against the will expressed in the provision. The will expressed in the provision, not being reflective of the will of the sovereign, has lost the force of law.

If courts were to act on the will expressed in the provision, they would be acting contrary to the will of the sovereign, contrary to law. Such behavior on the part of courts no doubt takes place, but such actions are clearly *ultra vires.* The will of the sovereign is determinative of law. If the will of the sovereign is clear, and a court knows that will and disregards it, for whatever reason, then that court has exceeded its legitimate authority and has acted illegally.

In many instances, of course, when a question comes before a court for decision the will of a consensus of the people may not be clear. It may be that people have failed to consider the issue or it may be that a consensus from a previous era is undergoing reexamination. In such cases, the role of the courts will be rather different than that described in this subsection. Such situations are discussed in the third subsection.

The second area in which important differences between the interpretivist and noninterpretivist versions of legal positivism appear is in the determination of the meaning of various constitutional provisions. For the positivist interpretivists, ideally, a constitutional provision wears its meaning on its sleeve. All that one need do in order to determine precisely what a constitutional provision requires is to read the provision.[35] When the meaning of a provision is unclear, then the courts should look to the legislative history of the provision to determine the original intent. If, as in the case of the liberty clauses of the Fifth and Fourteenth amendments, the meaning of the provision is unclear, and there is no legislative history indicating what the framers intended, the courts should refrain from imbuing the provision with their own values. Although there is a certain appeal to such a program, it has the unfortunate and unacceptable effect of deoperationalizing many important provisions in the Constitution.

Positivist noninterpretivism, on the other hand, has the court look to the understanding and will of a consensus of the people with respect to unclear constitutional provisions in order to determine the meaning of such provisions. The precise meaning of a constitutional provision depends upon the understanding of a consensus of the people with respect to that provision. As times change, and as the people's understanding of a constitutional provision changes, the legal requirements imposed by that provision change. An example of this sort of change can be seen in the attitudinal change with respect to equal protection that took place in the United States between 1896 (*Plessy v. Ferguson*) and 1954 (*Brown*). As the people, prompted by the courts, gradually came to the view that the requirements of the Equal Protection Clause were inconsistent with state-enforced racial segregation (a view shared by a consensus of the people at least by the late 1960s), the meaning of the Equal Protection Clause changed. That the framers of the Fourteenth Amendment did not intend to outlaw segregated public schools is of little importance. The will of the sovereign (the people) in 1954 was different than it had been in 1867. If the will of the people concerning a constitutional provision at one moment in history is at odds with the will of an earlier generation, so much the worse for the previous generation.

Sovereign will, for the positivist noninterpretivist, is determined through reference to a consensus of the governed. In order to make sense of the continued legal validity of old (sometimes ancient) statutory or constitutional provisions that cannot properly be understood to be a part of the will of the current sovereign, one needs a Lockean doctrine of tacit consent or tacit reauthorization. Unless the current sovereign specifically overrules actions of a previous sovereign, those actions remain in force. There are no major difficulties with this part of the consensus approach to sovereignty. Difficulties arise in determining what the consensus is on controversial issues like abortion. I address those difficulties in the third subsection. Assuming that I can construct a positivist theory of constitutional interpretation in which the concept of sovereignty is not tied to the intentions of the framers, what makes such a theory noninterpretivist? I address that question in the next subsection.

Determining the Values Courts May Impose

In the previous subsection I discussed modifications in the concept of sovereignty necessary to divorce the will of the sovereign from the will of the framers. So doing sets the stage for a positivist theory of constitutional adjudication that is noninterpretivist. The theory being developed is positivist in that it adheres to the sources thesis and, as will be demonstrated shortly, to the separability thesis. But it is also noninterpretivist.

The central feature of any noninterpretivist theory of judicial review is that the courts are empowered legitimately to impose extraconstitutional values—values that are not clearly stated in the Constitution nor intended by the framers to be imbedded in it. Because the concept of sovereignty outlined above locates sovereignty in the will of a consensus of the people, it should be clear that *legal* values need not be restricted to those expressly stated in the Constitution. The *text* of the Constitution simply is not the final word on questions of fundamental law.[36] Because law is but an expression of the will of the sovereign, for a norm to become law all that is required is that that norm be a part of the will of the sovereign. Thus, with certain exceptions, for a value to become law, all that is required is that that value become a part of the will of the sovereign. Even if these values are clearly extraconstitutional, such as the value of racial equality *vis-à-vis* the Fourteenth Amendment, that value becomes law, becomes legally binding, when incorporated into the value scheme willed by a consensus of the people. Once a value, even an extraconstitutional value, is so willed, the courts may legitimately apply that value. If and when a consensus determines that, say, equal protection of the laws is inconsistent with, *inter alia,* state-imposed racial discrimination, despite a deafening silence on such issues within the text of the Constitution, the value judgment adopted by the people becomes legally applicable by the courts. Accordingly, the version of positivism being considered here is noninterpretivist. One might worry that this theory runs roughshod over constitutional protection of minority rights against majority tyranny. In the last subsection I discuss this problem and a solution to it that involves restrictions placed on majority rule by the sovereign.

Care must be taken at this point not to confuse the positivist noninterpretivism that I advocate with the nonpositivist natural law theory advocated by Perry. In my view only those values that are part of the will of a consensus of the people are legally binding. If the people fail to incorporate a particular moral principle into their will, then that principle ultimately lacks legal force and can play, at most, a very limited role in legitimate judicial decisionmaking. That is not to say, however, that such a principle has no role at all, as will be discussed in the next subsection. To deny that principles, regardless of their moral validity, not willed by the sovereign lack legal force would be to deny both the sources and separability theses. That I am unwilling to do. Perry, on the other hand, straightforwardly denies the separability, and, *eo ipso,* the thesis. Perry argues that there are legally binding moral principles that exist and determine the correct answers to political-moral questions "independently of what a majority of the American people [believes or] comes to believe in the future."[37] And, for Perry, those principles should govern Supreme Court behavior when engaging in noninterpretive review.

Courts as Agents of Social Change

Even if one concedes that courts should apply the value scheme adopted by the sovereign as described here, it is not at all clear that there is a role for the courts to play as agents of social change. Moreover, it is unclear that there is any role for moral principles not incorporated into the will of the sovereign in judicial review. If one were to hold, as I do not, that the consensus on a particular moral question determinative of law at any given moment in history is the actual consensus of a prereflective or unreflective citizenry, neither of the roles mentioned above would exist. The courts would, in such a view, properly *reflect* change, but they would not initiate it. Moreover, such a view would result in the standards of constitutionality being held hostage by popular sentiment. In such a view, the decision in *Korematsu v. U.S.* might well turn out to be fully legitimate, the ruling reflecting the will of the majority at the time, while the decision in *Brown* would be illegitimate in that it failed, at the time the decision was made, to reflect a consensus.[38] Such results, however, can be avoided by allowing the courts to act as agents of social change, not merely as reflectors of it.

Claiming that there are instances in which courts should be allowed to act as agents of social change, where social change means a change in the will of the sovereign, has significant implications for legal theory. The claim suggests that a case sometimes comes before a court even though there is no clear law governing the case. The simple fact of the matter is that there are cases in which either the law is unclear or in which there is no law on the matter. Situations of this sort can arise when cases are unforeseen or when the people realize that what was once an accepted solution to a problem no longer "orders the phenomena justly and fairly." In either case, a court is faced with a very difficult task—it must decide a case[39] in the absence of clear law (perhaps in the absence of law at all).

This claim amounts to saying that there are gaps (lacunae) in the law that courts must attempt to fill.[40] A gap exists in the law whenever a case falls within the jurisdiction of a court and there are no clear legal rules for its resolution.[41] To be sure, the existence of legal lacunae has been much debated, and the existence or nonexistence of the same is a major question for legal theory. Even though this chapter is not a proper forum for exploring the issue of legal lacunae in depth, I do think it important to point out that my version of positivist noninterpretivism requires their existence. Moreover, positivist noninterpretivism makes it the province of the courts to fill such gaps.

When a court seeks to fill in a gap in the law, when it seeks to find/make the law, what the court must do is attempt to determine, or to help in the determination of, the will of a consensus of the people. If the court were to do otherwise, it would be abandoning the sources thesis and, accordingly, acting *ultra vires.* Thus saying that a court may, indeed has to, decide cases in the absence of law does not amount to a rejection of the sources thesis. In the absence of a clear consensus, in the absence of law, a court should attempt to determine the consensus or to shape it, whichever is appropriate to the case.

Determining the consensus of the people is never an easy task. The task is made all the more difficult when the issue involves a moral problem that the people have not subjected, or will not subject, to critical examination. The consensus determinative of law should be a reflective rather than a prereflective or unreflective one. It is in the provocation of critical reflection on difficult issues that the court has a role to play as an agent of social change. By tackling some tough issues, and attempting to find acceptable solutions to them, the courts have an extraordinary power to force critical evaluation or reevaluation of moral beliefs. The courts have the ability to act as *agents provocateurs* of a developing moral consensus. When there is no clear consensus on a particular moral question, or when the consensus appears to be unreflective, the task of the courts should be to try to determine an appropriate principle for resolving the issue and then see whether, upon reflection, a consensus develops that embraces the principle articulated. What is more, should a court fail to articulate a principle on which there is a consensus, or should it articulate a principle that runs counter to the reflective consensus, there are a number of ways in which such a principle can be denied legal force. Several examples should help clarify this point.

Three important cases dealing with difficult moral issues exemplify the nature of the role that courts should play as agents of social change. The cases are *Brown, Roe v. Wade,* and *Lochner,* representing, respectively, the court successfully acting as an agent of social change, the court urging a moral principle on which there is not yet a consensus, and the court urging a moral principle rejected by the people. Depending upon how one reads the social science data, a strong case can be made to the effect that in 1954 there was no consensus concerning racial equality and the Equal Protection Clause. The Court, however, saw that there was a need to address the issue of state-sponsored racial segregation and undertook to articulate a moral principle for dealing with the issue. To be sure, the principle articulated by the Court in *Brown* prompted neither instant nor universal assent, but it did force a critical evaluation of attitudes concerning racial discrimination. And, importantly, within twenty years a clear consensus had developed, a reflective consensus, agreeing with the principle articulated by the Court.

In clear contrast to the Court's success in changing social attitudes in *Brown* stands its limited success in dealing with the abortion issue. In *Roe* the Court accepted the task of attempting to articulate a moral principle for dealing with the problem of abortion that would be acceptable to a consensus of the people. The principle it articulated, however, far from coalescing a consensus, appears to have split public opinion. Few people are happy with the principle underpinning *Roe.* Those who favor the decision often feel that the right to abort should be stronger than the one the Court articulated; those who oppose the decision feel that there should be no such right. The ultimate fate of the decision still hangs in the balance, awaiting the development of a reflective consensus. The Court clearly succeeded in *Roe* in provoking critical examination of moral beliefs, but it has not yet and may never, succeed in discovering a moral principle governing the problem of abortion acceptable to a consensus of the people. Should a consensus fail to develop, the Court should return the issue to the states for determination in more homogenous forums. In my view the courts simply cannot provide answers to all questions and on those where they cannot, they should refer the questions to an organ of government more competent to decide.

Lochner provides a clear example of what happens when the courts identify a political-moral principle that is actually, or upon reflection, ultimately, rejected by the consensus. There are good reasons to believe that even in 1905 a majority of the people would have rejected the applicability of laissez-faire economics to many of the then current social problems. When the Court embraced laissez-faire, over Holmes's objections that the Constitution was written for people of fundamentally differing views, public rejection of the principle adopted by the Court was swift and overwhelming. Legislators continued to pass legislation that flew in the face of laissez-faire principles (much of it was subsequently struck), and President Harry Truman threatened to pack the Court with justices who would reverse *Lochner.* Within thirty years the Court saw the error of its ways and reversed. Had the Court not reversed, the people had and have other means at their disposal with which to reject court decisions (short of a court-packing plan). Perhaps the most powerful of these means is the amendment process.

One of the much overlooked features of the U.S. political landscape is the relation between the amendment process and rejection of Supreme Court decisions. There have been, of course, but twenty-six amendments to the Constitution of which ten accompanied the original document and were necessary for ratification, and yet another two were a serious mistake and its correction (prohibition). Of the remaining fourteen, five of the amendments are clear repudiations of Supreme Court decisions. The Eleventh Amendment reverses the decision in *Chisholm v. Georgia,*[42] the Thirteenth and Fourteenth reverse *Scott v. Sanford,*[43] the Sixteenth reverses *Pollock v. Farmer's Loan and Trust Co.,*[44] and the Twenty-sixth reverses *Oregon v. Mitchell.*[45] The amendment procedure is a powerful tool that the people can and have utilized to correct what are, in the eyes of the people, serious mistakes on the part of the Court when it comes to answering difficult political-moral issues. When the Court errs, there are remedies.[46]

Having outlined a theory of judicial review that is both positivist and noninterpretivist, and that retains a role for the courts to play as agents but not the sole determiners of social change, several problems remain to be considered. The problems addressed in the next subsection fall into two broad categories: those dealing with the determination of a consensus and those dealing with the problem of majority tyranny.

Difficulties with Positivist Noninterpretivism

The core of my positivist noninterpretivist theory of judicial review is the location of sovereignty in the will of a consensus of the people. Consensus theories, however, face several serious difficulties, not the least of which involves determining what the consensus is and whose views are to count toward the consensus. There are at least two approaches to determining a consensus: Everyone's views are to count and to count equally (a moral one-person, one-vote principle), or the views of some count more than, and perhaps to the exclusion of, the views of others. The former approach has been adopted by Edmund Burke and by Alexander Bickel in his later writings; the latter by modern-day contractarians, John Rawls, and others. Each of these approaches presents difficulties.

If, on the one hand, the views of some are to count more than the views of others in the determination of the consensus, two problems arise. First, as the views of some persons are valued more highly than the views of others, the charge that the consensus is elitist is hard to defeat. Even if those whose views are to be taken more seriously are identified as "competent judges" according to Rawls,[47] the consensus that emerges from the competent judges is in no way democratic. In a society at least nominally committed to democratic policymaking, this is a serious difficulty. The second difficulty involves the determination of who is to count as a competent judge in moral matters. The identification of competent judges in any area of inquiry often smacks of question-begging or stacking the deck. Determining who is a competent judge is often a question of power politics, a determination geared toward maintaining the status quo. Even in objective realms like physical science, Thomas Kuhn, Paul Feyerabend, and their followers argue that people who disagree with the majority power brokers are, despite their objective competence, ruled incompetent. Disagreement with the majority becomes a pretext for banishment to the gulag of incompetence. One should recall Bertrand Russell's conjugation of the highly irregular verb: I am firm, you are obstinate, he is a pig-headed fool. Although there may well be acceptable answers to the problem of determining who is to count as a competent judge (though I, I should confess, am dubious of even that modest prospect), I can see no way to counter the charge that entrusting policymaking exclusively to competent judges is inherently antidemocratic. It is, of course, disturbing that unqualified (not to say incompetent) persons take part in the democratic process, but democracy may well require not only a right to be wrong but a right to be stupidly wrong. To paraphrase Oliver Wendell Holmes, a commitment to democracy seems to require that the people are entitled to go to hell in a handbasket, so long as they vote themselves there.

Of course, embracing the other option, namely, that everyone's views count equally toward the consensus, poses a clear danger of majority tyranny. Burke noted long ago that there is nothing sacred in the concept of majority rule. It applies, where it does, as a result of history and habit, not because it is in any way an objectively superior form of government. Pure majority rule subjects the standards of legality and constitutionality to the sentiments rampant in the citizenry.[48] Protection of minority rights becomes, to put it mildly, a very serious problem.

Despite the serious nature of problems such as the protection of minority rights, my positivist noninterpretivist theory commits me to what Bill Nelson has called "radical democracy." Ultimately the exclusive determinant of what law is is the will of a consensus of the people. If the people will unwise, politically unsound, or clearly immoral laws into existence, then we are stuck with unwise, unsound, or immoral laws as sovereignty is located in the will of the people. As Justice Stewart said, dissenting in *Griswold v. Connecticut,* the silliness, or stupidity, or even asininity of a law does not, in itself, make such a law unconstitutional.[49] I wholeheartedly embrace Stewart's position. The courts simply are not the place within our system to seek protection from unwise, immoral, or blatantly discriminatory legislation. To be sure, such protection must be sought somewhere, but, as Learned Hand so ably argues: "This much I think I do know—that a society so riven that the spirit of moderation is gone, no court *can* save; that a society where that spirit flourishes, no court *need* save; that in a society which evades its responsibility by thrusting upon the courts the nurture of that spirit, that spirit in the end will perish."[50] To be sure, a society needs to try and protect itself against majority tyranny. But such protection lies chiefly outside the courts.[51] There is, however, a limited role for the courts to play in providing such protections.

One way the courts can aid in protecting society against majority tyranny is through the enforcement of self-imposed limits on majority power or action, that is, empowering courts to force the majority to abide by rules to which it, the majority, has agreed—rules that effectively disable the majority from asserting its will in certain areas. The restrictions on state and federal government actions found in Article I, Sections 9 and 10, and in the Bill of Rights count as instances of disabling rules that the courts could enforce. To be sure, such a move promotes protection of minority rights, but it does not guarantee them absolutely. Ultimately, of course, the protection offered by the courts is minimal in that the courts are empowered to enforce only those limitations on majority power that the majority accept. Should a super-majority (the two-thirds of the people needed to amend the Constitution—a number itself the product of self-imposed restraint) decide to free itself from the fetters of current constitutional restraints, then the courts can offer no protection.

Though I find the idea repugnant, I can see no good reason to suppose that the people could not free the states from the restrictions of the Fourteenth Amendment through the repeal process. If there were to be any protection from such action, it would lie outside the courts.

One thing that a positivist noninterpretivist theory of judicial review cannot guarantee, and does not pretend to guarantee, is that the courts will articulate correct moral values, or that the consensus that emerges will embrace correct values. There is no protection against morally bad, yet legally valid, laws. And there is no guarantee that a future decision like *Brown* would be legitimate while one like *Lochner* would be illegitimate. Those decisions and decisions like them stand on the same footing: Each is potentially legitimate. Where they differ is in the verdict history has passed on them. To ask for a guarantee that all decisions in cases of noninterpretive review will be morally correct is to ask too much from a theory of judicial review. To seek, as so many constitutional theorists seek, a theory that guarantees *Brown* while protecting against *Lochner* is truly the elusive quest.

NOTES

1. Alexander Bickel begins his classic defense of nonpositivist noninterpretive review, *The Least Dangerous Branch,* with the observation "The least dangerous branch of the American government is the most extraordinarily powerful court of law the world has ever known. The power which distinguishes the Supreme Court of the United States is that of constitutional review of actions of the other branches of government, federal and state." A. Bickel, *The Least Dangerous Branch: The Supreme Court at the Bar of Politics* (Indianapolis, Ind.: Bobbs-Merrill, 1963), p. 1.

2. Critics of judicial review (Ely among them) frequently fail to discuss one of the important functions of judicial review—legitimation. Whenever the Court upholds a legislative enactment (a far more common result than invalidation), that enactment gains an air of legitimacy. For a discussion of the legitimating function, see, A. Bickel, *supra* note 1, p. 29 ff.

3. J. H. Ely, *Democracy and Distrust: A Theory of Judicial Review* (New Haven, Conn.: Yale Univ. Press, 1980), p. 5.

4. For excellent contemporary statements of the positivist interpretivist position, see, R. Berger, *Government by Judiciary* (Cambridge: Harvard, 1977) and R. Bork, *Traditional Morality in Constitutional Law* (Washington D.C.: American Enterprise Institute, 1984); R. Bork, "Neutral Principles and Some First Amendment Problems," 47 *Indiana L. J.* 1 (1971). Excellent contemporary statements of the nonpositivist noninterpretivist position can be found in A. Bickel, *supra* note 1; M. Perry, *The Constitution, the Courts, and Human Rights* (New Haven, Conn.: Yale Univ. Press, 1977); T. Grey, "Do We Have an Unwritten Constitution," 27 *Stanford L. Rev.* 703 (1975).

5. *U.S. v. Butler,* 297 U.S. 1, 63 (1936).

6. One is reminded of the Vince Lombardi theory of equal protection. "Sure," Coach Lombardi is reported to have said, "I treat all my players equally. They're all scum." On a strict interpretivist reading of the Equal Protection Clause, as neither the language of the constitutional provision nor the intent of the framers

gives any guidance, a court would be compelled to rule a legislative equivalent to the Lombardi approach constitutional. Similarly, whenever a legislature says, "But that is all the process she is due," the court would be compelled to hold whatever minimal process the legislature provided as adequate.

7. See, for example, Lon L. Fuller, *The Morality of Law* (New Haven, Conn.: Yale Univ. Press, 1964); "Positivism and the Fidelity to Law," 71 *Harvard L. Rev.* 593 (1958).

8. Joseph Raz, "Legal Reasons, Sources, and Gaps," in Joseph Raz, *The Authority of Law* (Oxford: Clarendon Press, 1979), p. 53.

9. For a full statement of Kelsen's doctrines of authorization, see Stanley Paulson, "Material and Formal Authorization in Kelsen's Pure Theory," 39 *Cambridge L. J.* 172 (1980).

10. Jeremy Bentham, *Of Laws in General,* H.L.A. Hart ed. (Oxford: Oxford Univ. Press, 1970), p. 1.

11. *Ibid.*, pp. 18 ff.

12. For a discussion of the Constitution as *Grundnorm* see Paulson, *supra* note 9. Paulson makes the important point that the Constitution serves both a validating and an invalidating function; that is, the Constitution allows one both to determine which laws are invalid and which are valid. As noted above, the legitimating function of judicial review is a much neglected feature of the practice, neglected primarily by critics.

13. Robert Bork has noted that whenever possible judges talk as if they were searching for the intent of the framers ("Neutral Principles and Some First Amendment Problems," *supra* note 4 at pp. 3–4). Other authors insist that judges should be bound by the intent of the framers. Berger, *supra* note 4; T. Diamond, "Democracy and 'The Federalist': A Reconsideration of the Framers' Intent," 53 *Am. Pol. Sci. Rev.* 52 (1959); J. P. Frank and R. F. Monroe, "The Original Understanding of 'Equal Protection of the Laws,'" 50 *Columbia L. Rev.* 131 (1950); H. Morrison, "Does the Fourteenth Amendment Incorporate the Bill of Rights?: The Judicial Interpretation," 2 *Stanford L. Rev.* 140 (1949); C. Warren, "The New Liberty Under the Fourteenth Amendment," 339 *Harvard L. Rev.* 431 (1926). There are, of course, many who reject the quest for the original understanding. A. Bickel, "The Original Understanding and the Segregation Decision," 69 *Harvard L. Rev.* 1 (1955); P. Brest, "The Misconceived Quest for the Original Understanding," 60 *Boston Univ. L. Rev.* 234 (1980); A. S. Miller and R. F. Howell, "The Myth of Neutrality in Constitutional Adjudication," 27 *Univ. of Chicago L. Rev.* 661 (1960).

14. J. Bentham, "The Constitutional Code," in *The Works of Jeremy Bentham,* vol. 9, R. Bowring, ed. (London: Simpkin, Marshall, and Co., 1843), p. 121.

15. In large part I take my task here to be similar to that of Hart in his acceptance of a positivist theory of law while rejecting Austin's command theory of law and material reduction theory. I accept the basic Benthamite position on the nature of law, but I adopt a non-Benthamite, noninterpretivist theory of sovereignty.

16. One criticism of the interpretivist criterion of unconstitutionality is that it is too stringent. Felix Cohen argues that the interpretivist criterion, expressed in James Bradley Thayer's famous rule of clear mistake, amounts to a rule that what is rational is constitutional. "Taken seriously, this conception makes of our courts lunacy commissions sitting in judgment upon the mental capacity of legislators and, occasionally, of judicial brethren." F. Cohen, "Transcendental Nonsense and the Functional Approach," 35 *Columbia L. Rev.* 809, 819 (1935).

17. G. Sherman, "Keeping Alive a 2-century-old Document," *National L. J.*, Monday, October 13, 1986, p. 13.

18. One of the problems that one encounters in current debates about constitutional interpretation is that various theories of interpretation are often used to mask political convictions. The work of William Winslow Crosskey, for example, is almost totally ignored by current proponents of positivist interpretivism. This is odd in that Crosskey provides a careful and detailed study of the meaning of various constitutional provisions as they were understood by the framers in the context of the late eighteenth century. Crosskey's analysis, however, reveals that provisions like the Commerce Clause were originally intended to grant the federal government extraordinarily broad regulatory powers. Such a reading of the original intention of the Constitution is at odds with the political motives of many positivist interpretivists, so it comes as little surprise that Crosskey's work is virtually ignored. See, W. W. Crosskey, *Politics and The Constitution in the History of the United States*, 3 vol. (Chicago: Univ. of Chicago Press, 1980).

19. O. W. Holmes, "The Theory of Legal Interpretation," 12 *Harvard L. Rev.* 418 (1899). Crosskey, *supra* note 18, uses this quote from Holmes on the frontispiece of the first two volumes of *Politics and the Constitution.*

20. 5 U.S. (1 Cranch) 137 (1803).

21. 198 U.S. 45 (1905).

22. 347 U.S. 483 (1954).

23. 381 U.S. 469 (1965).

24. 367 U.S. 643 (1961).

25. 410 U.S. 113 (1973).

26. Perry, *supra* note 4, p. 93.

27. Perry does not subscribe to the view that there is a uniquely correct answer to each political-moral question—there may be several. Thus he rejects a moral version of Dworkin's right answer thesis. What Perry desires is a process of dispute resolution likely to reach one of the right answers to difficult political-moral questions. He believes that the process most likely to succeed is noninterpretive review.

28. Perry, p. 97.

29. Perry, p. 99.

30. Perry, p. 115. This passage in Perry clearly identifies his nonpositivist views. He requires neither that the moral values that underwrite correct legal decisions in hard human rights cases be enacted by the sovereign (made part of the law), nor that they be accepted by the sovereign. Such moral values exist and determine the correct answers to legal questions independently of what the sovereign believes or comes to believe. Perry thus rejects both the sources thesis and the separability thesis. Rejecting these theses identifies his view as one that is nonpositivist.

31. Perry, p. 102.

32. The positivist interpretivist's response to bad laws is "Get the legislature to change them." This view has been expressed in several important Supreme Court decisions concerning the standard of review. Justice Black, discussing a Kansas debt adjustment statute noted, "The Kansas debt statute may be wise or unwise. But relief, if any be needed, lies not with this body but with the body constituted to pass laws for the State of Kansas." *Ferguson v. Skrupa* 372 U.S. 726, 732 (1963). Similarly, Justice Potter Stewart said of Connecticut's birth control statute, "I think this is an uncommonly silly law. . . . But we are not

asked in this case to say whether we think this law is unwise, or even asinine. We are asked to hold that it violates the United States Constitution. And that I cannot do." *Griswold v. Connecticut* 381 U.S. 469, 527 (1965) (Justice Stewart dissenting).

33. H. Jones, "An Invitation to Jurisprudence," 74 Columbia L. Rev. 1023, 1031 (1974).

34. It should be noted that Jones's reference to state action doctrines implicitly endorses my view in that state action, as explicated for purposes of Fourteenth Amendment analysis, is a question of fundamental law.

35. Of course, such a reading of the First Amendment would support Justice Black's rather extreme view that "no law" means no law and, accordingly, that all libel and slander laws are unconstitutional.

36. The text is, however, the best place to start, and, frequently, the final word on the matter. The constitutional text has a very special place in U.S. political and legal theory, and any theory of judicial review that fails to take account of or that obscures that place is defective. Perhaps the single most devastating challenge that can be leveled against the American Legal Realists is that they give no account of the importance of legal texts, including the constitutional text, in their account of law.

37. Perry, *supra* note 4, p. 115.

38. Some constitutional theorists have managed to read the available social science data so as to find that in 1954 the decision reached in *Brown* was, in fact, reflective of an actual consensus existing in the U.S. public. Although I would like to believe that we do, in fact, live in an enlightened society, the data do not support such a belief. To be sure, there was in 1954 a growing uneasiness with state-enforced racial segregation, and the Court in *Brown* took an active role in the reconsideration of a social policy. I think it at best fanciful, however, to suggest that the *Brown* decision actually reflected the views of a consensus of the people at the time that the decision was handed down. The Court in *Brown* initiated and shaped a new consensus, it did not reflect a newly developed one.

39. The principal task of the judge is to decide cases properly brought before the court. One aphorism familiar to most beginning law students is that the judge is often in error but never in doubt. As disturbing as the claim may seem, a wrong decision from a judge is, for systematic reasons, better than no decision at all.

40. A full discussion of the problem of normative gaps or normative closure is far beyond the scope of the present chapter. For those interested in this problem, however, some of the leading works on the topic are Carlos Alchourron and Euginio Bulygin, *Normative Systems,* (Wein: Springer-Verlag, 1971); *Logique et Analyse N.S.* 9 (1966) is devoted to the problem; Joseph Raz, *The Authority of Law,* ch. 5; and Julius Stone, *Legal Systems and Lawyer's Reasonings* (Stanford, Calif.: Stanford Univ. Press, 1964).

41. One implication of embracing the existence of normative gaps in legal systems is that one must reject Ronald Dworkin's famous right answer thesis. The existence of legal gaps requires that there be cases within the jurisdiction of courts for which there is no uniquely correct legal resolution. Whether one treats the existence of gaps as a beneficial or detrimental feature of a legal system is a separate question. What one must do, however, is accept that there are cases for which there is no right answer.

42. 2 Dall. 419 (1793).

43. 19 How. 393 (1857).
44. 157 U.S. 429 (1895).
45. 400 U.S. 112 (1970).
46. One should also recall President Andrew Jackson's rebuff of Chief Justice John Marshall: "Mr. Marshall has made his decision, let him enforce it."
47. J. Rawls, "Outline of a Decision Procedure for Ethics," 60 *Phil. Rev.* 177 (1951).
48. Stability in law, particularly constitutional law, is a desirable trait. One does not want the standards of what is legal to change too rapidly. Accordingly, a tedious process like the amendment process, while allowing for expressions of the popular will, slows the rate of change.
49. See note 32, *supra.*
50. Learned Hand, "The Contribution of an Independent Judiciary to Civilization," in *The Spirit of Liberty,* I. Dillard, ed. (New York: Knopf, 1953), p. 165.
51. James Bradley Thayer, long an opponent of "judicial activism," argued at the turn of the century that "under no system can the power of courts go far to save a people from ruin; our chief protection lies elsewhere." Thayer, unfortunately, did not indicate just where "elsewhere" might be. J. B. Thayer, "The Origin and Scope of the American Doctrine in Constitutional Law," in *Legal Essays* (Boston: Boston Book Co., 1908), p. 39.

SIX

Toward a Public Values Philosophy of the Constitution

STEPHEN M. GRIFFIN

A relatively new type of constitutional theory involves applying moral and political philosophy to explain, justify, and criticize aspects of constitutional law. This chapter addresses a recent development in this category of constitutional theory—the effort to construct a public values or "neorepublican" philosophy of the Constitution.[1] The development of this philosophy is an attempt to articulate a distinct alternative to the democratic relativism that has dominated U.S. political and constitutional thought in this century.[2]

The proponents of a public values philosophy reject the political theory of interest group pluralism that awards political victory to the greatest aggregation of private preferences. They argue that the Constitution and the Bill of Rights presume "a conception of the political process as an effort to select and implement public values."[3] Public values can be understood as the common goals or aspirations of the American community, exemplified by the values contained in the Constitution. Despite the historical appeal of neorepublicanism, its proponents have not so far been able to provide much content to the concept of a public value.

A public values approach may also be usefully contrasted with traditional constitutional theory (which concerns itself with reconciling judicial review and democracy) in that this approach seeks not merely to influence the constitutional practices of government, but to find a new audience for constitutional discussion among the citizens of the United States. The general idea is that public discussion over issues of constitutional principle should be encouraged in the hopes of providing a more secure basis for the maintenance of freedom and equality. This encouragement of public discussion on constitutional matters can be regarded as a democratization of political and constitutional theory, the aim of which is a greater degree of awareness of constitutional values and participation in constitutional and political change.

The idea of a public values philosophy presents certain difficulties. For example, it is not immediately clear how the notion of a "public value" is to be distinguished from a purely private preference. Further, because the objective of the political process from a public values viewpoint is to select those values, the question arises as to the nature of the institutions and practices required to ensure that this process is not unduly influenced by powerful aggregations of private preferences. To see how these difficulties might be addressed and a public values philosophy elaborated, this chapter explores the public values alternative within the framework of Rawls's theory of justice.[4] Five main topics are considered: the justification of "public" values, the structure of Rawls's system of constitutional rights, the worth of liberty, whether judicial review can be justified within Rawls's theory, and the contrast between democratic relativism and a public values philosophy.

PUBLIC VALUES AND THE ORIGINAL POSITION

How are public values to be distinguished from mere preferences? Rawls's theory provides a straightforward solution to this problem: A public value is a value that would be affirmed from the perspective of the original position. Unfortunately, Rawls's idea of an original position has proved problematic, as it is the source of many misunderstandings. I will therefore offer an account of the original position that I hope will be less vulnerable to some standard objections.

The original position is a set of appropriate conditions to govern the selection of principles of justice for the basic structure of society. In trying to accurately and completely describe these conditions, the conception of the original position will inevitably appear as a philosophical ideal. But it is important to understand that the conditions specified are intended to be the restrictions on argument we try to adhere to every time we reason about questions of social justice.

When Rawls first introduces the concept of the original position, it is in terms of a social contract metaphor, an assembly of persons gathering to choose principles of justice.[5] In the main, he continues to use the original position as a social contract metaphor, speaking of "the parties" in the position and the like. But Rawls makes it quite clear that the original position should be interpreted so that anyone can assume its perspective at any time:

> [O]ne or more persons can at any time enter this position, or perhaps, better, simulate the deliberations of this hypothetical situation, simply by reasoning in accordance with the appropriate restrictions. . . . To say that a certain conception of justice would be chosen in the original position is equivalent to saying that rational deliberation satisfying certain conditions and restrictions would reach a certain conclusion. . . . It is important that the original position be interpreted so that one can at any time adopt its perspective.[6]

This is how I regard the original position: It is a collection of restrictions on the kinds of arguments we may use to advocate or oppose given principles of justice. If we find these restrictions persuasive, we will employ them in reasoning about questions of justice, and they will affect the arguments we make in a real and nonhypothetical fashion.

One may think that what is hypothetical about the original position is the agreement that is made there, the hypothetical contract Rawls speaks of.[7] Rawls is actually somewhat ambiguous on this point. When he tries to explain specifically why his theory is a social contract theory, he justifies the term by referring to the fact that the theory must apply to many persons, must be a public conception of justice, and that persons are expected to adhere to the agreed principles.[8] But all of these conditions can be built into the original position as appropriate conditions for argument without a contract ever occurring, real or hypothetical. Given the severe restrictions on information appropriate to reasoning about justice, there is no basis for bargaining or negotiation in the original position. The original position is thus the standpoint of one person, who by virtue of the restrictions imposed on his or her reasoning (some of which are inspired by the social contract tradition), can be assured that his or her favored principles would be chosen by anyone adopting that standpoint.[9]

It is thus misleading to characterize Rawls's theory as a social contract theory if what is meant is that the principles of justice are derived from or justified through a contract, real or hypothetical. If the question is one of justification, Rawls is not best understood as a contractarian, and his theory is not best understood as a social contract theory. The principles of justice do not acquire their initial justification from a hypothetical contract but from the moral force of the conditions on argument that make up the original position.

The condition on argument that ensures the values selected will be public values is the requirement that we must exclude the effects on our reasoning of information that prevents us from achieving an objective standpoint free of prejudice and bias (the "veil of ignorance"). It is not necessary to speak of hypothetical parties laboring under a sudden, mysterious denial of knowledge. We simply take care not to support the arguments we make in favor of our preferred principles of justice (public values) with certain kinds of information. The information that Rawls excludes essentially relates to the characteristics of persons that form the basis for personal preferences.[10] Due to this restriction on information, the values selected in the original position are substantially independent of existing preferences. They are public values.

For a public values philosophy, the question then arises whether the political system can be designed to approximate the fairness of the original position. If this can be done, the political system will be able to properly fulfill its role of selecting public values. The next three sections explore aspects of Rawls's constitutional scheme in order to determine how the political system must be structured to fulfill this role.

RAWLS'S SYSTEM OF CONSTITUTIONAL RIGHTS

Rawls's first principle of justice, the principle of equal liberty, states that the social primary goods known as the basic liberties should be arranged to form the most extensive set of liberties justifiable from the standpoint of the original position, and that the set of liberties should be distributed equally to all citizens. The content of the set of basic liberties is as follows: (1) liberty of conscience (including religious freedom); (2) the political liberties and freedom of association (including the right to vote, to run for public office, freedom of speech, press, and assembly); (3) the liberty and integrity of the person (including the right to hold personal property, freedom from slavery, and freedom of movement and occupation); and (4) the rights and liberties covered by the rule of law (including freedom from arbitrary arrest and seizure and all other liberties that may be usefully summarized under the heading of "due process").[11]

It appears that Rawls intends all of the basic liberties to be thought of as constitutional rights, rights that any just constitution must contain. As Rex Martin has observed, however, Rawls does not provide us with an account of what he takes a "right," constitutional or otherwise, to be.[12] Following Martin's Rawls-like theory of rights then, we may define a right for Rawls as "an individual's legitimate expectation as to what he would receive in a just institutional distribution of social primary goods."[13] Further, in virtue of the list of basic liberties Rawls gives, we may characterize rights as things that belong to individuals as persons, "which can be *individuated* (parceled out, equally, to the individuals within a certain class) in some *determinate* amount or to some determinate degree, under publicly recognized rules, such that the distribution of that [social primary] good can be *guaranteed* to each and every member of that class."[14] All of Rawls's basic liberties–constitutional rights meet these criteria.

In his most recent articles, Rawls has used the fundamental capacities and highest order interests of moral persons to have an effective sense of justice and to form, revise, and pursue a conception of the good to justify recognition of his general categories of constitutional rights.[15] Rawls tends to think in terms of three categories: rights that are supported by the interest in having an effective sense of justice; rights that are supported by the interest in having a conception of the good; and rights that are necessary so that the foregoing rights may be properly guaranteed.[16] Thus, the political liberties and freedom of thought are supported primarily on the basis that they enable citizens to express their sense of justice. Liberty of conscience and freedom of association are supported primarily on the basis that they enable citizens to have a conception of the good. The rights connected with the liberty and integrity of the person and the various due process rights are necessary if the other rights are to be guaranteed.[17]

Together, these different rights form a family or system of rights. As conflicts among the rights are inevitable, any right may be limited in the process of achieving a coherent system, and so no right is "absolute." There are no "preferred" rights in Rawls's theory. Further, Rawls does not assume that the entire system of rights can be derived solely from the universal interests of a moral person. Deriving a more specific system is a complex process involving arguments from the perspective of the original position, establishing scopes and weights for the different rights, taking into account constitutional considered judgments, and any appropriate facts and circumstances.[18] Rawls simply remarks: "The historical experience of democratic institutions and reflection on the principles of constitutional design suggest that a practicable scheme of liberties can indeed be found."[19]

Rawls therefore holds that the priority of the basic constitutional rights is not infringed by drawing limits to regulate them into a coherent system of rights. Rules of order and regulations of "time, place, and manner" are all appropriate. Rights may also be restricted, which is to say that they may be limited for the purpose of securing an even more extensive system of rights. There are two sorts of cases envisioned by Rawls: restrictions on the rights of political participation to protect other rights through the mechanisms of constitutionalism, and restrictions of an emergency nature necessary to protect the entire system of rights in time of war or other constitutional crisis.[20] Both cases are familiar enough in our constitutional law. Rawls sees "[t]he traditional devices of constitutionalism—bicameral legislature, separation of powers mixed with checks and balances, a bill of rights with judicial review"[21]—as being adopted for a just constitution on the grounds that by limiting majority rule, the system of rights is made more extensive or more secure. The restriction is thus built directly into the constitution.[22]

By contrast, restricting constitutional rights in an emergency involves interests extraneous to the system of rights, and such restrictions do not appear in the constitution. The sort of emergency Rawls has in mind is a very rare one, a constitutional crisis requiring "the more or less temporary suspension of democratic political institutions, solely for the sake of preserving these institutions and other basic liberties."[23] In a well-ordered society (or even in our own), such a crisis is unlikely to occur because such a society is a stable political order with a constitutional system flexible enough to handle "normal" emergencies such as foreign wars or even internal rebellions. Rawls is skeptical of Supreme Court decisions that imply such a crisis existed at some point in U.S. history, and he concludes that such a crisis is unlikely to ever occur in the United States or in any well-ordered society.[24]

THE WORTH OF LIBERTY

So in a Rawlsian well-ordered society, all citizens possess a determinate bundle of guaranteed constitutional rights. Given the inequalities in economic goods allowed by the second principle of justice, however, each citizen does not enjoy the same opportunity to exercise those rights. It appears that some citizens will be more able to pursue expensive conceptions of the good and that some citizens will have a greater ability to influence the political process. Rawls thinks of this difference between possessing a right and the ability to exercise it as a distinction between liberty and the worth of liberty. The basic liberties (or, as we have seen, all basic rights) are guaranteed to even the most poor and uneducated in an equal manner by the first principle of justice. The inequalities allowed by the second principle permit the worth of liberty to vary among the groups who possess different amounts of economic goods.[25]

It is at this point that egalitarian or Marxist critics of Rawls pose a strong objection. Rawls appears to assume too easily that inequalities in economic goods are compatible with equality in basic rights. What will the real "worth" of liberty be to someone who is one of the least-advantaged members of society? What will prevent powerful individuals or economic interests from unduly influencing the political process? Inadequate material means will often translate into a lack of political power. Why doesn't Rawls simply stipulate that all of the social primary goods be distributed so that the worth of the basic liberties is equal for everyone?

Rawls attempts to meet this objection through his guarantee of the "fair value" of the political liberties. In *A Theory of Justice,* his introduction of this idea seemed somewhat *ad hoc.*[26] Once we better understand the nature of Rawls's argument for the political liberties, however, we can see that his theory in fact *requires* that the worth of the political liberties be made as equal as possible for all. Further, the requirement that the equal worth of the political liberties be guaranteed has important egalitarian implications for Rawls's theory as a whole.

Although there are no rights with a preferred position in Rawls's system, the political liberties do hold a special place. If we keep in mind several themes in the preceding discussion, it is not hard to understand why this is the case. The moral interest that chiefly supports the political liberties is the interest in exercising our sense of justice. Our sense of justice is the capacity that allows us to attain the perspective of the original position and therefore to understand and apply the principles of justice. It thus has a central place in Rawls's theory. When we add to this the fact that the political process is responsible for the implementation of the two principles, the special role of the political liberties becomes apparent. So far as possible, we want the political process to mirror "the fair representation of persons achieved by the original position."[27] Allowing inequalities in the political process would be similar to allowing inequalities between persons in the original position. Such inequalities would be a severe violation of the equal status and dignity of individuals. Inequality would imply that those favored by it are somehow more worthy of exercising their sense of justice and governing society than those less favored.

We therefore arrive at the conclusion that the worth of the political liberties to all citizens must be equal, or as equal as possible. This guarantee of the "fair value" of the political liberties is similar to the idea of fair equality of opportunity in the second principle of justice.[28] Absolute equality is not to be expected, but we take whatever steps we can to ensure that everyone has a fair chance to hold public office, to be informed about political issues, to place items on the public agenda, and to generally influence the political process. Rawls suggests that the following measures be considered: "Property and wealth must be kept widely distributed";[29] and political parties must be kept independent of concentrations of private economic power, public financing of campaigns and elections, limits on political contributions, and subsidies to encourage a full airing of opinions on public issues.[30] He remarks

> Historically one of the main defects of constitutional government has been the failure to insure the fair value of political liberty. The necessary corrective steps have not been taken, indeed, they never seem to have been seriously entertained. Disparities in the distribution of property and wealth that far exceed what is compatible with political equality have generally been tolerated by the legal system. Public resources have not been devoted to maintaining the institutions required for the fair value of political liberty.[31]

The concept of guaranteeing the fair value of the political liberties is a powerful one. Under certain assumptions, it can become a mighty egalitarian engine. Rawls implies at some points that the inequalities allowed by the full operation of the second principle will still be too great to be tolerated under the fair value standard.[32] The fair value argument implies that if a completely equal distribution of social primary goods is the only means of attaining the equal worth of the political liberties, then that is what ought to be done. Perhaps this is why Rawls puts his main emphasis on policies that compensate for inequality (rather than working on inequality directly) in his suggestions for how to implement the fair value guarantee.

In any case, the fair value argument is an important one for a public values philosophy. For to carry out the public values vision, we must have a political process that is free of the distorting inequalities caused by private power.

The general character of Rawls's discussion suggests just how far our current political process is from ensuring the fair value of the political liberties, and thus just how much of a critical perspective a public values philosophy must have. A recent careful study of U.S. politics produced this sobering conclusion:

> The power shift that produced the fundamental policy realignment of the past decade did not result from a conservative or Republican realignment of the voters; nor did it produce such a realignment after the tax and spending legislation of 1981 was enacted. Rather, these policy changes have grown out of pervasive distortions in this country's democratic political process. These distortions have created a system of political decisionmaking in which fundamental issues . . . are resolved by an increasingly unrepresentative economic elite.[33]

Rawls's theory may be described in many ways, but one inappropriate description is that it is a defense of the status quo. It is quite clearly a powerful critique of our political system, a critique all the more compelling because its theoretical base is firmly within the domain of liberalism.[34]

JUSTIFYING JUDICIAL REVIEW

In designing just institutions for a Rawlsian constitutional system, the fundamental principle to bear in mind is the guarantee of equal, basic rights to all. All considerations of constitutional and political design are subordinate to this principle. The general objective is to establish a governmental system that will preserve the most extensive system of basic rights possible and lead to just legislation. To do this, we try insofar as possible to reproduce the fairness of the perspective of the original position within the constitutional system. As just discussed, this implies strong measures to keep the legislative-political process free from the influence of concentrations of private power.

As we have already seen, Rawls thinks it plausible that the traditional mechanisms of constitutionalism can be justified as desirable elements of a just constitution. Note, however, the nature of this justification. As *prima facie* restrictions on the equal political liberties, *all* of the devices of constitutionalism (a written constitution, bicameral legislature, separation of powers, a bill of rights, judicial review) are *equally* suspect. All must be justified on the ground that the restrictions they entail provide a greater degree of protection to the other liberties than would be available under a system of bare majority rule. Majority rule as such has no special place. It is dependent for its justification on the fundamental importance of the political liberties. If those liberties are not guaranteed, then the conditions of background political justice are not met, and the justness of any legislation enacted by the majority is in severe doubt.[35]

So judicial review is justifiable for Rawls if it ensures a more extensive system of rights. But can we be more specific than this? We must bear in mind that, at best, Rawls's theory can only provide us with a general justification for judicial review. This means a justification for a practice that allows the judicial branch of government to nullify acts of legislation.

Rawls's theory does not provide us with a basis for saying whether the judiciary should be elected, how it should construe the constitution, whether a special vote of the legislature could override certain judicial decisions, and so on. These are matters that lie beyond the theory of justice, matters of practical constitutional design.

We can say that, in comparison to the legislature, it is easier for the judiciary to mirror the fair representation of persons achieved by the original position. This is the ideal we are trying to achieve in designing the constitutional system. Striving for this ideal in the legislative process requires a complex system of restraints and compensatory devices. By contrast, the nature of constitutional adjudication is such that formally, persons are already equal. As Lawrence Sager has said of this process: "It is irrelevant that a claimant is despised or revered, or even that his is a claim shared by many or held in solitude."[36] Judges are commonly said to have a duty to act fairly, impartially, objectively, and to exercise their sense of justice wisely. This perspective is precisely the one persons adopt in the original position. If this perspective is already at least partially built into the institution of the judiciary, then we have strong grounds for saying that judicial review is compatible with Rawls's theory and stands on as firm a footing as the power of the legislature to enact legislation.

Of course, the courts cannot play the same role as the legislature in guaranteeing the system of rights. The courts cannot enact legislation or act on their own to create cases. Further, Rawls makes it clear that no branch of government has a monopoly on constitutional interpretation:

> In a democratic society, then, it is recognized that each citizen is responsible for his interpretation of the principles of justice and for his conduct in the light of them. There can be no legal or socially approved rendering of these principles that we are always morally bound to accept, not even when it is given by a supreme court or legislature. Indeed each constitutional agency, the legislature, the executive, and the court, puts forward its interpretation of the constitution and the political ideals that inform it. Although the court may have the last say in settling any particular case, it is not immune from powerful political influences that may force a revision of its reading of the constitution. The court presents its doctrine by reason and argument; its conception of the constitution must, if it is to endure, persuade the major part of the citizens of its soundness. The final court of appeal is not the court, nor the executive[,] [n]or the legislature, but the electorate as a whole.[37]

This is a very important point for my version of a public values philosophy. In a true constitutional *democracy*, constitutional interpretation is for everyone. Citizen discussion of and participation in such interpretation is required to guarantee that the system of rights is respected in everyday life, to ensure that appropriate constitutional change occurs, and to ensure that the government is held accountable on constitutional matters. The importance of a democratic attitude toward constitutional interpretation in a public values philosophy thus suggests the need for a reorientation of constitutional scholarship. The citizens of the United States are an appropriate audience for constitutional scholarship because ultimately they are the most important interpreters of the Constitution.

Rawls's way of justifying the mechanisms of constitutionalism places the traditional concern of constitutional theory in reconciling judicial review with democracy in a different light. According to Rawls's theory, judicial review is no more "deviant"[38] an institution than the other devices of constitutionalism; if judicial review stands in need of a justification, then so does the notion of a written constitution. If Rawls's principle of equal liberty bears the remotest relation to the Constitution, then the idea that "rule in accord with the consent of a majority of those governed is the core of the American governmental system"[39] is clearly untenable. It appears that the "counter-majoritarian difficulty"[40] is the difficulty of trying to reconcile judicial review with an implausible conception of democracy.

DEMOCRATIC RELATIVISM VERSUS A PUBLIC VALUES PHILOSOPHY

One of the reasons for the enthusiastic reception of Rawls's theory among legal scholars is that it was perceived as a theory that justified many aspects of the U.S. constitutional tradition. His later articles confirm this general impression. But strictly speaking, Rawls's theory is not meant as an interpretation of our Constitution. Rawls's principles of justice, and even his more specific arguments on the system of rights, are meant to establish a general framework for reasoning about questions of justice. Rawls remarks that his comments on U.S. constitutional law are not to be understood as answers to the questions that trouble judges, "but as a guiding framework, which if jurists find it convincing, may orient their reflections, complement their knowledge, and assist their judgment."[41] Rawls's theory of justice is relevant to U.S. constitutional law because it enables us to develop a normative constitutional theory (which I call a public values philosophy) that can simultaneously justify some of our most important convictions and practices and provide a critical perspective on our constitutional tradition. At least for that tradition, Rawls's theory does constitute an "Archimedean point" from which we may critically evaluate and seek to revise our constitutional law.

As a view about the Constitution—the values it contains and its role in our democracy—a Rawlsian public values philosophy is opposed by what may be called "democratic relativism."[42] Democratic relativism is the democratic theory that has had the most influence on constitutional practice in this century.[43] This theory strongly influenced such Supreme Court justices as Felix Frankfurter, John Harlan, and William Rehnquist; the constitutional scholar Alexander Bickel; and it is present in the recent work of John Ely and Jesse Choper.[44]

As its name implies, democratic relativism is a theory about what U.S. democracy is and the place of moral and political values within it. Democracy is characterized in terms of a free competition among politicians for the votes of citizens.[45] Democracy is thus equated with majoritarianism—the making of public policy on the basis of majority rule. Majority rule is particularly important to this theory because it sees no other reasonable way to make decisions. For a variety of reasons ranging from the impact of science to the critique of the natural law tradition by the legal realists, educated Americans in the middle of this century were made skeptical of any attempt to justify moral values.[46] In a free society, it thus appeared that the only way to resolve conflicts about values was through the majoritarian political process.

So construed, democratic relativism amounts to the contention that the U.S. constitutional order is best understood as a government designed for majoritarian moral skeptics. Because the Constitution does not appear to have been written by persons enamored of moral skepticism, democratic relativism is faced with certain problems. If the political process is all that matters, there is no particular reason to have a written constitution in the first place. Indeed, in this view, the U.S. Constitution does not contain any important values as values emerge only from the votes of the people. A further implication is that judicial review should be severely restricted or eliminated entirely. Constitutional rights have no greater intrinsic importance than the varying interests of society reflected in the political process.[47]

Because democratic relativism eschews moral theory, it cannot provide a normative lever or critical perspective on current institutions and so usually amounts to a defensive acceptance of the status quo. Moreover, in Rawlsian terms, the public conception of justice expressed by democratic relativism is extremely unstable. Our sense of justice is not affirmed as it is the object of skeptical indifference. Public institutions do not express respect for persons, but bury fundamental constitutional rights under the shifting sands of temporary majorities. A society without public values is not a community but a "private society," held together by the calculations of everyone that existing social arrangements are in their personal self-interest, not by considerations of justice.[48] The "competitive" theory of democracy cannot easily explain the public values the Constitution apparently contains. It cannot explain how the Constitution establishes a just order in a moral sense. In a private society, a political constitution can only be a *modus vivendi* between competing social groups with no shared aims, not even justice.

For a society whose constitution is taken to be an attempt to establish justice, democratic relativism is, at best, only relevant as an assertion that the basis for moral reasoning is not sufficiently understood. Rawls's theory of justice constitutes a decisive refutation of this assertion. His theory can be used to construct a constitutional philosophy—a public values philosophy—that has more justificatory and critical power than does democratic relativism.

A public values philosophy justifies the values the Constitution contains on the ground that they are moral values, values that can be affirmed by all citizens from a common perspective—the original position—that expresses our sense of justice. Among the most important of these values are our constitutional rights—social goods that affirm to each citizen his or her status as a free, equal, and moral person. Under normal conditions, and within their central range of application (after considerations of scope and weight are taken into account), these rights provide a secure base for the self-respect of all by guaranteeing determinate protection to the relevant activities.

One form of criticism a public values philosophy encourages is a familiar one: Our fundamental rights are not being adequately protected by current practices. But note that from a public values view, it is necessarily the practices of all social institutions that are open to examination, not simply the practices of the Supreme Court. More important, a public values view enjoins that social conditions and governmental institutions be structured so as to ensure that the political system is as free as possible to deliberate over public values from a moral perspective. In Rawls's terms, the "fair value" of the political liberties must be ensured through egalitarian social and economic policies and strong legislative measures to nullify the effects of concentrations of private power.

Because it has a significant potential to express the appropriate moral standpoint on questions of public value interpretation, a public values philosophy approves of judicial review. At the same time, it encourages a broader form of constitutional review that may be called constitutional politics. As free and equal moral persons, all citizens are responsible for assessing the justice of current practices and their obligation to respect those practices. To do so, they need the standards and conditions on argument that a public values view provides. One would hope that this democratization of constitutional interpretation will provide a basis for a widespread appreciation of constitutional values and a potential force for constitutional change. Because constitutional scholars have a special expertise in this area, it seems appropriate that they should devote some of their attention to the project of justifying and criticizing the Constitution to the people of the United States.

This project of justifying the Constitution may appear to be inappropriate. Isn't the Constitution already regarded as legitimate? What a Rawlsian view suggests is that it is not enough for free and equal moral persons to accept a constitution simply because it exists and appears to be working well. U.S. citizens normally demand a pragmatic justification for any significant government action. The Constitution should be no different. As the most fundamental act of government, its content and the practices it is said to allow deserve the closest possible scrutiny from a self-respecting citizenry. If we are committed democrats, we should condemn any form of "Constitution worship" and not fear the outcome of fair debate over the justification of the Constitution.

From the perspective of the tradition of moral and political philosophy, the sketch of a public values philosophy offered here may appear unremarkable. But once a public values philosophy is compared with democratic relativism, a theory that is very influential in U.S. constitutional law, the need for a constitutional theory of a Rawlsian character becomes apparent. Partly because of the influence of democratic relativism, many constitutional scholars and judges are extremely skeptical of the possibility of reasoning about moral values. A proper understanding of Rawls's theory may help to alleviate this skepticism. Judges and constitutional scholars cannot afford to ignore political philosophy as if it were a subject foreign to their way of thinking. In many decisions, judges in fact act as applied political philosophers, and how a judge construes U.S. democracy and its values has a profound influence on his or her judgments. Avoiding political philosophy means doing bad philosophy, not doing without it. Although it is unrealistic to expect judges to adopt Rawls's entire theory, it is not unrealistic at all to expect that Rawls's ideas, suitably transmitted, could eventually have an impact in constitutional cases. One would hope that the sympathetic interpretation of Rawls's theory presented here illustrates the ongoing relevance of political philosophy to constitutional law.

NOTES

1. See Frank Michelman, "Politics and Values or What's Really Wrong With Rationality Review," 13 *Creighton L. Rev.* 487 (1979); Owen Fiss, "Foreword: The Forms of Justice," 93 *Harvard L. Rev.* 1 (1979); Cass Sunstein, "Naked Preferences and the Constitution," 84 *Columbia L. Rev.* 1689 (1984); Cass Sunstein, "Interest Groups in American Public Law," 38 *Stanford L. Rev.* 29 (1985).

2. See E. Purcell, *The Crisis of Democratic Theory* (Lexington: Univ. Press of Kentucky, 1973); R. Smith, *Liberalism and American Constitutional Law* (Cambridge, Mass.: Harvard Univ. Press, 1985).

3. Cass Sunstein, "Naked Preferences and the Constitution," *supra* note 1, at 1694.

4. J. Rawls, *A Theory of Justice* (Cambridge, Mass.: Harvard Univ. Press, 1971).

5. *Id.* at 11–12.

6. *Id.* 138–139.

7. *Id.* at 11–13.

8. *Id.* at 16. See also J. Rawls, "Reply to Alexander and Musgrave," 88 *Q. J. Econ.* 633, 650–653 (1974).

9. J. Rawls, *supra* note 4, at 139. See also Jean Hampton, "Contracts and Choices: Does Rawls Have A Social Contract Theory?" 77 *J. Phil.* 315 (1980).

10. Under the veil of ignorance, the parties in the original position do not know the following: (1) their class position, social status, or anything of their place in society; (2) their fortune in the distribution of natural assets and abilities (including such qualities as intelligence, strength, age, sex, and race); (3) their conception of the good or rational plan of life; (4) any special features of their psychology, such as their aversion to risk or inclination to optimism or pessimism; (5) the particular circumstances of their society, the course of its history, its

economic and political circumstances, and its level of civilization and culture; (6) the generation to which they belong. See J. Rawls, *supra* note 4, at 137, 200.

11. *Id.* at 61; Rawls, "The Basic Liberties and Their Priority," in *The Tanner Lectures on Human Values*, vol. 3, pp. 3, 5, 50 (Salt Lake City: Univ. of Utah Press, 1982).

12. See R. Martin, *Rawls and Rights*, p. 26 (Lawrence: Univ. Press of Kansas, 1985).

13. *Id.* (footnote omitted).

14. *Id.* at 125–126 (emphasis in original).

15. See Rawls, "Kantian Constructivism in Moral Theory," 77 *J. Phil.* 515 (1980); Rawls, "The Basic Liberties," *supra* note 11.

16. Rawls, "The Basic Liberties," *supra* note 11, at 49–50.

17. *Id.* at 24–39, 49–50.

18. *Id.* at 9, 11–12.

19. *Id.* at 11–12.

20. See R. Martin, *supra* note 12, at 52–54.

21. J. Rawls, *supra* note 4, at 224.

22. R. Martin, *supra* note 12, at 53–54.

23. Rawls, "The Basic Liberties," *supra* note 11, at 70.

24. *Id.* at 63–72.

25. J. Rawls, *supra* note 4, at 204–205.

26. *Id.* at 224–226.

27. Rawls, "The Basic Liberties," *supra* note 11, at 45.

28. *Id.* at 42.

29. J. Rawls, *supra* note 4, at 225.

30. *Id.* at 225–226; Rawls, "The Basic Liberties," *supra* note 11, at 42–43, 73.

31. J. Rawls, *supra* note 4, at 226.

32. See, for example, Rawls, "The Basic Liberties," *supra* note 11, at 43.

33. T. Edsall, *The New Politics of Inequality*, pp. 241–242 (New York: Norton, 1984).

34. We may wonder why the fair value of the other liberties is not guaranteed. If we keep in mind the underlying structure of Rawls's view, the answer is fairly plain. The other liberties are primarily supported by the moral interest in forming a conception of the good. Unlike the sense of justice, conceptions of the good are not formulated and carried out from an objective perspective that is similar for all. Conceptions of the good are profoundly different, and different amounts of social resources are required to carry them out. There is no clear way to guarantee "equality" of resources to pursue conceptions of the good, at least no clear way that is preferable to the second principle of justice. See Rawls, "The Basic Liberties," *supra* note 11, at 44–45.

35. J. Rawls, *supra* note 4, at 224, 228–229, 356.

36. Sager, "What's a Nice Court Like You Doing in a Democracy Like This?" 36 *Stanford L. Rev.* 1087, 1099 (1984).

37. J. Rawls, *supra* note 4, at 390 (footnote omitted).

38. See A. Bickel, *The Least Dangerous Branch*, p. 18 (Indianapolis: Bobbs-Merrill, 1962) (" . . . judicial review is a deviant institution in the American democracy").

39. See J. Ely, *Democracy and Distrust*, p. 7 (Cambridge, Mass.: Harvard Univ. Press, 1980).

40. A. Bickel, *supra* note 38, at 16.

41. Rawls, The Basic Liberties, *supra* note 11, at 84.

42. I take the term from Rogers Smith, who characterizes the theory as "pragmatic democratic relativism." See R. Smith, *supra* note 2, at 169.

43. *Id.* See generally E. Purcell, *supra* note 2.

44. See the discussion of the opinions of Frankfurter and Harlan and "realist" democratic theory in M. Edelman, *Democratic Theories and the Constitution*, pp. 74–114 (Albany: State Univ. of New York Press, 1984). For a general discussion of democratic relativism under the name "democratic collectivism" and its influence on Chief Justice Rehnquist and other current members of the Court, see Elfenbein, The Myth of Conservatism as a Constitutional Philosophy, 71 *Iowa L. Rev.* 401 (1986). See also R. Smith, *supra* note 2, at 174–179; J. Ely, *supra* note 39; J. Choper, *Judicial Review and the National Political Process* (Chicago: Univ. of Chicago Press, 1980).

45. See M. Edelman, *supra* note 44, at 57, 69.

46. See E. Purcell, *supra* note 2, at 177–178, 205, 209.

47. See M. Edelman, *supra* note 44, at 96–97, 115–116.

48. J. Rawls, *supra* note 4, at 520–522.

SEVEN

Constitutional Integrity and Compromise

KENNETH HENLEY

The Constitution of the United States consists of a body of fundamental law rooted in a canonical text. The text of the Constitution is no more self-interpreting than is any other text—indeed, the interpretive enterprise is both unavoidable and unending. The interpretation of a written constitution must change for the same reasons that unwritten constitutions must change: New needs arise through social, economic, and political forces. The Equal Protection Clause of the Fourteenth Amendment cannot mean now what it meant in 1866—the United States is a very different nation than it was immediately after the Civil War, and a grudging admission to bare citizenship can no longer constitute equality. The earlier compromise, which interpreted the Equal Protection Clause to accommodate an unyielding practice of racial segregation, is supplanted by the present compromise, which interprets the Equal Protection Clause to accommodate an unyielding practice of economic segregation. Perhaps *San Antonio School District v. Rodriguez*[1] (constitutionality of higher funding for wealthy public school districts than for poorer districts) will someday seem as obviously biased against the poor as *Plessy v. Ferguson*[2] now seems biased against blacks. But such a change in perception will not likely occur until after much else has changed.

These compromises with the surrounding social order form only one of several kinds of compromise that mold constitutional development. There were compromises in the drafting of the original text; there have been compromises concerning institutional power among the three constitutional branches of government and between the federal government and the states; and, perhaps most pervasive, there are compromises among the justices as they blend individual lines of reasoning into opinions with the institutional authority of the Supreme Court. There is no doubt that compromises at times play an important causal role in the emergence of an authoritative interpretation of the Constitution.

But in the realm of principle, compromise has a bad name. Compromise with the social order is seen as either bad faith or cowardice; the original compromises of the framers are glossed over (except for the purged compromise over slavery). Compromises concerning institutional power are seen not as formative of the functional arrangement of constitutional power itself, but rather as mere temporary politics, leaving the Constitution unchanged. And the pervasive need for compromise within the Supreme Court is seen as something external to legal reasoning, rather than as both internal and crucial. As with compromises of institutional power, these judicial compromises are seen as mere temporary strategy; the Constitution itself remains intact.

What is this intact Constitution, unblemished by the many compromises of origin, implementation, and interpretation? Perhaps the most common understanding of the true Constitution identifies it with the intentions of the framers, which remain forever fixed despite politically compromised implementation or interpretation. Along with its more serious problems, this view must admit the existence of original compromises and must portray them as either trivial or as resting on a deeper coherence of intention—or as mere appearance to be discounted in light of the overriding intentions of the framers. Judicial compromise may be allowed as a practical necessity in this view; but such compromises can have no effect on the Constitution itself, for that can no more change than can a past event.

Ronald Dworkin has shown that this "historicist" account of the Constitution fails.[3] At its best, an understanding of the intentions of the framers reduces to something like Dworkin's own view: Intentions and convictions come in many levels of generality and specificity, of abstractness and concreteness, and so the best interpretation of intentions and convictions shares the structure of direct interpretation of the canonical text, seeking to understand the text in light of the principles that provide the best justification of it.[4] A constitution cannot come to us from the past in the same way that a physical object (James Madison's pen) can—though documents recording the text of a written constitution can. Taken alone, all that historical events fix definitively are the words. An appeal to intentions in order to fix meaning can be relevant only if the language of "intentions" is used to do the work of interpretation. And then it is not historical events *alone* that fix meaning, but rather the interpretation as a whole.

So, as Dworkin argues, constitutional arguments are interpretive, just as literary criticism is interpretive. Constitutional interpretation must take into account not only the text of the written Constitution, but the whole of the relevant legal practice that is built upon that text. Like all interpretation, legal interpretation has two dimensions: a dimension of "fit," so that as many elements of the text or practice as possible are consistent with the interpretation; and a dimension of justification, so that the text or practice is shown in the best light by the interpretation. Thus, an interpretation of a play should be consistent with as much of the play as possible while showing it in the best aesthetic light. And

Dworkin claims, an interpretation of legal text and practice should both fit and justify that practice—the justification here in political rather than aesthetic values.[5]

As a general interpretation of law, Dworkin develops his conception of "law as integrity," in opposition to conventionalist (positivist) and pragmatist (legal realist) conceptions. Law as integrity interprets legal practice as proceeding from the community speaking with one voice, expressing a commitment to coherent principles. Political integrity is a collective version of personal integrity, which consists in acting according to a coherent set of personal convictions even though those convictions are not universally shared. Dworkin writes: "Integrity becomes a political ideal when we . . . insist that the state act on a single, coherent set of principles even when its citizens are divided about what the right principles of justice and fairness really are."[6] This interpretive standard of integrity applies to the Constitution as well—thus Dworkin speaks of "constitutional integrity."[7] As interpretation always includes a normative dimension, constitutional integrity requires that the interpreter not only find a single, coherent voice of the community in the Constitution, but also that this voice be raised on the side of justice, fairness ("a matter of . . . the structure that distributes influence over political decisions in the right way"[8]), and procedural due process.

This normative dimension must, however, be balanced against considerations of fit, for the record of past political decisions (for instance, the text of the Constitution as amended and the precedents of constitutional case law) must itself be encompassed within the interpretation as far as possible. The fit will not be perfect because constitutional integrity will require that some past decisions be counted as mistakes. I assume, though I do not think that Dworkin explicitly says so, that the constitutional text itself is immune to such a finding of mistake.[9] This immunity is of little importance for interpreting the great abstract clauses central to much constitutional argument (including Dworkin's) as long as the interpretive argument does not require us to connect with more concrete clauses. But such connections are sometimes unavoidable, *especially* in the interpretive theory of integrity. These connections are important to my criticism of Dworkin's version of constitutional integrity, for they may require that the voice of the community endorse the kind of compromise of principle that Dworkin rules out. And there are other sources of genuine compromise of principle that Dworkin does not recognize as establishing constitutional law.

Dworkin's conception of constitutional integrity seems to share with the historicist, original intention approach the idea of the true Constitution, immune to real compromise of principle—though perhaps compromised in the actual political and judicial arena. In Dworkin's view, the Constitution consists of the best interpretation of text and practice—and there is a unique best interpretation, even though that interpretation will be controversial—and we are always fallible in thinking that we have found it. This may be too extreme a statement of Dworkin's commitment to what I call the idea of the true Constitution; strictly, he seems committed only to the view that it is muddled to say that there are never right answers to hard questions of constitutional (and other) law.[10] But Justice Hercules, Dworkin's mythical Supreme Court Justice of Integrity, seems at least heuristically committed to the full-blown conception that there is a unique best interpretation of the Constitution as a whole.[11] This heuristic commitment is what matters, for it encourages us to place too great an emphasis on the search for grand coherence and thus to slight the importance to constitutional law as such (rather than to mere external practicalities) of compromises of principle.

All compromise is not treated as mere practical strategy by Dworkin because he argues for integrity as a separate political ideal that must at times conflict with justice and fairness in a nonutopian state. A judge must at times compromise pure justice because of integrity, for the past political decisions of the community may not allow what is required by justice viewed apart from the context of that political history.[12] These, however, will be compromises not within the coherent principles discovered by applying the standard of interpretive integrity, nor compromises about the scope or reach of application of these principles. Rather, these will be compromises among competing ideals in the reasoning for adopting the principles. Integrity rules out "internal compromises"—compromises within the scheme of justice adopted by the political community. This is crucial for Dworkin, for it serves as an argument for the ideal of integrity and the underlying personification of the community. Dworkin claims that we should recognize a separate political ideal of integrity because it makes sense of our rejection of internal compromises, though such compromises would seem to treat divergent groups of conviction more fairly.[13]

I think that there are living internal compromises in the Constitution, compromises that, like the dead bargain over slavery, require that the best interpretation of the Constitution must be satisfied with less than full coherence at some deep level of principle. Considerations of fit require the recognition of several kinds of internal compromise of principle as constitutive of constitutional law. My argument builds upon Dworkin's general theory of interpretation and does not lead to a rejection of the idea of constitutional integrity—for the idea is illuminating. Rather, I suggest that constitutional integrity as an interpretive standard should not be pressed as far as Dworkin wishes to press it.

Dworkin seems to offer us only two alternatives within the interpretive conception he calls "law as integrity." The first alternative is a full-fledged interpretive commitment to bringing order to legal practice so that it can be perceived as the voice of a community of principle; this rules out all internal compromises. The second alternative is "internal skepticism," denying that legal practice can be seen as coherent and worthy.[14] There is room for a third alternative, though it is not clear to me how to categorize it within Dworkin's general account. Perhaps this third alternative could be situated within "law as integrity" as a form of moderate, limited skepticism—for my view is not fully skeptical, as I see a great deal of coherence in constitutional text and practice. To strike a more positive note, this might be called "limited integrity" as well as "limited skepticism."

But it may be better to categorize my view as an intermediate conception of constitutional law, rather than as a subspecies of law as integrity. For it does not really seem at all skeptical about the question of what constitutional law is, nor does it deny the worth of U.S. constitutional practice. The label of skepticism seems appropriate only because of the grand ambitions of the full-fledged commitment to uncompromised integrity. I wish to suggest a hybrid conception of constitutional law, combining elements of conventionalism (positivism) with a guiding interpretive approach that is still committed to integrity. Coherence of principle is not completely attainable in an interpretation of constitutional text and practice, unless we are willing very frequently to label past decisions as mistakes. Instead, the Constitution should be seen as dynamic. At any one time, the best interpretation of the whole of constitutional text and practice will recognize as binding various compromises of principle, in order to keep down to a moderate level the frequency of labeling past decisions as mistakes. Such compromised principles need not be seen as binding us forever. Future interpretation, building upon an expanded set of past decisions, may find that the cost in "mistake-labeling" is no longer prohibitively high.

So one index of how determined an interpreter is to construct an interpretation that expresses the coherence of a community of principle is his or her willingness to accept a high level of mistake-labeling. But this "high level" need not be a matter of frequency, for it is also reflected in the *kind* of past decisions labeled as mistakes. In constitutional interpretation, the highest level would be a direct denial of the force of a relatively concrete clause of the text of the amended Constitution. The lowest level would be ignoring an old, shaky precedent that had few if any progeny and concerned a subsidiary detail of the application of some larger doctrine. Between these extremes lies a continuum of triviality shading into marginal importance, and then into greater degrees of importance. None of these distinctions can be made mechanically, and there is room for much disagreement. But this, Dworkin would agree, is true of all interpretive questions of any significance. Dworkin argues persuasively that the dimension of fit and the dimension of justification are not really separable.[15] This will remain true within my hybrid interpretive conception of limited integrity. The difference is only that mistake-labeling is not embraced as willingly; on the conception of limited constitutional integrity, it is a presupposition of the process of interpretation (a heuristic principle) that there is only limited coherence of principle in the best interpretation of constitutional text and practice.

Why should an interpreter begin with the assumption of limited integrity? Dworkin argues that the normative dimension of interpretation leads toward constructing the best novel or constitution. But, of course, there is the other dimension—fit. It seems to me that a competent interpreter of the Constitution should bring to the task enough knowledge of constitutional history to make the grand ambition of uncompromised integrity unrealistic. This is not skepticism, but only facing up to the complexity of the practice under interpretation and to the diverse sources of its growth. Compromise, both conscious and hidden, marked that growth. Are interpreters to assume that a coherent, principled account can be given, connecting at the level of deep political justification all of the more localized elements that have resulted from this human history of compromise and adjustment? Such an account clearly is possible if the interpretation tolerates a very high level of mistake-labeling. But just as we may interpret a philosophical text such as *The Critique of Pure Reason,* recognizing from the beginning that the price of complete coherence of interpretation may be too high (in forced readings or in ignored passages), so we may come with the same recognition to the interpretation of constitutional text and practice. Indeed, interpreting our two hundred years of constitutional practice is more comparable to interpreting a historically extended philosophical tradition than a single work or even the entire corpus of a single philosopher. Only limited coherence is a realistic interpretive ambition. Beyond moderate pruning of "mistaken" past decisions lies constitutional law as it ought to be, rather than as it is. (Compare this with certain interpretations of Kant, or Spinoza, or Wittgenstein—more what these philosophers should have said than what they did say.)

I now turn to two applications of limited constitutional integrity as an interpretive conception. These have been chosen because I believe that the text of the Constitution limits the achievement of deep coherence of principle on these issues. Historic compromises and ancient practice, enshrined in concrete constitutional clauses, conflict with principles of justification underlying other elements of both text and practice. My argument is not the skeptical one that constitutional law is incoherent in these two areas. Rather, I argue that a less deep coherence—which Dworkin might call mere consistency[16]—is all we can have here. This leads to a form of conventionalism (positivism) on these issues, accepting as law rules that are specific and relatively limited in scope and that cannot be coherently justified at the deepest level, given other ineliminable elements of constitutional text and practice.

The first application is legislative apportionment. Until 1962 in *Baker v. Carr,*[17] it was settled constitutional law that legislative apportionment (except as it masked racial or other constitutionally impermissible discrimination[18]) was a matter for legislative not judicial determination. In respect to congressional districts, the "times, manner and places" clause of Article I, Section 4 of the Constitution established congressional power to correct inequities, if it ever wished to do so. Apportionment for state legislatures was a matter for the states themselves to decide. But after the interpretive break of *Baker v. Carr,* the doctrine has evolved that the Equal Protection Clause of the Fourteenth Amendment requires that the drawing of legislative districts should be based on population, so that each vote should count for roughly as much in selecting a representative as any other vote in any other district. (This is often phrased as "one person, one vote," though multiple voting has never been legal practice in the United States, unlike England.) In 1964 *Reynolds v. Sims*[19] ruled that even upper houses of state legislatures must be districted in such a way that population is the controlling consideration. The Equal Protection Clause, it is now declared, requires an equal voice for each qualified voter in the choice of all representatives. There is, of course, one great exception. The Senate of the United States cannot be proportionally representative of the people, for even an amendment to the Constitution cannot deprive any state of equal vote in the Senate without its consent (Article V of the Constitution).

In *Reynolds v. Sims* Chief Justice Warren discusses the Senate's special role in the federal system, for this had been used as an argument for allowing nonpopulation-based districting in upper houses of states. But the Chief Justice argues against the analogy. He discusses the origin of the Senate in the great compromise necessary to form the Union, and then points out that equal representation of each state in the Senate rests on state sovereignty. Because there are no sovereign political divisions within states, the analogy fails. Population must be the controlling consideration in districting (though political subdivisions may play some minor role) even in upper houses.

This distinction succeeds well enough to rebut the argument by analogy with the Senate. Limited integrity as an interpretive conception allows us to stop at this level of analysis. We can recognize the ineliminable, unamendable status of unequal popular representation in the Senate, while interpreting the Equal Protection Clause to require population-based districting in all other cases. Thus two rules are in force, each confined to its sphere. There is no inconsistency.

A full-fledged commitment to integrity must, however, seek to find a deeper coherence. And it is arguably not there to be found. *Reynolds v. Sims* detracts from robust state sovereignty, and yet an appeal to state sovereignty is necessary to defend the ruling from claims that the *federal* legislature displays a pattern permissible for the states. Justice and fairness are well-served by proportional representation, and so it makes interpretive sense to expand the Equal Protection Clause precisely up to the boundary of the concrete clauses of the Constitution. But why not then turn conventionalist and recognize that we are saddled with a compromised principle of equality? The "natural limits"[20] of the principle of equal representation would seem to include the Senate; but that natural understanding is ruled out by the text.

These points could be turned into an argument against *Reynolds v. Sims*, but I do not mean to criticize Chief Justice Warren's reasoning. The Fourteenth Amendment is a destabilizing addition to the federal Constitution, radically changing the arrangement of power within the federal structure. This implication was resisted for decades in a series of cases beginning with the Slaughterhouse Cases.[21] Proponents of original intention will argue that radical changes in the federal structure were not intended by the framers of the Fourteenth Amendment. As explained above, I agree with Dworkin's argument against this approach. An expansive interpretation is eligible because of the extremely broad and abstract language of the first section; case law in areas other than legislative apportionment pointed toward an expansive reading by the time of *Baker* and *Reynolds*. Both justice and fairness also support such an interpretation.

Dworkin could argue that there is no internal compromise of principle involved in *Reynolds v. Sims*, or more generally in the large range of cases where an expansive reading of the Fourteenth Amendment (including those that use the Due Process Clause to "incorporate" Bill of Rights protections) conflicts with the robust federal structure of the original antebellum Constitution. The model for this response is Dworkin's treatment of conflicting principles that compete with each other but are not contradictory. Dworkin insists that "the resolution of this conflict itself be principled."[22] In this approach the conflict between state sovereignty and an expansive federal protection of individual rights would call for a principled resolution as a part of the process of interpretation. The principled resolution of the conflict would then be applied across all areas of constitutional law. There would then be no *internal* compromise within the mid-level constitutional principle that the best interpretation of text and practice constructs.

Dworkin accepts that this interpretive avoidance of internal compromises of principle is not always available. Such an account could not be given of the original compromise concerning slavery.[23] Thus my argument is itself an interpretive claim that the original compromise concerning state representation in the federal legislature was, like that concerning slavery, a failure in what Dworkin calls "legislative integrity"; this failure of legislative integrity must, I think, be matched in our interpretation, setting a limit to adjudicative integrity. The destabilizing effect of the Fourteenth Amendment derives in part from its failure to address directly the question of state sovereignty. And, on the reasonable assumption that less populous states would withhold consent (one holdout would be decisive), no amendment can ever address the issue of representation in the Senate not being proportionate. Here there was, it seems, a successful attempt to make a mere bargain last forever. It is worth noting that the bargain concerning importation of slaves and the bargain concerning state representation in the Senate are included together as restrictions on amendment. The slavery bargain was unamendable until 1808, while the Senate bargain is eternal. As Dworkin notes, restriction to a given year is clearly arbitrary.[24] But is it not arbitrary to limit eternally the right of the sovereign people through the process of amendment to change the nature of the Senate? After all, individual rights are not at issue in this bargain between the states, and eternity is a long time.

A heroic effort of interpretation might be successful at constructing adjudicative integrity despite this eternal defect of legislative integrity. But I do not think so. State sovereignty can perhaps be given a principled justification, but equal state representation in the Senate is not a necessary concomitant of state sovereignty. So a constitutional interpretation that displays an underlying coherence of principle for the general federal structure, with separate state legal systems, will not so far have provided a principled justification for the eternal limitation of the scope of the principle of equality of representation for persons. It should be noted that Dworkin does encompass state sovereignty in his interpretation, even using Massachusetts as an example of a community that can be understood through personification.[25] Perhaps one could then argue, imaginatively, that equal representation of persons is not violated in the Senate, for the states are there treated as persons! (I do not mean to suggest that Dworkin would accept this imaginative interpretation—it is my creature.) But this is to confuse personification with personhood. And even if one accepted this too imaginative interpretation, there would surely remain a problem of coherent justification in principle for eternally forbidding a change in this arrangement.

After all, proportional representation in the Senate would still leave us with separate state legal systems. At the Constitutional Convention of 1787, the Virginia plan had called for both houses to be proportional (to either free inhabitants or amount of contribution). In *The Federalist* No. 62, Madison does rehearse the argument that equal representation in the Senate is justified by state sovereignty. But he frames this justification with disclaimers, noting first that the arrangement requires little attention because it is "evidently the result of compromise between the opposite pretensions of the large and the small States," and afterwards that "it is superfluous to try by the standard of theory" what was produced by an "indispensable" "concession."[26] Madison then turns to a discussion of the benefits of equal state representation in the Senate. The first consideration again relates to recognizing and protecting state sovereignty, and the second to "the additional impediment it must prove against improper acts of legislation."[27] Madison sees potential injuries as well as benefits from this arrangement. (Chief Justice Warren in *Reynolds v. Sims* seems to follow the line of reasoning in *Federalist* 62, for he distinguishes bicameralism in state legislatures from the special representation of sovereign states in the Senate. Madison treats bicameralism separately, and more enthusiastically, in the remainder of *Federalist* 62.)

Madison thus treats the Senate bargain as a mere compromise that yet can be defended; state sovereignty is represented and protected, and some improper legislation may be impeded (as well as some *proper* legislation). He does not, however, suggest that these arguments for the arrangement are conclusive. The second argument cuts both ways, and bicameralism would itself seem sufficient as a check on hasty legislation. And though the Senate bargain offers representation and protection of state sovereignty, it is clearly not a necessary feature of a federal system with state sovereignty.

There might be other arguments for the Senate bargain and its eternal limitation on representative democracy based on a principle of equality for natural persons. An interpretation of the Constitution is not constrained by *The Federalist*. But I cannot think of any other *kinds* of consideration that might justify the arrangement. And it seems to me that no considerations could justify in deep principles of political morality the unamendable character of the arrangement, even if the arrangement can be made to seem reasonable.

So I think that conflict resolution between abstract principles of deep political morality, issuing in a mid-level principle without internal compromise, cannot be used to construct deep coherence for U.S. constitutional text and practice in the area of equal political representation. At a level of analysis sufficient for the positive law, we can achieve what Dworkin calls consistency, but at a deeper level we can not construct an interpretation that shows the Constitution as proceeding from a community of principle. The people of the United States do not here speak with one coherent voice. To continue the personification, can one interpret the people to have given up their sovereignty on an issue unrelated to the individual rights of natural persons? Such an interpretation would, I think, warrant the judgment that the people must be seen as irrational. The attempt at grand coherence should be abandoned—all we have here is positive law. No principle of political morality of comparable importance can be constructed to vie with the principle of equal representation of natural persons, so the model of conflict resolution of abstract principles cannot be used. The struggle to construct an interpretation satisfying the ideal of integrity must end when we hit upon the brute historical fact of concrete positive constitutional law, unless we are willing to interpret away this impediment by ignoring the text and the practice built upon it. This is not conceivable in the case of the Senate bargain, for it is too massive a practice and too structural an element. However, even before the Civil War amendments, heroic efforts were made to interpret the Constitution so that it did not recognize the legality of the institution of slavery.[28] But the contrast in Article I, Section 2 between "free Persons" and "all other Persons" logically implies a legally recognized category of persons who are not free, as does the language of "importation" in Section 9, and, less undeniably, the language of Article IV, Section 2, Clause 3. The question of the constitutional recognition of the institution of slavery is different from those raised in *Dred Scott*, among them the question of the extension of slavery to the territories. Even if *Dred Scott* was incorrectly decided, the institution of slavery in the original slave states was clearly constitutional until the radical changes during and after the Civil War.

Can the more concrete clauses of the Constitution ever be ignored as we seek the best interpretation of the whole text and the practice built upon it? Might the normative dimension of interpretation warrant such an extreme use of mistake-labeling, where the clause is not related to the structure of the Constitution and the matter is morally very serious? On balance, I think that the best interpretation must respect such concrete clauses. But the second application of my conception of limited constitutional integrity will test this view. And my commitment to the result is less than wholehearted.

The second application is the question whether the death penalty is constitutional. The interpretive conception of constitutional integrity directs us to answer this question by constructing an interpretation that both fits and justifies the text of the Constitution and the practice built upon it. This interpretation is not constrained by the concrete intentions of the framers—the historical fact that they would not have considered the death penalty cruel and unusual punishment is no more relevant than the fact that the framers of the Fourteenth Amendment would not have considered segregated public schools unconstitutional. Dworkin vividly describes the kind of interpretive argument that might serve to strike down the death penalty: "If the Court finds that the death penalty is cruel, it must do so on the basis of some principles or groups of principles that unite the death penalty with the thumbscrew and the rack."[29] The concept of "cruel and unusual punishment" must be applied through a coherent, principled conception of what constitutes something as cruel and unusual; this conception need not be the one held by the framers of the relatively abstract clause. Apart from the death penalty, the distinction must be accepted, as everyone would now count as cruel and unusual various forms of punishment that the framers would not have.

I think that the death penalty counts as cruel and unusual punishment under any conception that can now be given a principled justification and consistent application. Justice Brennan has so argued from his concurring opinion in *Furman v. Georgia*[30] through his dissenting opinions since the validation of refurbished death penalty statutes by the Court. Only Justice Marshall now agrees, though on somewhat different grounds, that the death penalty *as such* is cruel and unusual.[31] The death penalty is, arguably, uncivilized in the same sense as the rack and the thumbscrew. This has consistently been Justice Brennan's claim. He has interpreted the prohibition of cruel and unusual punishment as resting upon a conception of human dignity. This respect for human dignity is denied by an unusually severe punishment that is selectively visited upon a few, while society is unwilling to subject all similarly situated to the same severity.[32] The refurbished death penalty statutes have not corrected this defect, for only a fraction of murders lead to the death sentence, and only a fraction of those sentences lead to execution. Despite all of the guidelines for juries and judges, surely no one would argue that something morally significant distinguishes the small number of those executed from the large number not executed. Although much could be done to make the arbitrariness less extreme, it seems to me that society would not stand for the number of executions required by a truly principled application of the death penalty. If this is true, then under current social conditions the few who are executed really are subjected to cruel and unusual punishment, and Justice Marshall's claim seems plausible that the enactment of the new statutes does not conclusively establish that an informed public finds the death penalty morally acceptable.[33] The public may support the death penalty only insofar as it is applied very selectively—too selectively to satisfy the requirement that it be principled.

This interpretive argument may be flawed, but my point does not turn on whether it is accepted. For there are much more specific, concrete clauses in the text of the written Constitution that seem to give constitutional recognition to the death penalty. The Fifth Amendment requires indictment by a grand jury for "capital, or otherwise infamous crime." Both the Fifth and the Fourteenth amendments protect life, liberty, and property from deprivation without due process of law. This seems logically to imply that life can be taken as long as there is due process of law. This point was made by the dissenters in *Furman*, and again in the opinion announcing the judgment of the Court in *Gregg*. If we see this as barring an interpretation of "cruel and unusual punishment" that includes capital punishment, even though a principled interpretation would have that result, then once again integrity is limited by the brute fact of positive law. This limited integrity is morally more serious than the Senate bargain—if one thinks that capital punishment is inconsistent with principles of human dignity. But in one way it is less serious, for it could be cured by constitutional amendment, or, less decisively and less durably, by statutory change. The people could seek legislative integrity where adjudicative integrity has been blocked by the past. It is also possible to switch ground, arguing that the death penalty cannot be applied so as to satisfy the requirement of due process. But that is a separate interpretive argument. This argument, however, would also seem to go aground on the specific mention of "life" in the Fifth and Fourteenth amendments, for there seems to be an implication that there can be such a thing as deprivation of life that satisfies due process, though whether a *particular* case does so can be in question.

So it may not be possible to do as Dworkin says we might, interpreting the death penalty as unconstitutional "on the basis of some principles or groups of principles that unite the death penalty with the thumbscrew and the rack." However, I am not sure that mistake-labeling is really so farfetched here. The use of "life" and "capital" in these clauses is merely formulaic, inherited from centuries of English common law and, in the case of "life," from some political philosophers who built theories on that tradition. An interpreter could read "life, liberty, or property" and "capital and otherwise infamous" as units. The first basically means the same thing as the generic concept of serious punishment, a kind of idiom that is to be understood without division into parts. (Or it could be said to mean nothing more specific than does "ruined" in the provision of the *Magna Carta*, surely an ancestor of these clauses, that no free man should be "in any way ruined . . . except by the lawful judgment of his peers or by the law of the land.") "Capital and otherwise infamous" means no more than "infamous" alone—by internal logic. Another approach would be to construe the clauses in the light of their purpose. The purpose of each is clearly to secure the rights of those prosecuted, and as life is one of the things in need of protection given the common law and practice, it is mentioned. But it is completely outside of the purpose of these clauses to set a seal of approval, with the authority of the Constitution, upon the death penalty. "Life" and "capital . . . crime" are mentioned only to secure the protection of due process and of grand jury indictment, respectively, not to make a point about the death penalty. Here the text stutters.

Through such interpretive points I think that a case could be made for interpreting "cruel and unusual punishment" to include the death penalty in spite of these clauses. The use of "life" and "capital" has no structural role in the clauses themselves, though the clauses are constitutionally important. The constitutionality of the death penalty plays no essential role in our constitutional system. But here there arises a connection between my two applications of limited constitutional integrity. For it can be argued that what is really at issue is not the constitutionality of the death penalty, but rather the legislative authority of the states and Congress to impose the death penalty (as long as the people do not exercise their legislative authority to forbid this by constitutional amendment). Thus state sovereignty over ordinary criminal law (as well as other structural elements of our system) would be weakened if the death penalty *as such* were ruled unconstitutional. By itself this point is not conclusive, for I think that on the dimension of moral justification there is a strong argument for considering capital punishment "cruel and unusual" in this society. Furthermore, a weakening of legislative authority has often been a price of securing constitutional rights. But then there is the recalcitrant text of the Constitution, with its mention of "life, liberty, or property" and "capital . . . crime." Though the offending words can be interpreted out, I think that on balance we had better read the text more straightforwardly, out of concern for the separateness of state criminal law as an aspect of state sovereignty. (This aspect is surely more crucial to sovereignty than is the eternal bargain for equal state representation in the Senate. And without state sovereignty the Constitution makes little sense.) The potential for destabilization by the Fourteenth Amendment should again be noted, for it is through "incorporation" of the Eighth Amendment in the Due Process Clause of the Fourteenth Amendment that cruel and unusual punishment is forbidden to the states. This mechanism of interpretation places special emphasis on the implication of the use of "life" in the Fourteenth Amendment Due Process Clause: A state can take a life as long as it observes due process. This implication limits coherence of principle in our interpretation of the prohibition on cruel and unusual punishment. The grand jury clause of the Fifth Amendment has not been incorporated in the Fourteenth Amendment Due Process Clause. Given the strong argument of coherent political morality against capital punishment, I think that the maneuvers above might suffice to block a straightforward reading of "capital and otherwise infamous," for state sovereignty is not at issue in interpreting this clause.

As with the limit on the principle of equal political representation, I do not think that this limit on a principled understanding of "cruel and unusual punishment" can be justified at any deep level of political morality. I think that what we have is a compromised principle of justice, rather than the resolution of conflicting principles. Remove the word "life" from these two clauses, and the best interpretation of constitutional text and practice would result in ruling the death penalty unconstitutional. The word "life" is there as a mere historical accident, not as an expression of, for instance, some retributive theory of punishment. All we have here is positive law, limiting the construction of an interpretation that reveals a community of principle.

It is state sovereignty that tips the balance in favor of a straightforward reading, though congressional legislative authority is also relevant. But whatever the principles of fairness underlying state sovereignty, they would take second place in any conflict resolution with justice on such an issue as capital punishment.[34] It is the attraction of the straightforward reading of these clauses *taken together* with the principles of political morality underlying state sovereignty that supports this interpretation. Interpreting away the specific, separate force of "life" and "capital" is an extreme form of mistake-labeling (even though it can be done without directly saying so and with some interpretive rationale). Under the interpretive conception of limited integrity, the price of achieving deep coherence of principle is here too high.

My judgment that matters of principle are constrained here by a recalcitrant text is itself an interpretive judgment, inevitably controversial. This judgment is guided by limited integrity as a heuristic assumption. Justice Hercules works on a different assumption—full integrity. Which heuristic assumption is better depends upon the quality of the interpretations produced. So there can be no quick and general way of deciding between them.

But, nonetheless, let me add a nondecisive general comment. I see no reason why political integrity should be more perfect than personal integrity. A biographer interprets the life of a person. Suppose that the biographer comes to his or her subject with the initial judgment that that individual was a good person, whose life can be seen as expressing personal integrity. Yet the biographer would not expect perfect integrity, nor feel justified in forcing his or her materials into a portrait of perfect integrity. This should also be our initial assumption when we use the conception of political integrity—specifically, *adjudicative* political integrity—to construct an interpretation of law. (I speak here of "inclusive integrity,"[35] for that is the interpretive conception relevant to the question what the law is. Personal integrity is also "inclusive"—the coherence is not that of pure justice or pure goodness, but a more particularized, contextual, and historical matter. There is no reason to assume that perfect inclusive integrity can be found in any life or any legal system. So we should *sometimes* stop short of full coherence in our interpretation.)

The Constitution is the product of a continual process of compromise. The effective and authoritative constitutional law of any one time shows the marks of these compromises. Regardless of such origin in compromise, some of the marks can be encompassed within an interpretation that displays them as coherent at a level of deep political morality. But some of them cannot. Some of this residue of legal doctrine without deep principled support can be dealt with by mistake-labeling. Some, I have argued, cannot. The Constitution is human, just as its framers, interpreters, and subjects.

NOTES

I am grateful to the National Endowment for the Humanities for a Summer Seminar for College Teachers fellowship in 1985, which allowed me to begin the research leading to this paper. Professor Walter F. Murphy, director of the seminar, structured the fundamental questions of constitutional interpretation so that my initially blurred vision came into some focus.

1. 411 U.S. 1, 93 S. St. 1278, 36 L. Ed. 2d 16 (1973).
2. 163 U.S. 537, 16 S. Ct. 1138, 41 L. Ed. 256 (1896).
3. Ronald Dworkin, *A Matter of Principle* (Cambridge: Harvard Univ. Press, 1985), pp. 38–57.
4. Ronald Dworkin, *Law's Empire* (Cambridge: Harvard Univ. Press, 1986), pp. 361–363.
5. Dworkin, *A Matter of Principle*, p. 160.
6. Dworkin, *Law's Empire*, p. 166.
7. Dworkin, *Law's Empire*, pp. 397–398.
8. Dworkin, *Law's Empire*, p. 404.
9. This immunity is not absolute, for I think that in very special cases an interpreter might *in effect* judge that a minor, nonstructural element of the constitutional text is a mistake. This, however, must be done indirectly, by a special sort of interpretation. See the discussion within the chapter about capital punishment and the text of the Constitution. It could be argued that this kind of interpreting away *has* been done to the impairment of contracts clause in

Home Building & Loan Association v. Blaisdell (the Minnesota moratorium case), 290 U.S. 398, 54 S. Ct. 231, 78 L. Ed. 413 (1934), and that this clause now has little significance in our constitutional practice. My argument requires that the immunity to "mistake-labeling" only be seen as a *strong* presumption.

10. Dworkin, *Law's Empire,* p. 412 (where he is discussing law in general with the clear implication that constitutional law is included). For a clear, precise analysis of this point, based on Dworkin's articles before *Law's Empire,* see Leon Galis, "The Real and Unrefuted Rights Thesis," *The Philosophical Review,* 93 (1983):197–221.

11. Dworkin, *Law's Empire,* p. 398: "The American Constitution consists in the best available interpretation of American constitutional text and practice as a whole. . . ." In Dworkin's view, many controversial judgments, including ones of political morality, must necessarily bear upon Justice Hercules's interpretive conclusion that one account is best. But Dworkin has continually insisted that controversial moral and legal questions can have right answers. See "Can Rights be Controversial?" ch. 13 of *Taking Rights Seriously* (Cambridge, Mass.: Harvard Univ. Press, 1978); "Is There Really No Right Answer in Hard Cases?" (ch. 5 of *A Matter of Principle*); and especially the section on "Objectivity" in "On Interpretation and Objectivity" (ch. 7 of *A Matter of Principle,* pp. 171–174), which is substantially followed in *Law's Empire,* pp. 81–83.

12. Dworkin, *Law's Empire,* pp. 176–177, and the distinction between pure integrity and inclusive integrity, pp. 404–407. It is, of course, inclusive integrity that serves as Dworkin's conception of law, and that can lead a judge to compromise pure justice and the pure integrity built solely upon justice. My two applications below are of conventionalist compromises within the law, preventing the achievement of full inclusive integrity.

13. Dworkin, *Law's Empire,* pp. 178–184.

14. Dworkin, *Law's Empire,* pp. 78–80 for the general distinction between internal and external skepticism, and pp. 266–268 for internal skepticism regarding the law.

15. Dworkin, *Law's Empire,* p. 257.

16. See Dworkin's distinction between consistency "narrowly understood" and the "wide-ranging and imaginative . . . search for coherence with fundamental principle" encouraged by integrity, *Law's Empire,* p. 220.

17. 369 U.S. 186, 82 S. Ct. 691, 7 L. Ed. 2d 663 (1962).

18. *Gomillion v. Lightfoot,* 364 U.S. 339 (1960).

19. 337 U.S. 533, 84 S. Ct. 1362, 12 L. Ed. 2d 506 (1964).

20. Dworkin, *Law's Empire,* p. 179: "Each point of view must be allowed a voice in the process of deliberation but . . . the collective decision must nevertheless aim to settle on some coherent principle whose influence then extends to the natural limits of its authority." Dworkin later claims that the Fourteenth Amendment "is now understood to outlaw internal compromises over important matters of principle" (p. 185).

21. 16 Wallace 36, 21 L. Ed. 394 (1873).

22. Dworkin, *Law's Empire,* p. 436, and see pp. 268–280 as well as Dworkin's way of dealing with Critical Legal Studies at pp. 443–444.

23. Dworkin, *Law's Empire,* p. 184 and p. 436, note 9.

24. Dworkin, *Law's Empire,* p. 436, note 9.

25. Dworkin, *Law's Empire,* p. 172 for the personification of Massachusetts. For a general recognition and discussion of state sovereignty within the federal system, see pp. 185–186. It is clear, given this discussion, that Dworkin would

accept the general possibility of the kind of appeal to state sovereignty that I use in my example of capital punishment later in the paper. However, he would presumably not use it, as I do, to argue for *limited* integrity. I suppose that Dworkin's rebuttal must take the form of the treatment of abortion on p. 186. But Dworkin does not *endorse* that treatment, and as he indicates "a question of integrity remains: whether leaving the abortion issue to individual states to decide differently if they wish is coherent in principle with the rest of the American constitutional scheme, which makes other important rights national in scope and enforcement" (p. 186). The same question would be even more pressing in the case of capital punishment, for, unlike abortion, there are specific clauses in the text of the Constitution that, in some interpretations, imply recognition of capital punishment. At the same time, the "cruel and unusual punishment" clause can, under current social conditions, be interpreted to establish a right against capital punishment that must be "national in scope." The dispute has a more *textual* basis in the case of capital punishment.

26. James Madison, *The Federalist* No. 62, *The Federalist Papers,* 2d ed., Roy P. Fairfield, ed. (Baltimore: The Johns Hopkins Univ. Press, 1981), pp. 182–183.

27. Madison, *The Federalist* No. 62, in *The Federalist Papers,* p. 183.

28. See Robert M. Cover's discussion of Lysander Spooner (who published *The Unconstitutionality of Slavery* in 1845) in *Justice Accused: Antislavery and the Judicial Process* (New Haven, Conn.: Yale Univ. Press, 1975), pp. 156–158.

29. Ronald Dworkin, *Taking Rights Seriously,* p. 136.

30. *Furman v. Georgia,* 408 U.S. 238 (1972).

31. See Justice Marshall's dissent in *Gregg v. Georgia,* 428 U.S. 153, 96 S. Ct. 2909, 49 L. Ed. 2d 859 (1976).

32. See Justice Brennan's concurring opinion in *Furman v. Georgia.* I here paraphrase and slightly modify his reasoning.

33. See Justice Marshall's dissent in *Gregg v. Georgia.*

34. Where important individual rights are at issue, Dworkin seems to allow only a subsidiary role to the ideal of fairness (which concerns the structure of political decisionmaking, including some preference for majority rule). See, for instance, *Law's Empire,* p. 250 and p. 377.

35. Dworkin, *Law's Empire,* pp. 404–407.

SELECTED BIBLIOGRAPHY

Dworkin, Ronald. 1978. *Taking Rights Seriously.* Cambridge, Mass.: Harvard Univ. Press; especially ch. 5, "Constitutional Cases."

———. 1985. *A Matter of Principle.* Cambridge, Mass.: Harvard Univ. Press; especially Part Two, "Law as Interpretation."

———. 1986. *Law's Empire.* Cambridge, Mass.: Harvard Univ. Press; especially ch. 2, "Interpretive Concepts"; ch. 6, "Integrity"; ch. 7, "Integrity in Law"; and ch. 10, "The Constitution."

Ely, John Hart. 1980. *Democracy and Distrust: A Theory of Judicial Review.* Cambridge, Mass.: Harvard Univ. Press.

Fiss, Owen M. 1982. "Objectivity and Interpretation." *Stanford L. Rev.* 34, pp. 739–763, and, immediately following, a comment by Paul Brest.

Hart, H.L.A. 1983. "American Jurisprudence through English Eyes: The Nightmare and the Noble Dream." In H.L.A. Hart. *Essays in Jurisprudence and Philosophy.* Oxford: Clarendon Press. Originally published in *Georgia Law Review* 11 (1977), pp. 969–989.

"Interpretation Symposium." 1985. *Southern California L. Rev.* 58, nos. 1 and 2; especially David Couzens Hoy, "Interpreting the Law: Hermeneutical and Poststructuralist Perspectives," in no. 1; and David A.J. Richards, "Interpretation and Historiography," in no. 2.
Mitchell, W.J.T., ed. 1983. *The Politics of Interpretation.* Chicago: Univ. of Chicago Press.
Perry, Michael J. 1982. *The Constitution, the Courts, and Human Rights.* New Haven, Conn.: Yale Univ. Press.
Powell, H. Jefferson. 1985. "The Original Understanding of Original Intent." *Harvard L. Rev.* 98, pp. 885–948.
Rehnquist, William H. 1976. "The Notion of a Living Constitution." *Texas L. Rev.* 54, pp. 693–706.
Smith, Rogers M. 1985. *Liberalism and American Constitutional Law.* Cambridge, Mass.: Harvard Univ. Press; especially ch. 5, "Voting Apportionment."
Tushnet, Mark V. 1983. "Following the Rules Laid Down: A Critique of Interpretivism and Neutral Principles." *Harvard L. Rev.* 96, pp. 781–827.

PART FOUR

Current Issues in Constitutional Law

Introduction to Part Four

DIANA T. MEYERS

The U.S. constitutional tradition has roots in the classic liberalism of John Locke, who based his political theory on an individualistic conception of natural rights. For Locke, the rights to life, liberty, and property authorize people to pursue their own projects as they see fit provided that their activities do not violate the rights of others. Rights protect people from others' unwanted incursions, but they do not supply any positive benefits. People are entitled to noninterference (for example, the right to life entitles people not to be killed), but people are not entitled to aid (the right to life does not entitle anyone to the means of subsistence). Likewise, natural rights are equal rights since all people possess these rights and since no one's rights are weightier than anyone else's. But Locke regarded the equality of natural rights as formal rather than substantive. Respecting natural rights does not require equality of outcomes; it requires observing impartial procedures.

This Lockean view of rights continues to dominate jurisprudence in the United States. Constitutional rights are seen as negative rights that guarantee spheres of personal liberty by forbidding unwarranted forms of government interference, including censorship, establishment of religion, and deprivation of life, liberty, or property without due process of law. The business of providing such benefits as public education, pollution control, and shelter for the homeless is seen primarily as a legislative matter. Yet, there is controversy about the adequacy of this negative, individualistic interpretation of constitutional rights, and, even if one accepts this general view of constitutional rights, there is controversy about how to analyze them.

The chapters in Part 4 take up various aspects of these controversies. Virginia Held disputes the appropriateness of a negative analysis of free speech in the context of modern communications systems. Michael Mc Donald defends the tenability of a nonindividualistic conception of freedom of religion. Carl Wellman inquires into the basis of the right to privacy. Michael Bayles proposes a revised analysis of the circumstances triggering due process of law. Christopher Gray defends a robust conception of the exclusionary rule for illegally obtained evidence.

In "Access, Enablement, and the First Amendment," Virginia Held denies that standard philosophical and legal conceptions of free expression are adequate for contemporary cultural realities in advanced societies. These standard accounts take the orator in a public square as a model of free speech. This individual has the means to express his or her ideas, and all that government need do to guarantee this individual's free speech is to refrain from interfering. But modern means of communication—mass electronic and print media—do not fit this model. They are so pervasive that they control what people think about and the terms in which people reflect on issues. They are also expensive to use, and they constitute a profitmaking industry. Held advocates increasing the cultural independence of the media and reducing the tie between business interests and expression in order to enable the media to perform their traditional function of social criticism. Held concludes by reviewing the current state of U.S. law regarding free speech and by defending "enabling rights" to access to the media.

Michael Mc Donald takes up another dimension of the First Amendment, namely, freedom of religion. In particular, Mc Donald addresses the question of the state's support for religious schools in "Respect for Individuals versus Respect for Groups: Public Aid for Confessional Schools in the United States and Canada." In contrast to the U.S. Constitution, which prohibits government funding of religious schools, Canadian constitutional law requires public funding of religious schools for some religious groups. These include Roman Catholics, Anglicans, along with various other Protestant sects, and, in one province, the Salvation Army. Mc Donald asks what principle underlies these divergent traditions regarding the relation between church and state. He maintains that the Canadian approach rests on the historic recognition of religious groups as having collective rights, whereas the U.S. approach can best be understood in terms of respect for individual rights. Although both societies are pluralistic, they differ dramatically with respect to their views of community and therefore with respect to their support for communities within the larger nation.

Carl Wellman's essay, "The Right of Privacy and Personal Autonomy," affirms that a long line of decisions has established a constitutional right to privacy; he asks how that right is related to personal autonomy. Noting that David A.J. Richards defines the right to privacy in terms of autonomy while Hyman Gross completely rejects this account, Wellman points out that these differing interpretations have significant implications for judicial decisions regarding homosexual rights and abortion. Wellman then turns to legal precedents with the aim of extracting a unified account of privacy. Wellman argues that the right to privacy is properly understood as a "claim-right against governmental intrusions into that area of an individual's life where personal decisions lie." Thus, the right to privacy does not protect personal autonomy directly; it protects personal autonomy indirectly by securing areas of life in which the individual is free to act autonomously.

In "Procedural Due Process," Michael Bayles asks when the Fifth and Fourteenth amendments require due process of law—that is, observance of procedural safeguards designed to protect individuals' rights. The texts appear to limit due process to situations in which life, liberty, or property is at stake; however, many commentators have taken a broader view. Bayles defends an analysis that focuses on when deprivation occurs, rather than on whether the deprivation is of life, liberty, or property. He distinguishes four types of decisions: burden-imposing decisions, burden-relieving decisions, benefit-conferring decisions, and benefit-terminating decisions. Deprivation involves harm and makes a person worse off. Bayles maintains that burden-imposing decisions and many benefit-terminating decisions involve deprivation and require due process. Bayles applies his analysis to the cases of revocation of parole, dismissal from employment, and government entitlement programs.

Christopher Gray's paper, "The Exclusionary Rule as Constitutional Renewal: U.S. Integrity and Canadian Repute," focuses on court procedures. In both the U.S. and Canadian legal systems, courts refuse to admit evidence that has been obtained illegally. For example, evidence that has been obtained in a search of private premises conducted without a search warrant cannot be presented to a jury. Gray examines the basis for this rule. He traces the U.S. legal practice to the doctrine of judicial integrity and the Canadian legal practice to the doctrine of judicial disrepute. He then undertakes to interrelate these two doctrines urging that integrity does not allow the courts to disassociate themselves from the questionable activities of other branches of government, that the courts' condoning such activities would bring them into disrepute, and that the disrepute of the courts would undermine the rule of law.

EIGHT

Access, Enablement, and the First Amendment

VIRGINIA HELD

In the discussion that follows I take a commitment to free expression as given. I shall not address questions concerning the justification of free expression. Arguments for it are often based on deontological principles concerning autonomy, or on consequentialist claims that free expression is conducive to true belief; we can well argue for free expression on both of the above grounds and on some additional ones.[1] In this chapter I shall explore instead what a conception of free expression adequate for our time and place should include: What would it mean to be able to express oneself "freely" in a society such as that of the United States? What would a conception of "free expression" suitable for the kinds of culture that now exist include? And what would a "right to free expression" adequate for the kind of society we live in provide?

It seems clear that standard current philosophical and legal treatments of free expression do not adequately address these questions. Complaints about the unsatisfactory state of recent judicial determination of First Amendment issues abound. Benno Schmidt recently wrote that "the judicial decisions that make up the body of First Amendment law are most notable for an absence of unifying theory and a disinterest in confronting basic assumptions."[2] And Archibald Cox has written that "the first amendment decisions of the 1970's seem to me to bear the marks of an exceedingly pragmatic and particularistic jurisprudence."[3] Of one opinion he said it "underscores the problems of the Burger Court in developing a coherent approach to the first amendment."[4] Decisions since then have, if anything, aggravated the problem.

Current philosophical and legal discussions deal almost exclusively with problems of interference with expression, seeing rights to free expression as rights to express oneself without governmental restraint. What arguments are devoted to questions of access, or to whether one has the capacity to express oneself, focus unduly on what should or should not count as a public forum in which such expression may take place. Almost all discussions merely assume that people already have the means with which to express themselves if only they are not interfered with.[5]

This assumption is in large measure false. Although there are, of course, many other problems with which theories of free expression must be concerned, such as problems of defamation, obscenity, privacy, and the like, I shall focus on the questions of access and enablement.[6]

THE ORATOR IN THE SQUARE

The image that pervades the philosophical and legal literature is the image of an orator on a soapbox in a public square. This orator has a constitutional right not to be interfered with by government officials, and most writers might also want to say that this is a moral right. Occasionally, the orator becomes a citizen with a handbill to distribute or post, but this is about as far as the images at the heart of the standard treatments of free expression have gone to catch up with modern technological and cultural realities. Questions that have been considered by the courts are whether a given locus, such as car cards in a public vehicle[7] or walkways in a shopping center,[8] do or do not constitute a public forum where speech in the traditional sense will be protected from unjustified interference. But in virtually all the legal and almost all the philosophical discussions, the capacity to speak is presumed: The orator has his own voice, the leafleteer her mimeographed handout. If the issues concern access to advertising space, it is presumed that the persons wishing to express themselves in an advertisement have the economic resources with which to purchase space.[9] And if the issues concern the speech heard on television, or the words printed in newspapers, virtually the same presumptions are made. The bearer of the right to free expression, the contents of which right may be carefully discussed in other ways, is assumed to possess the means to express himself, the way an orator already possesses a voice or the way the leafleteer already has her handbills. The ability to speak is presumed, and the debate revolves around the appropriateness of the forum in question for the application of rights worked out conceptually for the speaker in the public square.[10]

Related issues that have been addressed have concerned whether newspaper publishers and broadcasters should possess the same First Amendment guarantees against government interference or regulation as ordinary citizens possess.[11] Or they have dealt with whether First Amendment guarantees of free speech should be extended to the "commercial speech" or advertisements of corporations. The issues presume, again, that the means to speak are available to the person or entity claiming the right to free expression; otherwise, the issues whether one is being interfered with, or has a right not to be interfered with, do not arise, as far as the standard treatments of freedom of expression are concerned. And in the absence of interference, no problem of free expression is recognized.

CONTEMPORARY REALITIES

What are some of the current realities of expression and communication? Some writers suggest that our society can increasingly be characterized as a "media culture." As one account has it, in place of the religious worldview that prevailed through the eighteenth century, and in place of the scientific worldview that has been dominant from the nineteenth century until recently, we are becoming a society shaped by the media. We increasingly see the world through the lenses of the media and interpret reality within the framework the media constructs.[12]

Whether we welcome or resist such sweeping characterizations, we can agree that the mass media are an enormously influential feature of contemporary society. The media have a compelling place in the cultural and political landscape. Their messages are pervasive, their sounds and images hard to escape. What is "real" for many people may be what is reported in the media. It is widely thought that politicians can no longer be elected without some ability to communicate through television. And what gain attention as cultural symbols, as role models, as the sources of the social evaluations that culture has a function to provide, are to a large extent the symbols and celebrities that permeate the culture through the mass electronic and print media of television, radio, recordings, movies, magazines, and newspapers.

The word *culture* has in the past been used by anthropologists to refer to virtually everything that occurs in the societies they have studied. But in recent years, some agreement has evolved on connecting the word *culture* with questions of meaning. Culture, then, is what gives meaning to what occurs and comprises the ideas, attitudes, and meanings created by humans in societies. Sociologists and social anthropologists usually distinguish culture from social structure, that is, from the systems of authority and the institutions that allocate power and organize economic activity.[13] In contemporary developed societies, a distinction is often made between "high culture"—the art in museums and the concerts of symphony orchestras—and the "mass culture" or "popular culture" of television, radio, and the like, though it is increasingly claimed that with postmodern culture, this distinction breaks down.[14] Without being able to develop any of these concepts here, I shall discuss culture as something that is at least potentially different from and more symbolic than social structure. And I shall focus on the culture of societies like that of the United States where the mass media are a salient feature of the culture.

As presently constituted, the U.S. mass media are first and foremost businesses whose primary objective is economic gain. In some cases they achieve such gain by appealing directly to mass audiences, in other cases by bringing audiences to the advertisements of others, and thus serving their own economic interests by effectively serving the economic interests of others.

Advertising is at the heart of the media and of the culture. In a recent review of a book on the history of U.S. advertising, Andrew Hacker suggested that advertising may be the country's "most characteristic institution."[15] Certainly, advertising is, as Raymond Williams puts it, "the official art of modern capitalist society: it is what 'we' put up in 'our' streets and use to fill up to half of 'our' newspapers and magazines; and it commands the services of perhaps the largest organized body of writers and artists, with their attendant managers and advisers in the whole society."[16] In the United States, commercial television and radio get virtually all of their revenues from advertising. Newspapers get from 60 to 80 percent, and magazines get up to 100 percent (though small magazines may have no advertising).

The primary objective of television programming is to build audiences for the messages of advertisers. Programs exist for the sake of advertisements, not the reverse.[17] This view is not held solely by media critics. Even those who are entirely satisfied with current arrangements agree that, as one account states, "TV programs are packages for commercials," and "since the primary aim of television is to sell products to a mass market, television must design . . . programs that hold an audience up to and through a commercial message."[18] As a Carnegie Commission report phrased it, "commercial broadcasting's entire output is defined by an imperative need to reach mass audiences in order to sell products."[19] News programs are not significantly different. They, too, are designed to be, most importantly, entertaining, and to hold their audiences for the rest of the evening's programs and thus advertisements.[20]

Newspapers also are first of all businesses for whom advertising revenue is central. According to a past president of the American Society of Newspaper Editors who has headed four leading newspapers, "the profit response to the First Amendment is often much stronger than the journalistic response," both in the print and the electronic media. "The underlying purpose," he writes, "is to create an uncritical, permissive buying mood for the benefit of advertisers." As he puts it, "the main goal of the news media conglomerates must be mass advertising."[21]

According to one study of the media, which describes monopolies in the media in the United States, "Increasingly, editorial content of publications and broadcasting is dictated by the computer printouts on advertising agency desks. . . . When there is a conflict between the printout and an independent editor, the printouts win."[22] Television programs are chosen to win rating wars and boost advertising revenues. And editorial content in magazines is chosen to gain "the right kind of readers," meaning those with higher incomes and other demographic characteristics that advertisers like.

In sum, in the current broadcasting industry there is little room for cultural independence, that is, for making decisions in such a way that aesthetic and distinctively cultural values are given priority over considerations of economic gain. And the realities of the print media are increasingly similar.[23]

THE QUESTION OF PRIORITIES

Instead of putting cultural values first, and economic necessity second, the most important forms of cultural expression available in our society today serve business interests. With very few exceptions, those who create the images and symbols of the society can only choose between serving one commercial interest or another. And with very few exceptions, those who receive such images and symbols can only choose to receive them from one commercial source or another.

I want to emphasize that the issue is one of priority. Making a television program or writing an article that is thoroughly admirable and also a financial success does not indicate subservience to commercial interests. If it has been made because it is aesthetically pleasing or culturally interesting, and if these have been the primary objectives, commercial success need not in itself be questionable. But if commercial success supersedes cultural value in the making and distributing of cultural products, this may be the reverse of what culture ought to strive to provide. It is comparable to elevating commercial convenience over the findings of an independent scientific view in arriving at an accurate estimate of, say, the environmental damage caused by the dumping of certain chemicals. Nearly everyone would recognize that such an ordering of priorities in scientific research would be faulty.

Clearly, the primacy now accorded to commercial interests over distinctively cultural considerations could be changed. Our society could give priority to cultural rather than commercial goals, and the arguments in favor of striving to achieve such a liberation of expression seem overwhelming.

An important question to consider about any society is the relation between its culture and its political economy. Most agree that a culture ought to provide evaluations of a society's social structure and not merely reflect or reinforce existing configurations of power. To the extent that contemporary cultures are subservient to commercial interests, they may fail to perform this important cultural function. Just as "free inquiry" has had to free itself from religious and political control, it seems clear that cultural expression in our own time and place should free itself from commercial control.[24]

There is no doubt that we are, to a large extent, a commercial society, a society in which the values of business predominate and in which the social structure and the culture reflect to a high degree the interests of business. Perhaps we will continue to be a commercial society by choice. Perhaps the values of business are those that persons, if given real and meaningful choices, would choose, both as creators and receivers of cultural messages. But then business need have no fear of the liberation of culture. If a culture freed from commercial control chose the values of business, these values would have a legitimacy they cannot now have. For we cannot know what people would choose if their culture were free of commercial control because they are not now in such a position.

Arguments for greater cultural freedom should not be confused with arguments for "high art" distinct from "mass culture." Comparisons between programming that appeals only to relatively small and well-educated audiences, and popular commercial programming, are not relevant to this argument. Rather, we should contrast noncommercial and commercial programs at a given level of audience appeal. Noncommercial programs such as "Sesame Street" can reach large numbers of children, as can commercial programs for children, but the latter are increasingly composed of dramatizations of manufacturer's products such as dolls and toy weapons and thus amount to little more than program-length advertisements.[25] Sophisticated movies can be presented either on noncommercial channels without interruptions for advertising, or on standard channels with breaks for commercials every few minutes. These are the relevant comparisons. There is no reason to associate noncommercial broadcasting with so-called elitist tastes, except to distort the public's views of the alternatives to commercial broadcasting.

ON THE LIBERATION OF CULTURE

Recent popular criticism of the organization of the media has been sparse. What criticism there has been has largely focused on the dangers of monopoly and the need for competition. But if competition is solely among commercial enterprises, this may contribute nothing toward the goal of putting noncommercial values ahead of commercial values.

In the United States the pattern has repeatedly been that of a few giants coming to dominate the airwaves; as questions have been raised in Congress and in public discussion about existing arrangements, the complaints have crystallized into complaints about a lack of competition.[26] Discussion has characteristically focused on how to increase competition in the marketplace, while ignoring the more fundamental issue of whether the marketplace is where so much of our culture should be determined.[27] Questions of commercial control versus noncommercial broadcasting have simply not been discussed. The Federal Communications Commission (FCC), charged with regulating broadcasting "in the public interest," has characteristically concerned itself with how to serve the economic interests of the industry as a whole. But these interests are still economic interests and hardly equivalent to the interests of the public or to more distinctively cultural interests. There has been virtually no popular discussion of how commercial competition may not be the right way to decide the content of culture.

Almost everyone engaged in popular debate about either free expression or the media seems imprisoned in Oliver Wendell Holmes's metaphor of the "marketplace of ideas";[28] this commerce of culture, they argue, should be our goal. That one of the ideas in that marketplace should be to take culture out of it doesn't seem to occur to any of the participants. As one observer has noted about the FCC, "the FCC has refused to even broach the issue of commercialism in any serious way. . . . The FCC, by its silence, has from the beginning served to uphold the interests of the networks by ensuring the corporate, profit-making structure of the broadcast system."[29] Publicly funded, noncommercial broadcasting is never mentioned by the FCC and has often been ignored by most of those who discuss the problems of the media.

Clearly there is a need to raise more fundamental questions about mass culture than to ask how to ensure that it be subject to market competition, though problems of monopoly and interlocking directorships are also serious. The society might demand that a substantial proportion of mass culture obtain operating revenues from public support, which would enable it to put cultural values ahead of commercial ones. In the United States almost all agree broadcasting should be free of political control. We could agree that it should also be free of commercial control.[30]

THE QUESTION OF PROFESSIONAL STANDARDS

To foster the growth of a culture that is guided by independently developed cultural values, the professional standards of those engaged in cultural activities may have to address themselves far more than they have to the problem of independence. The ethical and professional standards of journalists, editors, producers, writers, artists, and actors could be written to demand freedom from commercial control as well as freedom from government censorship or interference. Independence from commercial control could be an intrinsic part of the professional standards by which those engaged in cultural activities evaluate each other and evaluate those to whom they give the rewards of jobs, advancement, and praise. Independence from commercial control could be included in the standards by which working conditions are compared. The chance for independence could come to be more highly regarded than a mere increase in salary. And a professional association of journalists or broadcasting artists could censure those newspapers or broadcasters that fail to provide journalistic and artistic independence the way the American Association of University Professors censures educational institutions that violate academic freedom.

Currently, academic freedom protects, at least relatively, the independence of those supported by universities; similarly, a comparable standard of freedom from outside control could be demanded by those who work in the areas of culture that are distinct from education, even in the area of popular culture. And institutional arrangements could be developed to support cultural independence, so that the preconditions for such independence would not be limited to those who have them through such accidental and unrelated occurrences as inherited wealth.

When the church was dominant in a society and able to deprive dissenters of their livelihoods and even their lives, cultural critics saw it as their responsibility to resist this domination so that objective or scientific inquiries could proceed. Where the party or the junta is dominant, and dissenters disappear or are sent to insane asylums, cultural critics see it as their task to resist this domination so that free inquiry can take place. And where economic power dominates cultural life, leaving those who dissent from the dominant commercial values of the society and culture unemployed or unable to be heard, cultural critics should see it as their task to remedy this situation.

Perhaps the most important element in encouraging independence would be making independence a standard and part of the criteria by which those concerned with cultural expression evaluate themselves and others. This reform could proceed long before the social structures of the society had changed significantly in the direction of greater independence for cultural activities. The standards of "artistic integrity" now recognized for high art could well be extended to the media or at least certain portions of it. Even U.S. culture does not (yet) frame the art in its museums or the concerts of its symphony orchestras with commercials for soft drinks. It does not need to accept that the news of war and of fateful governmental decisions, or the major images and dramas by which its members understand and shape their lives, are subordinated to commercial interests.

Cultural critics cannot escape their own histories or their own times and places. But where the church or the party or economic power control the culture, it is possible to see this domination, and to see it from within the society in which one is immersed. It is possible to make comparative judgments, noting the relative independence the pursuit of knowledge has at universities and the relative lack of independence other cultural activities confront.

Those engaged in cultural expression need not agree on most moral or political positions or on cultural values themselves. But they could come to agree that such values ought to be developed from positions free of domination by sources of power outside the realm of culture, and that those sources of power can be economic as well as political. And they could build such views into the professional standards by which they are guided.

INDIVIDUAL RIGHTS TO FREE EXPRESSION

Having outlined some arguments for a culture freed from outside control, I would now like to distinguish a culture that is free in some collective sense from an individual right to free expression. A culture as a whole—to whatever extent one can make sense of such a notion—might theoretically be free from outside control while being internally organized in some quite hierarchical and repressive way. One can, for instance, imagine a "culture czar" not subject to political or commercial control, but able to dispense jobs and praise as he and his closest advisers see fit. One can therefore imagine a kind of culture free from outside control but without strong individual rights to free expression.

On the other hand, in a society in which much of the culture is not free from outside control, there might be some individual rights to free expression; this is the current situation in the United States. And, too, adequately developed individual rights to free expression might exist in a culture truly independent from outside domination; this is the goal I seek to outline.

The following discussion explores some questions concerning individual rights to expression and what they should include. I said at the outset that the contemporary philosophical and legal literature seems inadequate for dealing with this topic. Let's consider a few important, central examples of how individual rights to free expression are conceptualized in this literature.

RECENT DISCUSSIONS

In a recent paper, which will no doubt be widely cited, Thomas M. Scanlon suggests a division of "the interests with which freedom of expression is concerned" into "the interests of participants, the interests of audiences, and the interests of bystanders."[31] Participant interests are characterized as those interests people have in expressing themselves on such matters as religion, politics, and commercial matters. Scanlon discusses freedom of expression as "a right" on which we agree because "we believe that limits on the power of government to regulate expression are necessary to protect our central interests as audiences and participants. . . ."[32] Scanlon fleetingly mentions the issue of equity in the access to means of expression.[33] Allen Buchanan, commenting on Scanlon's paper, says that it would follow from Scanlon's positions that there would have to be positive enabling rights and not only an absence of governmental interference.[34] But nowhere in Scanlon's discussion does he consider the issue of enabling rights—of the empowerment of those not now having access to the means of expression to obtain such means—or of any of the implications of this sort of concern. The capacity to express oneself is presupposed, not considered, and the discussion only addresses appropriate protections of capacities already possessed, or limits on the exercise of those capacities. Anyone lacking the capacity for expression is not covered by Scanlon's theory of freedom of expression.

Although Buchanan recognizes that any concern with fairness would seem to lead to positive enabling rights, it is unclear whether this observation is offered as a recommendation that we explore the implications of such a view, or as a warning against pressing this line of thinking about expression. "I would suggest," he says, "that if the commitment of the fairness principle to equal access were taken seriously, the result would be a complex of redistributive measures which would make current welfare programs look extremely modest."[35] He himself does not pursue these issues. But we can note that if structural differences between those in a position to express themselves to millions and those almost completely unable to gain a hearing for their views do not benefit the least advantaged groups in the society—and how could they?—then, on such grounds as those of Rawls's difference principle, we could criticize such differences as unjust.[36]

However, it is questionable whether principles of justice appropriate for the distribution of wealth and income are those that should guide arrangements for the creation of culture. If the arguments that culture ought to be out of the marketplace rather than in it are persuasive, then we do not necessarily improve the culture in the most appropriate way merely by making the marketplace a more egalitarian market.[37]

In another major treatment of freedom of expression, Archibald Cox is as silent as Scanlon about the problem of access for those who do not already possess the means to express themselves.[38] He does briefly consider some questions about reporters' possible rights of access to judicial proceedings, but the issues revolve around whether the courtroom is like a public square or forum. We have already seen how deficient this metaphor is for dealing with the realities and problems of contemporary forms of expression. In *Richmond Newspapers*[39] decided in 1980, Justice Stevens, in a concurring opinion, thought the Court was acknowledging a right of the press to "the acquisition of newsworthy matter." Cox, however, disagrees. He does not think that any such right of access or right to know has been established.[40]

In this case Chief Justice Burger refers to "streets, sidewalks, and parks" as "places traditionally open, where First Amendment rights may be exercised";[41] he considers whether a trial courtroom is also a public place where reporters have a right to be present. Cox makes the following comment on the Court's decision that in this case reporters should be admitted: "A municipality need not create parks or auditoriums for speakers, but if they exist and have long been so used, the municipality cannot without specific overriding justification withdraw them from particular speakers or subjects of discussion."[42] So, if courtrooms have traditionally been open, they cannot be closed without good reason. But from this we learn nothing about anyone's right of access to anywhere they have not traditionally been accustomed to having access, such as to the electronic and print media.

Laurence Tribe seems to think that the Supreme Court may have established a First Amendment right to a public forum.[43] Cox does not agree.[44] In any event, the cases in which this right may or may not have been recognized involved assembly in such semipublic institutions as hospitals and welfare offices, which can exclude demonstrators "provided that alternative channels remain open."[45] Based on decisions made so far, there is no indication that any such right to a mass media forum has been suggested by the Court, and perhaps the Court will not take seriously, as Tribe thinks it should, the requirement that "alternative channels" be of comparable suitability. Tribe wondered where else one could effectively demonstrate against a welfare requirement or treatment of patients than in a welfare office or in a hospital. But Cox, and presumably the courts, would probably maintain that the streets outside such places are suitable enough as an alternative forum.

Cox thinks that "the chief danger to freedom of expression by the poor, the unorthodox, and the unpopular," lies in local restrictions on picketing, marches, and demonstrations.[46] Such a view takes the poverty of the poor as no bar to free expression and assumes that it is perfectly proper for demonstration to be the only avenue of expression open to them.

It is clear, however, that the major bar to expression by the poor, the unorthodox, and the unpopular is that demonstrations are the only means of expression open to them. The overwhelmingly more influential avenues of the electronic and print media are not part of the "public forums" to which these individuals have been deemed to have a traditional right of access. And the standard philosophical and legal treatments of the issues do not question whether all persons might be thought to have rights to be heard by media audiences, as they have rights to be heard by bystanders in the park, or whether it is only the rich, the powerful, and the successful who have rights to be heard by media audiences.

That demonstrations will sometimes receive news coverage does not remedy the situation for those whose only means of expression is through demonstration, for it leaves the question of coverage entirely to broadcasters and publishers. Those trying to express themselves have little power in deciding which images and messages will be transmitted and which ignored.

As for the question whether citizens have a "right to a forum" even in the traditional sense of a public place to speak and be heard or to hand out a leaflet, Cox thinks that "the availability of a wide variety of public forums has made it unnecessary to put the question to a test."[47] Thus even a writer such as Cox, whose primary professional concern is freedom of expression, can in a book on the topic simply overlook the enormous problem of access to the media or even of access itself. He simply assumes it is not a problem.

THE FORUM AND THE AUDIENCE

Let's return to the image of the public square. Restrictions of time, place, and manner have been recognized as legitimate regulations of expression. Thus, licenses for the use of streets or parks can be required as long as the restrictions are not based on the content of the speech but only on such considerations as traffic control, public safety, and the protection of participants. But the concept of a right to express oneself in a public forum makes certain assumptions about the likelihood of an audience. If a municipality required that demonstrations take place in a nearby forest where the only recipients of the messages would be trees, those wishing to demonstrate in a more inhabited area could certainly find a sympathetic hearing in the courts. Or if a town's officials decreed that the only picketing they would allow against some policy they had adopted would be silent picketing between 3:00 and 4:00 in the morning, the courts surely would find such a restriction on expression unreasonable.[48]

But then the argument should apply on a wider scale. If one can only picket and demonstrate with a message against X, while the airwaves reaching millions of listeners are saturated with messages in favor of X, one is as disabled as if one were required to picket silently between 3:00 and 4:00 A.M.

The right to free expression is in part a right to express oneself to an audience. It is at least in part a right to communicate. For most expression, the audience must be free to walk away, or not to have its senses unduly assaulted, as by a painfully loud noise or obscenely offensive depictions. But the audience should not have to make special efforts to obtain the expression before the expression is protected. The right to free expression is a right to express oneself in a forum where the public may be found. Hence the image of the public square. If we consider the implications of these aspects of expression for contemporary society, we may have to conclude that if people are likely to be in front of a television screen rather than on the street, then a right of expression may be a right to express oneself via a television screen, not only on the street.

A public forum need not be an open space or meeting hall. In a society where communication through the mass media is pervasive, free expression through the mass media must in some way be connected with the rights of individual persons. But can such rights be spelled out in some plausible way?

ACCESS TO THE MEDIA

One way to recognize individual rights to free expression in a culture dominated by the media would be to take the issue of access seriously. The FCC has evolved the Fairness Doctrine, requiring broadcasters to (1) cover controversial issues of public importance, provide a reasonable opportunity for the presentation of contrasting viewpoints, ascertain the needs and problems of the community and offer programming to meet them; and (2) provide those attacked on the air a right of reply. The Supreme Court in *Red Lion* in 1969 has upheld the FCC's authority to demand that stations meet these requirements.[49]

The FCC has made almost no demands that the first part of the doctrine be carried out, and only the most modest demands that those attacked by a broadcaster be permitted to reply. This has led broadcasters to argue in favor of abolishing the Fairness Doctrine on the grounds that it only promotes blandness. If anyone attacked can respond, stations will avoid attacking.

But the solution might be a much more vigorous enforcement of the first part of the Fairness Doctrine rather than abandonment of the second part. It would be possible for the FCC under present law to insist on far more opportunities than now exist for programming participation by a wide variety of individuals and groups. Stations could be required to set aside some percentage of time every day for open access, for noncommercial programming for children, for public service and creative programming aimed at children's development, citizens' enlightenment, and artistic achievement. Stations need not be permitted to use virtually all broadcast time for the commercial gain of sponsors and stations.

Defenders of the Fairness Doctrine have suggested that "fair but content neutral regulation of access is a real possibility."[50] Some have offered a variety of proposals to ensure "fairness in communication on controversial issues of public importance" and to bring it about that all citizens have "equal access to 'the indispensable instruments of effective political speech.'"[51] One proposal would require that a certain amount of time on each broadcast frequency be designated as "access time" to be allocated "according to criteria of representation. Speakers who are representative of a substantial group of citizens in a signal area shall have a right of access. . . ."[52] Access would mean to have one's message aired, like commercials, many times, and to reach an audience, like commercials do, whether or not the audience sought out the message. Another proposal would require that broadcast frequencies become semicommon carriers that would auction program periods for a given season and reserve a substantial percentage of program access for nonprofit groups that demonstrate support by membership or petition.

Proposals such as these emphasize the role of representation in public debate and argue that the media must be included in the system of democratic discussion in which citizens' views are aired and represented. The Supreme Court has declined to extend the arguments of *Red Lion* to the print media. Newspapers are thus permitted to cover or not cover whatever viewpoints they please, and it has been ruled unconstitutional for newspapers to be required to accord those they attack a right of reply.[53] But suggestions to provide public subsidies for alternative nonprofit newspapers that would offer possibilities for access comparable to those discussed for broadcasting could be pursued.

Thomas Emerson, in his study *The System of Freedom of Expression* published in 1970, recognized that "in general, the government must affirmatively make available the opportunity for expression as well as protect it from encroachment. This means that positive measures must be taken to assure the ability to speak despite economic or other barriers."[54] Although he did not pursue in depth what this might require, he noted that "government funds that enable private individuals or groups to engage in expression are being made available in many fields. . . . Even government subsidies of newspapers are being seriously proposed."[55]

In the years since his book appeared, and especially in the Reagan era, developments have gone largely in the other direction, both in reduced government efforts to increase opportunities for expression, and in scholarly discussion. But the arguments in favor of access remain both valid and available.

Some of those who recognize the problem of access construe it as a problem of private "censorship" comparable to government censorship.[56] Protections are needed against both forms. Although this view is an improvement over views that see no problem at all, it would be better still to confront the inadequacy of notions of freedom that see threats to freedom only in interference.[57] Current problems of free expression need to be seen in terms of positive enablements. Empowering many of those who now lack the means of expression could avoid conflicts with First Amendment protections already in place. Recent Supreme Court decisions leave little room for substantial regulation of the commercial press, such as regulations requiring meaningful access. The view that government should not determine the content of expression even where regulation is permitted is well established. It may inhibit the extent to which further FCC oversight of commercial broadcasting can be developed. But nothing in First Amendment law would conflict with an expansion of the kinds of efforts made through the National Endowment for the Arts,[58] or the National Endowment for the Humanities, or the Corporation for Public Broadcasting, to extend the possibilities for expression. Enabling more creative and independent work than at present in the broadcasting and print media would be entirely consistent with standard interpretations of the First Amendment.

A promising mechanism may be found in enlarged support for existing public access systems. Over 600 public access television systems now operate in the United States. Starting in 1972, cable systems have been required by the FCC to provide channels for public access, that is, cable companies should make airtime and equipment available to anyone who wishes to use them on a first-come, first-served basis. For the most part, disorganized and unprofessional expression fails to gain an audience and sours many potential viewers to public access channels. But the opportunities are considerably more interesting than has been recognized. In Austin, Texas, for instance, surveys indicate that from 10,000 to 30,000 Austin viewers watch at least one public access television program every night.[59] Philosophy professor Douglas Kellner is among those donating their time to produce "Alternative Views," which has produced several hundred hour-long programs shown in Austin and available for viewing on public access channels around the country. The programs include informal but intense conversations with various social critics and activists. Such developments illustrate the potential of public access,[60] but as long as there is no substantial public funding for the production and promotion of such programs, the disadvantages of public access television in competing with commercial television for viewers remain serious. The disparities between those with vast economic resources and those without them still distort one's ability to express oneself to an audience in the kind of culture that now prevails.[61]

Our society has permitted its airwaves to be used almost entirely for commercial development and gain. It could regain these airwaves or part of them for public benefit and enjoyment. As a Carnegie Commission has recommended, it could at least charge commercial broadcasters for the use of the airwaves and use the money for public broadcasting.[62] It could tax the profits of commercial broadcasters. And it could decrease the deductions now granted for advertising and for corporate cultural production and consumption.[63] At present, in the United States, more than $35 billion a year is spent on advertising.[64] In answering the question where the funds for expanded cultural subsidies can be found, it is important to keep in mind what the society is already spending on cultural production. Vast sums are now being spent on the production, promotion, and distribution of commercial entertainment and commercial advertising. What is required is a redirection of some of what is already being spent, not a shifting of expenditures from noncultural spending to cultural spending.

Many persons have been misled by the argument that the only alternative to commercial control of the media is governmental control. Between the two, they prefer commercial control. But public funding for universities and individual students is compatible with academic freedom. Public funding of cultural expression could also be compatible with a comparable freedom. Boards independent of governmental control could run noncommercial cultural institutions, including those directed at mass audiences, as such boards now run institutions of higher education that depend on governmental funding while respecting academic freedom.

EXPRESSION AND EDUCATION

Although thinking in terms of representation may be appropriate for political debate, it may not be suitable for much artistic and cultural expression. The very notion of creative expression may include being novel, unique—not, or at least, not yet representative.

My own interpretation of access to expression would suggest that we pursue an analogy between a right to expression and a right to education. This does not mean that cultural expression should be thought to be *like* education. Artistic expression may not be cumulative in the way that knowledge is, and the primary faculty for cultural expression may be imagination rather than the faculties needed for either political representation or the developing or imparting of knowledge. But like a right to education, a right to free expression should be an enabling right, a right to have access to the means to educate or express oneself, and it should ensure access to institutional structures free from the outside control of both political *and* commercial sources of power.

In a developed culture, persons need to be enabled to obtain education. A right to an education cannot be a mere liberty to try to pay for it in a "free market" in education. A right to education must enable one to acquire an education, and society must devise ways to provide public education open to all.

In the nineteenth century the United States developed a massive scheme of public education so that education was no longer as dependent as it had been on the possession of economic advantages. Gradually, access to even higher education has become less a privilege of the rich, and more a right that those who can meet the academic qualifications are enabled to exercise. We need a comparable development of large-scale possibilities for individual and group cultural expression.

Chances to express oneself to media audiences should depend on talent and imagination, not economic resources. Access to contemporary means of expression should include gaining the needed training to express oneself effectively, and it should include access to the materials with which to reach media audiences. Producing high-quality television documentaries, or performances with first-rate talent, or magazines and newspapers, is very expensive. U.S. society currently expends enormous sums on the images and programs and cultural productions favored by those whose primary goal is commercial gain. We could redirect some of these sums to allow for the development of substantive enabling rights to free expression.

In the case of education, we did not close down the great private universities or schools but we developed public alternatives and provided funding for individual students to enable them to attend either public or private educational institutions. Comparable developments for expression would be the public funding of adequate alternatives to the major networks and publications, and subsidies to individuals to enable them to engage in cultural activities for outlets appropriate to their work. Of course not everyone can go to either Harvard or the City University of New York. But admission should be based on talent and effort, not wealth. Similarly, not all who wished to would be able to express themselves on national television, but at least some decisions on access should be made on the basis of cultural merit, judged by independent review boards, not on the basis of how much a corporation will pay for an advertisement, or how much a performer will contribute to the commercial gain of a network.

At present we fall far short of actually ensuring adequate enabling rights to education. Even when two groups of children are of equal intelligence, the children of rich parents in the United States are twelve times as likely to complete college as the children of poor parents.[65] Professional education often serves to perpetuate class disparities and uphold traditional privilege rather than to promote the public interest, let alone the general good.[66] Rights to even elementary education have not yet been recognized as constitutional rights in the U.S. legal system;

enabling rights even to basic necessities sufficient to maintain life have, to our shame, continued to be unrecognized as fundamental legal rights.[67] In the absence of more satisfactory judicial interpretations of fundamental rights—interpretations that will begin to include the enablements and capacities essential to the assurance of various rights[68]—arguments must be made in terms of social policies and moral obligations. The discussion of rights in these terms is inadequate but apparently the most that can be expected in the near future. It is by no means unimportant.

We understand, conceptually, that a right to education must be an enabling right, that it must include a right of actual access to classrooms and libraries, not merely a right to buy an expensive education if one has the economic resources to do so. Education should be open to everyone on the basis of ability, not ability to pay. Policy decisions at many levels are made on the basis of such a shared standard. By and large, we understand what rights to education we *ought* to provide. We have *no* comparable notions of enabling rights to free expression. We *ought* to develop them.

NOTES

This essay was written while the author was a fellow at the Center for Advanced Study in the Behavioral Sciences in Stanford, California. I am grateful for financial support from the center, from the Andrew Mellon Foundation, and from Hunter College of the City University of New York. I am also grateful to the many persons who offered helpful comments when the paper was presented at philosophy department colloquia at the University of Pennsylvania, Tufts University, UCLA, UC San Diego, UC Davis, and the University of Massachusetts at Amherst, especially Rogers Albritton, Fred Berger, Norman Daniels, David Gauthier, Edward Lee, and Warren Quinn. I thank the members of the Law and Philosophy Colloquium at New York University, where the paper was discussed, especially Paul Chevigny, John Kleinig, Sylvia Law, Thomas Nagel, and Lawrence Sager. The comments of many AMINTAPHIL members who discussed and commented on the paper at the 1986 meeting and later were especially useful, and I thank, in particular, Randall Curren, Joseph Grcic, Martin Gunderson, Ken Kipnis, Bruce Landesman, Diana Meyers, and Carl Wellman. Finally, I thank Serafina Bathrick, Matt Fenner, Charles Firestone, Phil Jacklin, Douglas Kellner, Judith Lichtenberg, and Amelie Rorty for useful suggestions.

1. For discussion, see John Stuart Mill, *On Liberty*, edited by C. Shields (Indianapolis: Bobbs Merrill, 1956); Thomas M. Scanlon, "A Theory of Freedom of Expression," *Philosophy and Public Affairs* 1 (1972):204–226; Fred Berger, ed., *Freedom of Expression* (Belmont, Calif.: Wadsworth, 1980); Frederick Schauer, *Free Speech: A Philosophical Inquiry* (Cambridge: Cambridge Univ. Press, 1982); and Paul Chevigny, *Dialogue Rights and Modern Liberty* (Philadelphia: Temple Univ. Press, 1987).
2. Benno C. Schmidt, Jr., *Freedom of the Press vs. Public Access* (New York: Praeger, 1976), p. 3.
3. Archibald Cox, *Freedom of Expression* (Cambridge, Mass.: Harvard Univ. Press, 1981), p. 88.

4. *Ibid.*, p. 32.

5. There is by now a considerable literature on what is called "access," but it deals almost entirely with whether persons should or should not be thought to have a right to buy advertising time or space. The issue of access to the broadcasting or print media for those who lack the means to pay for such expression is almost never considered. For an extended bibliography up to 1973, see David L. Lange, "The Role of the Access Doctrine in the Regulation of the Mass Media: A Critical Review and Assessment," *North Carolina L. Rev.* 52 (1973–74):1–91, note 5. See also Nicholas Johnson and Tracy A. Westen, "A Twentieth-Century Soapbox: The Right to Purchase Radio and Television Time," *Virginia L. Rev.* 57 (1971):574–634; Kenneth L. Karst, "Equality as a Central Principle in the First Amendment," *Univ. of Chicago L. Rev.* 43, no. 1 (Fall 1975):1–68; Benno C. Schmidt, Jr., *op. cit.*; and Benno C. Schmidt, Jr., "The First Amendment and the Press," in Elie Abel, ed., *What's News: The Media in American Society* (San Francisco: Institute for Contemporary Studies, 1981). In a book entitled *Free Speech: A Philosophical Inquiry* (Cambridge: Cambridge Univ. Press, 1982), Frederick Schauer devotes only a few paragraphs to problems of access, seeing only the ways in which "the speculative benefits seem hardly worth the cost" (p. 128). He relies on the traditional distinction between "liberty and the conditions for its exercise," relegating problems of access to the latter, and thus considering them beyond the reach of a theory of free speech.

In his book, Schmidt does mention the question of access for those who lack the resources with which to buy advertisements, but he does so primarily to sketch out some "absurd" forms of such a possible right and to contrast it with the kinds of access to which he does devote serious attention: the possible right to buy advertising; whether a court can order a publication to publish the court's judgment that the publication has defamed someone; and the requirement that if a broadcaster gives time to one candidate for public office, it must give time to others.

Experience has shown how unsatisfactory it is to think of access only in such terms. Those offering more than superficial challenges to existing social structures and practices are much more likely to be impoverished than to be denied advertising space, and much more likely to be ignored than attacked. Their views are simply not on the agenda of discussion in the mass media.

6. For reasons that I hope may be suggested though not developed in this chapter, I disagree with Benno Schmidt's view that arguments for access are more questionable if the case for free expression is based on autonomy rather than on the Holmes and Brandeis position. This position, derived from Mill, holds that a multiplicity of views is instrumentally conducive to arriving at the truth. On the contrary, I shall try to show why access must be a part of an individual right to autonomous self-expression in the kind of society that now exists.

7. *Lehman v. City of Shaker Heights,* 418 U.S. 298 (1974).

8. See, for example, *Lloyd Corporation v. Tanner.* For discussion, see William Van Alstyne, "The Recrudescence of Property Rights as the Foremost Principle of Civil Liberties," *Law and Contemporary Problems* 43 (Summer, 1980):66–82.

9. Even Jerome Barron, the foremost advocate of "access," deals in his relatively innovative discussion with no more radical an issue than whether people have rights of access to advertising space or time for which they are willing and able to pay, or rights to have a letter on a controversial public topic published in the letters to the editor column of a newspaper. See Jerome A.

Barron, *Freedom of the Press for Whom? The Right of Access to Mass Media* (Bloomington: Indiana Univ. Press, 1973).

10. For further discussion, see "Recent Discussions" in this chapter.

11. The courts have generally treated print and electronic media differently, ruling against the regulation of print and continuing substantial Federal Communications Commission regulation of broadcasting. Originally, the justification given for the regulation of broadcasting was the scarcity of usable frequencies, an argument that did not apply to print media. With recent technological developments such as the growth of cable channels, this rationale is partially undercut, though it is useful to recognize that scarcity exists whenever demand is greater than supply, which is still the case for all broadcasting opportunities. An effort to provide an alternative rationale than the traditional one for the difference of treatment of print and electronic media is offered by Lee Bollinger in "Freedom of the Press and Public Access: Toward a Theory of Partial Regulation of the Mass Media," *Michigan L. Rev.* 75 (1976–77):1–42.

12. Robert P. Snow, *Creating Media Culture* (Beverly Hills, Calif.: Sage, 1983).

13. See especially Clifford Geertz, *The Interpretation of Cultures* (New York: Basic Books, 1973). Geertz writes that "a great deal of recent social scientific theorizing has turned upon an attempt to distinguish and specify two major analytic concepts: culture and social structure," and he provides extended references (p. 361). "Within this two-sided development," he writes, "it has been the cultural side which has proved the more refractory and remains the more retarded. In the very nature of the case, ideas are more difficult to handle scientifically than the economic, political, and social relations among individuals and groups which those ideas inform" (p. 362).

14. *Ibid.*, p. 361.

15. Andrew Hacker, review of *The Mirror Makers*, by Stephen Fox, *New York Times Book Review*, June 24, 1984, p. 1.

16. Raymond Williams, *Problems of Materialism and Culture* (London: Verso, 1980), p. 184.

17. For a discussion of some implications of this, see Virginia Held, "Advertising and Program Content," *Business and Professional Ethics Journal* 3, nos. 3 and 4 (Spring/Summer 1984).

18. Robert P. Snow, *op. cit.*, pp. 127 and 147. See also Les Brown, *Television. The Business Behind the Box* (New York: Harcourt, 1971), especially pp. 15–16.

19. *A Public Trust. The Report of the Carnegie Commission on the Future of Public Broadcasting* (New York: Bantam, 1979), p. 10.

20. See William A. Henry III, "News as Entertainment: The Search for Dramatic Unity," and Edward Jay Epstein, "The Selection of Reality," in *What's News: The Media in American Society.*

21. J. Edward Murray, "Quality News Versus Junk News," *Nieman Reports* 38, no. 2 (Summer 1984):14–19.

22. Ben Bagdikian, *The Media Monopoly* (Boston: Beacon Press, 1983), p. 113. See also Donald McDonald, "The Media's Conflict of Interest," *The Center Magazine* 9, no. 6 (November/December 1976):15–35; and Donald McDonald, "Coverage and Candor: An Editor's Testament," *The Center Magazine* 17 (November/December):43–46.

23. On these issues, I would especially like to recommend the journal *Media, Culture, and Society;* a text by Denis McQuail called *Mass Communication Theory: An Introduction* (Beverly Hills, Calif.: Sage, 1983); James Curran, Michael Gurevitch, and Janet Wollacott, eds., *Mass Communication and Society* (London:

Arnold, 1977); and Michael Gurevitch, Tony Bennett, James Curran, and Janet Wollacott, eds., *Culture, Society, and the Media* (New York: Methuen, 1982).

24. For further discussion, see Virginia Held, "The Independence of Intellectuals," *The Journal of Philosophy* 80, no. 10 (October 1983):572–582; and Virginia Held, *Rights and Goods. Justifying Social Action* (New York: Free Press/ Macmillan, 1984), especially ch. 12.

25. See, for example, Claudia Mills, "Children's Television," in *QQ. Report from the Center for Philosophy and Public Policy,* Univ. of Maryland (Summer 1986):11–14.

26. See, for example, Thomas Streeter, "Policy Discourse and Broadcast Practice: The FCC, the U.S. Broadcast Networks and the Discourse of the Marketplace," *Media, Culture, and Society* 5 (1983):255.

27. Even as astute a critic of the media as Ben Bagdikian focuses primarily on the problem of concentration and lack of competition between commercial conglomerates. See Ben Bagdikian, *The Media Monopoly.*

28. See *Abrams v. United States,* 250 U.S. 616, 630 (1919).

29. Thomas Streeter, *op. cit.,* p. 259.

30. On these issues, see *A Public Trust,* p. 10.

31. T. M. Scanlon, Jr. "Freedom of Expression and Categories of Expression," *Univ. of Pittsburgh L. Rev.* 40 (1979):519–550; this at 520.

32. *Ibid.,* p. 536.

33. *Ibid.,* pp. 536 and 545.

34. Allen Buchanan, "Autonomy and Categories of Expression: A Reply to Professor Scanlon," *Univ. of Pittsburgh L. Rev.* 50 (1979):556.

35. *Ibid.,* p. 557.

36. John Rawls, *A Theory of Justice* (Cambridge, Mass.: Harvard Univ. Press, 1971).

37. One might have expected that an article with the title "Equality as a Central Principle in the First Amendment" might address this issue, but the article is, instead, a defense of the view that all *views* must be treated equally. The implication of the "equality principle" according to the author is that government must not become involved in choosing between views being expressed: "The core of the principle of equal liberty of expression is that government action may not favor or disfavor expression because of its content" (Kenneth L. Karst, *op. cit.,* p. 53). There is no discussion in the article of the inequalities inherent in arrangements that make it possible for those with vast economic power to express themselves to millions, while those without such economic power are unable to reach more than a handful of listeners. Although the author does consider the requirements of one person/one vote, he fails to see the implications of such a notion of equality for expression. Arguing in the other direction we could ask: If current arrangements for expression are not violations of principles of equality or liberty, why shouldn't those with great wealth have many more votes than those with little wealth? The reason one person should have one vote is that political power should not be a function of economic power, that rights to vote should be outside rather than inside the market. Similar arguments can be made for rights to free expression and the means to exercise those rights.

38. Archibald Cox, *Freedom of Expression.*

39. *Richmond Newspapers, Inc. v. Virginia,* 200 S. Ct. 2814 (1980).

40. Cox, *op. cit.,* pp. 25–28.

41. *Richmond Newspapers* at 2828.

42. Cox, *op. cit.*, p. 28.
43. Laurence H. Tribe, *American Constitutional Law* (Mineola, N.Y.: The Foundation Press, 1978), §§12–21.
44. Cox, *op. cit.*, p. 56.
45. Tribe, *op. cit.*, p. 691.
46. Cox, *op. cit.*, p. 49.
47. *Ibid.*, p. 87. In fact, shopping malls have often been closed to demonstrators. Although it would seem especially appropriate to see shopping malls as contemporary analogues of the traditional public square, the owners of malls have claimed rights to restrict expression on their property. See Van Alstyne, *op. cit.*
48. See, for example, Kenneth L. Karst, *op. cit.*
49. *Red Lion Broadcasting v. Federal Communications Commission*, 395 U.S. 367 (1969).
50. Charles Firestone and Phil Jacklin, "Deregulation and the Pursuit of Fairness," *Telecommunications Policy and the Citizen*, Timothy Haight, ed. (New York: Praeger, 1979), p. 125.
51. *Ibid.*, p. 131.
52. *Ibid.*, p. 132.
53. *Miami Herald Publishing Co. v. Tornillo*, 418 U.S. 241 (1974).
54. Thomas I. Emerson, *The System of Freedom of Expression* (New York: Vintage, 1970), p. 629.
55. *Ibid.*, pp. 650 and 652.
56. See, for example, Lange, *op. cit.*
57. For further discussion, see Virginia Held, *Rights and Goods*, ch. 8.
58. For discussion, see, for example, W. McNeil Lowry, ed., *The Arts and Public Policy in the United States* (Englewood Cliffs, N.J.: Prentice-Hall, 1984).
59. Douglas Kellner, "Public Access Television: Alternative Views," in *Making Waves. The Politics of Communications*, Radical Science Collective, ed. (London: Free Association Books, 1985), p. 83.
60. See especially Douglas Kellner, "Network Television and American Society," *Theory and Society* 10 (1981):31–62.
61. The idea that public access cable television "demonstrates" the unworkability of serious access rights is another faulty argument that serves commercial interests. (For this kind of dismissal, see Martin Mayer, *About Television* [New York: Harper & Row, 1972], p. 388). For a short time after 1972, cable systems were required to have a minimum capacity of twenty channels and to reserve one for public access. Unions, religious groups, and organizations of various kinds could use, without cost, public access time to communicate with their members or the public. Funding for the production of programs came largely from foundations, but was often not continued. (See Benno Schmidt, *Freedom of the Press vs. Public Access*, ch. 13.) A significant problem, of course, was attracting audiences, and much available access time remained unused. This hardly means that with better funding and more experience, open access could never produce interesting and professional programs or sustained audiences. See "Access to the Media."

Cable channels themselves can, of course, and usually have, become as dominated by commercial interests and as inhospitable to genuine cultural and political diversity as noncable broadcasting.

62. *A Public Trust*, pp. 16 and 139.
63. See Ben Bagdikian, *The Media Monopoly*, ch. 8.

64. Stanley J. Baran, Jerilyn S. McIntyre, and Timothy P. Mayer, *An Introduction to Mass Communication* (Reading, Mass.: Addison-Wesley, 1984), p. 199.

65. Richard DeLone, *Small Futures. Children, Inequality, and the Limits of Liberal Reform* (New York: Harcourt, 1979).

66. See Virginia Held, *The Public Interest and Individual Interests* (New York: Basic Books, 1970).

67. See, for example, Louis Henkin, "Rights, American and Human," *Columbia L. Rev.* 79 (April 1979):405–425; Virginia Held, *Rights and Goods*, especially chs. 8 and 10; Henry Shue, *Basic Rights: Subsistence, Affluence, and U.S. Foreign Policy* (Princeton, N.J.: Princeton Univ. Press, 1980); James Sterba, *The Demands of Justice* (Notre Dame, Ind.: Univ. of Notre Dame Press, 1980); and James W. Nickel, *Making Sense of Human Rights* (Berkeley: Univ. of California Press, 1987).

68. Much of the world recognizes the necessity of this inclusion, as reflected in the *International Covenant on Economic, Social, and Cultural Rights* (see Nickel, *ibid.*) and the *European Social Charter* (Strasbourg, France: Council of Europe, Directorate of Press and Information, 1981).

SELECTED BIBLIOGRAPHY

Carnegie Corporation. 1979. *A Public Trust. Report of the Carnegie Commission on the Future of Public Broadcasting.* New York: Bantam.

Emerson, Thomas I. 1970. *The System of Freedom of Expression.* New York: Vintage.

Gurevitch, Michael, Tony Bennett, James Curran, and Janet Wollacott, eds. 1982. *Culture, Society, and the Media.* New York: Methuen.

Held, Virginia. 1984. *Rights and Goods. Justifying Social Action.* New York: Free Press/Macmillan.

Media, Culture, and Society. Journal available through Sage Publications, London.

NINE

Respect for Individuals Versus Respect for Groups: Public Aid for Confessional Schools in the United States and Canada

MICHAEL MC DONALD

This chapter might well be entitled, "A Tale of Two Judges," for it had its original impetus in a classroom discussion of Ronald Dworkin's mythical judge Hercules and my invention of his Canadian counterpart Hercule. In "Hard Cases," Dworkin has Hercules consider the following:

> Suppose there is a written constitution in Hercules' jurisdiction which provides that no law shall be valid if it establishes a religion. The legislature passes a law purporting to grant free busing to children in parochial schools. Does the grant establish a religion? The words of the constitutional provision might support either view. Hercules must nevertheless decide whether the child who appears before him has a right to her bus ride.[1]

For Dworkin this requires Hercules's construction of "a full political theory that justifies the constitution as a whole" and "fits the particular rules of this constitution," namely, one that does not "include a powerful background right to an established church." But Dworkin says that such a constitution might be grounded either on avoiding social tensions or on "the background right to religious liberty." To resolve the hard case before him, Hercules will have to decide between these two possible justifications of the constitution. Dworkin believes that political arrangements can only be just if they show "equal concern and respect" for the individuals governed by them. Following recent decisions in U.S. law (as discussed below), Hercules would rule that using tax revenues to provide bus service for parochial school students shows a lack of respect for the fundamental convictions of nonbelievers.

What would his Canadian counterpart Hercule decide? After all, Canadians do not have an "antiestablishment" clause; quite the contrary, we have a number of explicit guarantees of the right to denominational education. Yet if Dworkin is correct in contending that equal concern and respect for individuals is a fundamental juridical value, then our judge Hercule may well feel compelled to rule as his U.S. counterpart Hercules would.

Even if we reject Dworkin's natural law view that all constitutional adjudicators must reason from the same value of equal concern and respect for each individual and adopt a more positivistic position, it still remains that written or unwritten constitutions often do and ordinarily should reflect fundamental social values. And it is highly plausible to claim that the assigned protector of that constitution—be it the judiciary or Parliament itself—has a legal and moral obligation to revert to these fundamental values in extending the constitution to hard cases.[2] The question that prompts this chapter, then, is what are the fundamental values that differentiate Canadians from U.S. citizens?

FUNDAMENTAL VALUES

In five Canadian provinces, confessional schools receive public funds. In the main, this funding is *constitutionally guaranteed.* Here, Canadian constitutional principles differ sharply from U.S. ones, in particular the First Amendment of the U.S. Bill of Rights that states "Congress shall make no law respecting an establishment of religion." The First Amendment effectively blocks the use of tax money to support confessional (religious) schools. In the recent case of *Grand Rapids v. Ball,* Justice Brennan said, "Although Establishment Clause jurisprudence is characterized by few absolutes, the Clause does absolutely prohibit government-financed or government sponsored indoctrination into the beliefs of a particular religious faith."[3]

The issue in *Grand Rapids* was whether the First Amendment was violated by the public provision of a secular core curriculum (reading, mathematics, art, music, and physical education) to denominational school students. The classes were given by public school teachers in classrooms leased from the denominational schools. Brennan argued that such arrangements failed to pass the three-part test devised in *Lemon,* namely, "purpose, effect, and entanglement": "First, the statute must have a secular legislative purpose; second, its principal or primary effect must be one that neither advances nor inhibits religion . . . ; finally, the statute must not foster 'an excessive government entanglement with religion.'"[4] Regardless of whether one thinks this case was rightly decided,[5] it still would be true that under the First Amendment it would not be possible in the United States to have the full-fledged support for confessional schools that exists in Canada.

This difference between Canadian and U.S. constitutional provisions could be investigated in a number of ways—historical, sociological, jurisprudential, and so on. I propose to look at the difference from a normative perspective. My aim is to identify the fundamental norm or norms that underlie Canadian constitutional guarantees for confessional schools. My main claim is that the rights in question are collective rather than individual; hence, the underlying principle is that of showing respect for groups. This is in sharp contrast to the principle that seems to underlie U.S. law, that is, as Rawls and Dworkin proclaim, a Kantian principle of respect for individual autonomy.[6] In his concern with the "symbolic union of church and state," Brennan's opinion in *Grand Rapids* emphasized respect for individual persons. Brennan argued that such a union is "likely to be perceived by adherents as an endorsement, and by nonadherents as a disapproval of their individual choices."[7] He worried, too, that the disputed classes were offered in a setting (for example, Roman Catholic schools with crucifixes on the walls) that "convey[ed] a measure of state support for religion to students and the general public."[8]

My contention is that the Canadian conception of pluralism offers what the U.S. conception does not, namely, pluralism for groups and not just for individuals. That is, we Canadians are willing to give legal and moral standing to collectivities to an extent that U.S. citizens are not. The U.S. system is primarily aimed at individuals; whereas, Canada also recognizes collectivities. While I do think our arrangements are preferable (I am a Canadian by choice and not by birth), I am doubtful that they are transplantable. Our slow and at times painful *evolution* as a Confederation of provinces is vastly different than the U.S. *revolutionary* past. Where U.S. constitutional history begins with a declaration of inalienable rights, Canadian history commences with a desire for much more limited goals of "peace, order, and good government." Where the U.S. one dollar bill proclaims a "new order of time," the Canadian dollar has a portrait of the Queen.

The central and distinguishing feature of Canadian history has been the relationship between our two founding "races"—the French and the English. No wonder then that collective rights are not alien to our constitutional history. Even though U.S. legal history begins in the Declaration of Independence with an assertion of a collective right of self-determination,[9] the end of that self-determination has been the protection of individual rights. Indeed, it has been argued that the U.S. Constitution is based on a Jeffersonian and Madisonian idea of the republic—an idea that it is claimed

> did not adequately take into account the identity of groups, communities, and institutions (families, churches, schools, businesses). . . . No effort was made to give constitutional recognition of any "subjects" other than "individuals" and the "political entities" through which they were publicly organized. Thus when, under the influence of Jefferson and others, the republican idea of public education began to grow, it only took into account the needs of "individuals" in the context of a "universal republic," not the responsibilities of families, churches, and schools as nonpolitical entities in which individuals also find themselves involved as social creatures.[10]

I will now proceed in three steps. First, I will discuss the concept of a collective right. Second, I will advance a collective rights interpretation of Canadian constitutional guarantees of tax support for religious schools. Third, I will address a number of philosophical and political objections.

COLLECTIVE RIGHTS

By a "collective right," I mean (1) a right that is held and/or exercised by a group per se, that is, the group acts as a claimant of the right (with the option of exercising it), and (2) a right that is held and/or exercised for the intended benefit of the group itself, that is, the group is the beneficiary of the right. Derivatively, I include as collective rights those rights in which individuals are claimants or beneficiaries simply by virtue of their membership in the given collectivity.[11] In describing the right to confessional education as a "collective right," I mean to distinguish the right from any rights members of the collectivities exercise or enjoy simply as individuals, for example, the right to equal treatment under the law (the so-called rule of law). Thus, in describing this right as collective, I do not mean the sum of rights possessed by individual members of a particular religion, in particular their rights as parents to have their children educated in state-supported schools. Instead, this right is one they possess as a group per se or as members of a group.[12]

While I would insist that collective rights are not reducible to individual rights, I would emphasize that the logic of collective and individual rights is the same; they are but two species of the genus. This aspect is especially important in order to identify who can be (1) a claimant and (2) a beneficiary of a right. Claimants, whether individual or collective, must have the capacity for exercising the rights in question. Following Feinberg, this means being able to do what counts as "exercising the right" under the rules in question (namely, moral or legal rules).[13] To take a simple example of a positive *in personam* right: If Jones has a right to $10,000 from Smith, then we understand that Jones is or could become aware of Smith's indebtedness to him, Jones is able to oblige Smith to repay, and if Smith does not, then Jones can engage in those procedures requiring payment (he can sue Smith). And if Jones lacks these capacities himself, someone can be found who has these capacities and who can act in his stead—a trustee or guardian. That is, we attribute to Jones a capacity for intelligent activity under the rules in question. Now for all I have said, Jones could be a collective rather than an individual claimant, that is, a corporation, clan, or community.

To be the beneficiary of a right, one must be taken to be able to benefit in some (standard) way from that right; the aim of the right's fulfillment is then the provision of that benefit. In the case above, Jones the natural person, Jones, Ltd., or the Jones family is the beneficiary of the right in question; to count as such we have to agree that repayment of the money is at least *ceteris paribus* of benefit to Jones. Thus, Jones, the individual or the collectivity, will be better off with the loan's repayment than without it.

Thus, the interpretation of the right to confessional education in Canadian law as a collective right involves a twofold implication that religious groups can act as claimants and beneficiaries. How? In the ordinary case, their situation as claimants is recognized by giving members of the group resident in a given school district the right to jointly require the election of a school board for that area with a right to directly (through school taxes) or indirectly (through provincial subsidies) raise money for schools.[14] The intended beneficiaries of these constitutional provisions are both individual students and religious groups. The religious group gains because an important means of recruitment (acculturation) is placed at its disposal; thus, there clearly is a collective beneficiary.[15]

CANADIAN CONSTITUTIONAL ARRANGEMENTS

In a recent case, *Reference re an Act to Amend the Education Act,*[16] the majority in the Ontario Court of Appeal said

> The Constitution of Canada, of which the Charter is now a part, has from the beginning provided for group collective rights in §§ 93 and 133 of the *Constitution Act, 1867.* As Professor Hogg . . . has expressed it: these provisions amount to "a small bill of rights." The provisions of this "small bill of rights," now expanded as to the language rights of § 133 by §§ 16 to 23 of the Charter, constitute a major difference from a bill of rights such as that of the United States, which is based on individual rights. Collective or group rights, such as those concerning language and those concerning certain denominations to separate schools, are asserted by individuals or groups of individuals *because of* their membership in the protected group. Individual rights are asserted equally by everyone *despite* membership in certain ascertainable groups. Collective rights protect certain groups and not others. To that extent, they are an exception from the equality rights provided equally to everyone.[17]

As this passage makes clear, we must address Canada's constitutional situation both before and after the adoption of the new constitution, the Canada Act 1982.[18] Before the Canada Act, the main constitutional document in Canada was the British North America Act (BNA Act) of 1867.[19] The BNA Act stated that education is a provincial and not a federal responsibility (a. 93) so that federal action in the area of education would be *ultra vires.* However, this provision was subject to the important qualification that the provinces were not permitted to make any law that "shall prejudicially affect any Right or Privilege with respect to Denominational Schools which any Class of Persons have by Law in the Province at Union" (a. 93.1). Thus, Québec and Ontario, which had tax-supported denominational schools (Protestant and Roman Catholic) at the time of Confederation (1867), had to maintain those schools under provisions no less favorable than at Confederation.[20] In Ontario, this meant that public support of Roman Catholic schools to grade 8 was constitutionally required. This requirement was extended to grades 9 and 10 in later years.[21] Most recently, in a very controversial move, it is being extended to grades 11 and 12.[22] New Brunswick, Nova Scotia, Prince Edward Island, and British Columbia did not have publicly supported religious schools when they entered Confederation in 1867 and so were exempt from funding them.[23] In Manitoba a Privy Council ruling exempted the province from its obligation to support Roman Catholic schools.[24] Alberta and Saskatchewan were similar to Québec and Ontario; Alberta and Saskatchewan also had such schools and so were brought into Confederation in 1905 under the same type of arrangement. When Newfoundland joined Canada in 1949, the Terms of Union guaranteed protection of no less than five denominational school systems: Anglican, Roman Catholic, United Church, Pentecostal, and Salvation Army! (Newfoundland has no nondenominational school system.)[25] In the 1982 Canada Act, Canada constitutionally entrenched a bill of rights entitled the Canadian Charter of Rights and Freedoms. Section 29 of the Charter specifically embeds the protections of the BNA Act: "Nothing in this Charter abrogates or derogates from any rights or privileges guaranteed by or under the Constitution of Canada in respect of denominational, separate or dissentient schools."

Let us now imagine that Hercule, the ideal Canadian judge, is faced with a hard case involving the constitutional right to confessional schools. According to Dworkin, he will have to construct a political theory that best fits Canadian constitutional history. Like his U.S. counterpart, Hercules, he will rest this construction on a right rather than a goal.[26] However, Hercule will differ from Hercules in asserting that this fundamental right is collective rather than individual. Hercule will not be perturbed by the fact that in many cases it is individual parents who claim this right for their children; for he will understand that a fundamentally collective right can in some cases be claimed by individual members of the collectivity in question. Hercule realizes that the right to a confessional education is historically, practically, and intentionally a collective right. It arose out of a historic compromise between two religious majorities—the Catholics in Québec and Protestants in Ontario, each of which was trying to protect their coreligionists in the other province. Outside the context of private tutorials, Hercule sees that the practice of education requires a collective context—a classroom and school. Finally, the intent of the historic guarantee was to allow the minority religious group to preserve its character over time without assimilation. In brief, Hercule will realize that the primary intended beneficiaries and claimants of these rights are groups and that individuals are considered only in virtue of their group membership.

Up to now, the contrast between Hercule's and Hercules's rulings is unsurprising; for in one jurisdiction the legal materials lend themselves to a collectivist reading while in the other they prompt an individualistic interpretation. But, it might be argued, there is one crucial feature of the Canadian guarantee of confessional educational rights that should greatly disturb Hercule. This feature is that historically rights have been limited to only a few determinate groups, mainly Roman Catholics and mainline Protestants. Jews, Anabaptists, Jehovah's Witnesses, Moslems, Fundamentalists, and so on may not claim this right. Hercule may ask if like cases are being treated alike here, especially in the light of § 15.1, which rules out governmental discrimination on religious grounds.[27] To answer, Hercule will have to decide whether the historic difference between those groups guaranteed these rights and those denied them is a difference that his political theory can countenance.[28] Hercule would *not*, I think, have a hard time convincing himself that at least some rights depend on historic features; that is, he would not be an ideal judge if he thought that all fundamental legal rights are necessarily ahistorical human rights, that is, rights pertaining to persons individually or collectively on the basis of purely ahistorical (or "patterned") characteristics.[29] Still, we would hope that Hercule's ideal construction would treat people with respect—in this case it would respect the need of groups linked by fundamental convictions to acculturate their young. Because my focus is on the contrast between individual and collective rights, I will not offer any predictions of Hercule's ultimate disposition of this equal rights' challenge to religious educational rights.

Thus far, I have pointed out that the Canadian Constitution unlike the U.S. Constitution requires the public provision of confessional schools for some religious groups. This provision rests on the historic recognition of certain religious groups as themselves bearers of rights. If Dworkin's analysis of the U.S. Constitution is correct in showing that it rests on a principle of respect for persons, I would argue that the Canadian Constitution rests on a principle of respect for religious groups.[30] In other parts of the Canadian Constitution, other groups are similarly protected: aboriginal peoples (§§ 25, 35) and linguistic groups (§§ 16–23). If I am correct, then there both is and ought to be a very different approach to religion, politics, and pluralism in Canada than in the United States.

PHILOSOPHICAL OBJECTIONS

A number of major questions might well be raised about the thesis advanced in this chapter.[31] Some of these questions will be addressed below.

Negative Rights. It might be objected that the real difference between U.S. and Canadian positions on public aid to denominational schools lies in the distinction between negative and positive rights, rather than in the distinction between individual and collective rights.

This distinction belies the general provision of public education from the primary to the postsecondary level throughout the United States.

And, unless I misunderstand U.S. constitutional history, it would also have to ignore a long series of decisions by the Supreme Court regarding the provision of public education to minorities—in particular, *Brown v. Board of Education.*[32]

Parental Rights. A second objection is that the real right at issue in Canadian constitutional practice is a right of parents rather than a right of religious groups.[33] One might argue then in favor of a voucher system in education.[34]

Now I would not deny that the decision to send their children to a denominational or a nondenominational school rests with the parents. By law, however, the child has a right to attend the denominational school in question only if the child is a member of that denomination; in Ontario, the parents have had to be registered as Separate (Catholic) School supporters.[35] But whether the denominational school in question is publicly supported rests, I have shown, on a constitutional guarantee of a collective right.

Secular Versus Confessional. It might also be argued that in my brief portrayal of the U.S. position on public aid for religious schools I haven't really captured the spirit of the U.S. debate about the separation of church and state. State governments in the United States have tried to extend public aid to those attending confessional schools. But the rationale for doing so has been on grounds of individual, rather than collective, rights. In *Grand Rapids,* Justice Brennan ruled that the Community Education Program violated the First Amendment provision for neutrality between church and state. The proponents of such programs argue that they in fact preserve this neutrality. Thus, one might plausibly claim that invalidating such programs evidences hostility rather than neutrality on the part of the state.[36]

This defence is predicated on the idea that one can, as it were, separate religious from nonreligious components of confessional education and avoid violating the First Amendment by subsidizing only the latter. A collective rights approach does not pretend to make such an artificial division—a division that I think proponents of religious education would candidly want to reject. A collective rights approach does not then divide the child into religious and nonreligious components; instead, it treats the child as a whole. And yet at the same time, this collective rights approach does not establish any religion as a state religion; therefore, it is pluralistic.

Respect for Individuals. One important concern about the collective rights thesis is that in respecting the autonomy of various collectivities we might fail to respect the autonomy of individuals per se. This is the most difficult objection to answer both in terms of theory and practice.[37] Nevertheless, I would offer this suggestion—again a provocative one—that it is a mistake to adopt a normative view that treats individuals apart from their groups, in particular those groups that provide for the individuals in question a horizon of meaning and a focus of identity.[38]

For many people, this meaning and identity are provided by religious groups; others find roots in nonreligious communities—for example, occupational, familial, national, or linguistic groups.

This suggests one important complication in both theory and practice, namely, that it is not always easy to know which collectivities are the most significant for a people.[39] For example, Québec has tried to reorganize education along linguistic rather than religious lines. This attempt has been struck down by the Québec Superior Court.[40] Yet, this ruling may well fail to respect the most significant collectivities in question—which in Québec are linguistic rather than religious. The same problem of identifying the ultimate claimants and beneficiaries of a right can arise with regard to individual rights as well. Even though the rights may be controversial, the important thing is to have rights that show respect for people, taken both individually and, I have argued, collectively.

Reductionism. At this stage, philosophers will want to raise "the big objection," namely, that the rights of a group can be "reduced to" the rights of the individual members of that group.[41] Thus, the right of Ontario Roman Catholics to their own school system would be nothing but the several rights of individual Roman Catholics to such a school system. If this is correct, it would seem to undermine my main thesis concerning group rights. Such an objection is hard to answer without a fairly precise statement of the kind of individualistic reductionism being advanced. In my brief response, I survey three kinds of reductionism: analytical, descriptive or explanatory, and normative.

An analytical reductionist would claim that statements about group rights are equivalent to some combination (a product or sum) of the members' rights. Sometimes we do think this way; for example, the constitutional right of citizens to vote in a democracy is simply the right of each citizen to vote. But sometimes the reduction fails; thus, the right of a jury to convict or acquit is not analyzable into the rights of individual jury members to convict or acquit. In the section on collective rights, I argued that in Canadian constituional law certain religious groups were collective right-holders in two respects: (1) as claimants and (2) as beneficiaries. As claimants, these religious groups act collectively through various decision procedures, for example, electing a confessional school board. Here, just as in the jury example, we can't reduce the collective right of the voters to elect representatives to the several individual members' rights to vote; for the individual's right to vote is only a right to take part in a collective decision and not a right to make the decision on his or her own. A parallel argument can be made regarding collective benefits. Thus, for example, a company like General Motors may grow richer even though its employees, managers, and shareholders do not.

Even if analytical reductionism fails, one might still claim that descriptively or explanatorily it succeeds. That is, the objection would be that I am simply misdescribing the differences between the Canadian and U.S. legal systems when I differentiate them in terms of respect for groups as opposed to respect for individuals. Ultimately, the issue can only be decided by comparing alternative ways of reading Canadian and U.S. law and jurisprudence.[42] Suffice it to say that I think I have a fairly strong case here.

Finally, and perhaps most interestingly, a normative reductionist might insist that group rights are only justifiable in terms of individual rights. In some cases, such normative reductionism is both natural and compelling. For example, one primary justification of the common law right to a jury trial in criminal cases is the individual right of each accused person to a fair trial; given this rationale, the collective right of juries to decide such cases appears as a means and not an end. If rights are justified in terms of the interests they serve, then the normative reductionist would probably argue that collective rights are only ultimately justifiable in terms of individual, but not collective, interests. Insofar as this is taken as a truism (that is, as resting on the claim that only individuals but not groups can feel and think), then it may not cut any ice; for attachments to groups are in fact crucial to almost all human beings. If on the contrary the claim is taken as stating a profound "truth" (as opposed to a truism) that such attachments are always mistaken and should be subordinated to purely selfish interests, then that "truth" is clearly false.[43]

To begin to adequately address the issues raised by normative reductionism, I would have to consider the nature of practical justifications. For example, it will matter greatly whether we think there are first principles of practical or moral reason to be found (or invented?). A more plausible view is that practical justification is context- and audience-relative. If so, then justifying rights is likely to be a two-way street: Sometimes the justificatory appeal is best made to individual rights and the interests they protect, and at other times it is best made to collective rights and interests. In similar ways, analytical and descriptive reductionism raise parallel concerns about the nature of analysis and explanation.

Education for Citizenship. Walzer has argued that schools, like neighborhoods, should ideally contain a representative selection of the total population. He sees schools preparing children for their future roles as citizens, which in a pluralistic society involves interaction with members of diverse groups. For this reason, he condemns ethnic and racial—specifically black—schools as exemplifying "separatism."[44]

Let me respond briefly. First, Walzer's ideals of citizenship and public schools are self-consciously American.[45] The Canadian experience has been different. For example, it might be argued that Canadian history manifests a degree of regionalism that was effectively eradicated in the United States by the Civil War; thus, for many Canadians, allegiance may be as much or more provincial than national. Second, education is not just for citizenship, it is also for group membership. That is, groups more homogeneous than the national community and local groups less heterogeneous than the neighborhood also have a social stake in basic education. Although Walzer admits this, he seems to imply that in the event of conflict the "national" and "neighborhood" suits always trump the minority suit. Finally, one may ask who is ultimately to come to the adult political arena: Only individuals, or are groups to be admitted as well?

National Unity. Finally, it might be argued that in protecting the rights of groups we lose a significant means of holding together a pluralistic society.[46] Will there be one society and one polity if there are no common loyalties? And how can we reasonably expect common loyalties if we not only permit but also encourage divisions in such a vital area as education through the provision of collective rights? Preexisting religious divisions will be reinforced and new divisions will be created by perpetuating and extending collective rights in education.[47]

These are, I admit, important questions that must be addressed. Canada is a large country with deep internal divisions posed by geography, language, and history. Matters are not made easier by the proximity of the most powerful nation on earth—a proximity that is in no way balanced by our traditional European ties and our growing Asian connections. Yet it seems to me these questions may overstate the actual and potential divisiveness of public support for confessional education. Beyond that they may also underrate seriously the advantages of a multicultural society—a Canadian mosaic rather than a U.S. melting pot, that is, greater adaptability.[48] In any case, the hard reality for us is that we are not one people but many. Given the regional character of these differences, it is unlikely that an assimilationist program would work.

CONCLUSION

The range of objections to this collective rights thesis have not been exhausted. My aim here is the more modest one of offering a philosophical account of an important difference between U.S. and Canadian constitutional arrangements. To close, I offer a suggestion about the larger philosophical and political agenda. My collective rights thesis presents an alternative to prevailing individualistic models of rights. For it challenges the individual rights model on two fronts: first, in terms of descriptive adequacy; and second, in terms of its ability to give expression to the deep human need for community.[49] Politically, this need for community provides a rationale, perhaps the best one for Canada's continued existence as a nation: not as a community itself, but as a "community of communities."[50]

NOTES

This work has been generously supported by Research and Leave Grants from the Social Sciences and Research Council of Canada. I am also deeply indebted to Professor Carignan (Faculty of Law, University of Montreal) for his work on the topic of collective rights and for the time he has taken in discussing his research with me. See Pierre Carignan, "De la notion de droit collectif et de son application en matière scolaire au Québec," *Thémis* 18 (1984):3–103, Faculty of Law, University of Montreal. This paper was first presented at the University of Dayton's 1985 colloquium, "Religion and Politics in a Pluralistic Society." I am also indebted to Robert Van Wyk (University of Pittsburgh, Johnstown) for his comments at that colloquium. The paper was also presented to the 1986 meeting of the Canadian Society for Political Philosophy and Philosophy of Law in Winnipeg.

1. Ronald Dworkin, "Hard Cases," in *Taking Rights Seriously* (London: Duckworth, 1977), p. 106.

2. This reading of Dworkin is supported by his latest and, in my opinion, best book *Law's Empire* (Cambridge, Mass.: Harvard Univ. Press, 1986). In the discussion of courtesy (ch. 2), Dworkin much more clearly emphasizes the extent to which the interpreter of a legal system is bound to the shared practices that constitute that system and also bound to try to make of them a unified whole (ch. 6).

3. *Grand Rapids School District of the City of Grand Rapids et al. v. Phyllis Ball et al.*, 53 LW 5006 (June 25, 1985), at 5009.

4. *Ibid.*, at 5008.

5. It can be argued that First Amendment jurisprudence combines two incompatible views of the separation of church and state: On the one hand, there is the secularist view that "government may not aid the religious enterprise and must leave that area for private sponsorship," and on the other hand, the protectionist view, that the First Amendment does "not demand neutrality as between religion and non-religion, but set[s] aside a protected sphere in which religion might flourish untainted by the defilement of state meddling." Lorraine E. Weinrib, "The Religion Clauses: Reading the Lesson," 8 *Supreme Court L. Rev.* 507, at 510 (1986).

6. I am aware that both Rawls and Dworkin might be read as claiming that the Kantian principle is a universal and not just a U.S. principle. I see three problems with such a reading. First, if I am right in what follows, one could not use this principle to reach a reflective equilibrium (Rawls) or "concept of the principles that 'underlie' or are 'embedded in' the positive rules of law" (Dworkin, p. 105), in at least this case. Second, for reasons that Van Dyke has given, I am not satisfied with the individualism that the Kantian principle manifests. Here, see Vernon Van Dyke, "Justice as Fairness for Groups," *American Political Science Review* 69 (1975), p. 607. Finally, the texts may not support such a universalistic reading. See Wesley Cragg, "Two Concepts of Community or Moral Theory and Canadian Culture," *Dialogue* 25, no. 1 (Spring 1986):31–52. See also John Rawls, "Justice as Fairness: Political not Metaphysical," *Philosophy and Public Affairs* 14 (1985):223–251.

7. *Grand Rapids*, at 5010.

8. *Grand Rapids*, at 5012.

9. I owe this point to Chris Morris (Bowling Green). I see no inconsistency here in the assertion of the collective right of the colonists to secede and in the subsequent denial of minority collective rights, for the U.S. founders assumed an essentially homogeneous population. John Hart Ely, *Democracy and Distrust:*

A Theory of Judicial Review (Cambridge, Mass.: Harvard Univ. Press, 1980), p. 79.

10. Rockney McCarthy, James Skillen, and William Harper, *Disestablishment A Second Time* (Washington, D.C.: Christian Univ. Press, 1982). I owe this reference to my commentator at Dayton, Robert Van Wyk.

11. I would submit that "group" membership (for example, being an Acadian) can be distinguished from "set" membership (being tall) in a way that supports describing the former but not the latter as a potential ground for a collective right. The latter unlike the former is essentially a *self-collecting* unit. Here, see my essay "Collective Rights and Tyranny," in *Pouvoir et Tyrannie*, Guy Lafrance, ed. (Ottawa: Univ. of Ottawa, 1986), pp. 115–124, and simultaneously in the *Univ. of Ottawa Quarterly*. Hereafter, Mc Donald, 1986.

12. In Upper Canada, the establishment of a religious school required five Roman Catholics or twelve Protestants; that is, there would be no religious school unless a specified number of people wanted it (Carignan, p. 65, n. 152). I take this as a clear case of a right possessed and exercised by a group per se.

13. Joel Feinberg, "The Nature and Value of Rights," in *Rights, Justice, and the Bounds of Liberty* (Princeton, N.J.: Princeton Univ. Press, 1980), pp. 143–158.

14. Carignan, p. 52 ff. See *A.G. Québec v. Greater Hull School Board* (1984) *SCR*, p. 577, especially p. 593.

15. Because a collective right is *shared* or *social*, it belongs only to groups with some social unity (see n. 10). Thus, a random collection of people (for example, every third person listed in the Toronto phonebook) would not count as collective right-holders. See Mc Donald, 1986.

16. *Reference re an Act to Amend the Education Act*, 53 O.R. 2d, 513 (1986).

17. O.R. 566 (1986).

18. See Peter Hogg, *Canada Act 1982, Annotated* (Toronto: Carswell, 1982). For the history of the act's adoption see Roy Romanow, John Whyte, and Howard Leeson, *Canada . . . Notwithstanding: The Making of the Constitution 1976–1982* (Toronto: Carswell/Methuen, 1984).

19. Now officially known as the Constitution Act 1867 (see § 60 the Canada Act 1982). A complete schedule of constitutional documents is given in § 53.2. It should be noted that the first part of the Canada Act 1982 is the Canadian Charter of Rights and Freedoms.

20. Robert F. Cummings, "Religious Pluralism in Education: Pressures for Public Financing and Implementation," in H. A. Stevenson and J. D. Wilson, eds., *Precepts, Policy and Process: Perspectives on Contemporary Canadian Education* (London, Ontario: Alexander Blake and Associates, c. 1977), pp. 98–99.

21. J. B. St. John, "Separate Schools in Ontario," reprint from the *Globe and Mail* (Toronto, pamphlet, 1963), pp. 19–21.

22. See the *Globe and Mail* (Toronto) for Friday, July 5, 1984, pp. 1 and 4. Also see Mark Holmes, "Funding Catholic Schools: The Implications," *CT Reporter* (December 1984):11–13. The Ontario Court of Appeal ruled in favor of extending tax support to grades 11 and 12. The case has been appealed to the Supreme Court of Canada.

23. In fact, British Columbia like Manitoba funds Roman Catholic schools on the same basis as other private schools in the province.

24. Joseph Magnet, *Constitutional Law of Canada: Cases, Notes, and Materials*, vol. 2 (Toronto: Carswell, 1985), pp. 785–786.

25. Even in provinces outside these constitutional protections, public aid is provided for denominational schools; for example, in British Columbia and Alberta funds are provided for textbooks. See "Review of Educational Policies in Canada," *Western Region Report* (1975), p. 29. In Nova Scotia, New Brunswick, and Prince Edward Island school buildings are designated for denominational use (Cummings, p. 98).

26. This is, I think, not a necessary feature of legal interpretation but one that obtains in virtue of a positive commitment to fundamental rights in the specific legal system.

27. Hercule would want more than the bare assertion (by the Ontario Court of Appeal) that collective rights unlike individual rights "protect certain groups and not others" (53 O.R. 2d, 566). For he will want an argument for this alleged asymmetry between collective and individual rights. That is, he will make a distinction between a right-holder as a group or individual and whether the class of right-holders is defined in a principled or unprincipled way (here see *Law's Empire* on checkerboard laws, pp. 178–184).

28. One possibility here is a *selective* amelioration argument, namely, that §15.2 of the Charter allows a government to improve the condition of *some* disadvantaged groups but does not require that it thereby improve the situation of all similarly situated groups. The U.S. Supreme Court dismissed a selective amelioration defence of public aid to religious schools in *Aguilar et al v. Betty Fulton et al.*, 53 LW 5013 (June 25, 1985), at 5014. It is also worth noting that the minority in the Ontario reference case, *Re Education Act*, has recently argued that this extension of aid violates both the equality provision in the Charter, § 15, and the provision for multicultural heritage rights, § 27 (53 O.R. 2d [1986], 552–557 and 562).

29. Robert Nozick, *Anarchy, State, and Utopia* (New York: Basic Books, 1974), pp. 153 ff.

30. Dworkin, pp. 105–106.

31. For reasons of space, I have had to largely ignore a number of relevant concerns, in particular questions of implementation. For such issues, see Stephen B. Lawton, "The Funding of Roman Catholic Separate Schools: Issues and Implications," *Ontario Education* (March-April 1985):6–14.

32. 347 U.S. 483 (1966).

33. In arguing in favor of provincial support for Christian schools, John Olthius appeals to the parents' right to determine in what schools their children shall be educated. He appeals both to the U.N. Declaration of Human Rights (Article 26.3) and Vatican II. H. A. Stevenson, Robert M. Stamp, and J. D. Wilson, eds., *The Best of Times, The Worst of Times: Contemporary Issues in Canadian Education* (Toronto: Holt, Rinehart, and Winston, 1972), ch. 5, pp. 203–204. Interestingly, Mel Shipman, a defender of "alternative and independent" schools, initially takes a similar approach. But under criticism from Penny Moss, an opponent of funding for nonpublic schools, Shipman adopts a more collective rights' perspective. Mel Shipman, "Funding Independent Schools" (February 1985) and "A Reply to Penny Moss" (April 1985), *Orbit* 74:8–10 and 15–16. Penny Moss, "'Funding Independent Schools'—A Reply to Mel Shipman," *Orbit* 74 (April 1985):14–15.

34. Like Michael Walzer, I think such a system would expose children "to a combination of entrepreneurial ruthlessness and parental indifference." Michael Walzer, *Spheres of Justice* (New York: Basic Books, 1983), p. 219. I also accept Walzer's claim that such a system completely ignores the community's and, I would add, a minority's collective stake in education.

35. It is now being proposed that the former requirement be abandoned, so that Separate Schools would have to accept children of all confessions. The schools would, nonetheless, remain Catholic in content and direction.

36. See note 2.

37. Think of the difficult issues posed in *Wisconsin v. Yoder*, 406 U.S. 25 (1972). In that case the desire of Amish families to remove their children from school after grade 8 conflicted with the state's rule of mandatory attendance to age sixteen. The state argued that the mandatory attendance law protected the student's autonomy. From the Amish point of view, the law undermined group solidarity through a policy of assimilation. The U.S. Supreme Court ruled in favor of the Amish. The deeper issues raised in *Yoder* and in related cases (particularly, *Bob Jones University v. United States*, 103 S. Ct. 2017 [1983]) are brilliantly discussed by Robert Cover in "Nomos and Narrative," 97 *Harvard L. Rev.* 4 (1983).

38. The "mistake" I criticize here is that individuals both can and should detach themselves from their cultures and find some privileged, acultural perspective from which to assess the world, for example, Henry Sidgwick's utilitarian "point of view of the Universe" or John Rawls's contractarian "Archimedean point." The philosophical issues raised by such "detachability" claims are too profound and complex to be adequately considered here; see Cover, *op. cit.*, and Sabina Lovibond, *Realism and Imagination in Ethics* (Oxford: Blackwell, 1983). For example, if such detachability were possible, what reasons other than culturally rooted ones could be given for so detaching oneself? See also Ronald Garet, "Communality and Existence: The Rights of Groups," 3 *Southern California L. Rev.* 1001–1075 (1983).

39. One of Canada's leading constitutional experts, Professor Noel Lyon of Queen's University, has recently argued the following: "Preserving separate schools in public education would . . . seriously impair the viability of the multicultural, pluralistic vision of the 1982 Constitution. The Court's [Supreme Court of Canada] only alternative for reconciling the old and new is to separate language and religion and to treat language as the real source of Québec's concern. The Catholic-Protestant dichotomy no longer goes to the cultural duality of Canada. Denominational rights, but not language rights, must yield to the new pluralism." "Group rights in the New Canada," paper delivered at the Duke University, Durham, N.C., symposium on "Canadian Law and Legal Literature: The Commonwealth Perspective," May 29–30, 1987.

40. See *The Globe and Mail* (Toronto, June 26, 1985), p. 3.

41. In fact, the anonymous referee for this chapter did raise this objection. For a more complete response than I give here, see my paper "Collective Rights and Tyranny," *supra* n. 11.

42. On issues of legal interpretation, see Dworkin's *Law's Empire, supra* n. 2, and by contrast Cover, *supra* n. 36.

43. Here see Neil MacCormick's splendid essay "Nation and Nationalism" in his book *Legal Right and Social Democracy* (Oxford: Clarendon Press, 1982), pp. 247–264.

44. Walzer, p. 223.

45. Bickel's objections to Walzer's emphasis on the rights of citizens versus the rights of persons should be noted. Alexander M. Bickel, "Citizen or Person: What Is Not Granted Cannot Be Taken Away?" in *The Morality of Consent* (New Haven, Conn.: Yale Univ. Press, 1975), pp. 31–54.

46. Holmes, p. 13.

47. One critic argues that "the risk that a school system segregated by race, language or religions may give rise to or reinforce social and economic inequality is widely recognized. At a time when Canadian provinces are facilitating such segregation, numerous nations, including nations as diverse as the United States, Singapore and France, are fighting these 'centrifugal' forces lest the fabric of their nations be pulled apart" (Lawton, p. 9).

In *Grand Rapids*, Justice Brennan presented the following rationale for the First Amendment: "For just as religion throughout history has provided spiritual comfort, guidance and inspiration to many, it can also serve to powerfully divide societies. The solution to this problem adopted by the Framers and consistently recognized by this Court is jealously to guard the right of every individual to worship according to the dictates of conscience while requiring government to maintain a course of neutrality among religions, and between religion and non-religion."

48. Lawton, p. 12.

49. Here, I want to ally myself with contemporary communitarians. Michael Sandel, *Liberalism and Its Critics* (New York: New York Univ. Press, 1984).

50. I intend more than an echo here of guild socialism. See Ernest Barker, *Political Thought in England 1848–1914*, 2d ed. (Oxford: Oxford Univ. Press, 1963), p. 201.

SELECTED BIBLIOGRAPHY

Carignan, Pierre. 1984. "De la notion de droit collectif et de son application en matière scolaire au Québec." 18 *Thémis* 1.

Copp, David. 1984. "What Collectives Are: Agency, Individualism, and Legal Theory," *Dialogue* 23, no. 2 (June):249–270.

Cover, Robert. 1983–1984. "Nomos and Narrative." 97 *Harvard L. Rev.* 4.

Mc Donald Michael. 1986. "Collective Rights and Tyranny," published simultaneously in *Pouvoir et Tyrannie*. Guy Lafrance, ed. Ottawa: Univ. of Ottawa, 1986; and in the *University of Ottawa Review* 56 (April-June 1986):115–123.

Palley, Claire. 1978. *Constitutionial Law: Minorities*. London: Minority Rights Group.

Pfeffer, Leo. 1984. *Religion, State and the Burger Court*. Buffalo: Prometheus Books.

Sigler, Jay A. 1983. *Minority Rights: A Comparative Analysis*. Westport, Conn.: Greenwood Press.

Van Dyke, Vernon. 1985. *Human Rights, Ethnicity, and Discrimination*. Westport, Conn.: Greenwood Press.

TEN

The Right to Privacy and Personal Autonomy

CARL WELLMAN

It is now unreasonable, I presume, to question the existence of a constitutional right to privacy, for it is deeply embedded in a long line of decisions of the Supreme Court of the United States. But it is not too late to ask how this right is best defined, for its interpretation remains controversial and cases continue to arise to which its application is contested. One of the most difficult problems in the interpretation of the constitutional right to privacy is understanding the precise relation between privacy and autonomy. On the one side we find Professor David A.J. Richards, who defines the right to privacy in terms of autonomy.

> In such cases, where reasonable moral argument no longer can sustain absolute prohibitions and the issue in question is one among the fundamental life choices, the constitutional right to privacy, understood as a right of personal autonomy, finds its natural home. It is natural to call this autonomy a right of privacy in the sense that moral principles no longer define these matters as issues of proper public concern but as matters of highly personal self-definition ("Sexual Autonomy and the Constitutional Right to Privacy," 30 *Hastings Law Journal* 1000).

On the other side stands Hyman Gross, who completely rejects the attempt to conceive of privacy in terms of autonomy.

> In speaking of privacy and autonomy there is some danger that privacy may be conceived as autonomy. Such confusion has been signaled in legal literature by early and repeated use of the phrase "the right to be let alone" as a synonym for "right to privacy." The United States Supreme Court succumbed completely in 1965 in its opinion in *Griswold v. Connecticut*, and the ensuing intellectual disorder warrants comment ("Privacy and Autonomy," 100 in *Nomos XIII: Privacy*, edited by J. Roland Pennock and John W. Chapman).

In this chapter I will comment on this intellectual disorder and attempt to find some hidden order within it.

Philosophical disagreements about the proper definition of the constitutional right to privacy have practical implications for the legal application of this right to particular cases before the courts. David Richards, as one would expect, believes that the Supreme Court ought to extend the line of privacy cases to protect the right of consenting adult homosexuals to engage in the form of sex they find natural (pp. 957–958). Because he believes that previous decisions in the privacy cases have established a right to sexual autonomy, he concludes that the Court erred in its summary affirmance in *Doe v. Commonwealth's Attorney for the City of Richmond* (403 F. Supp. 1199). Presumably he would object, on similar grounds, to the refusal of the Court in *Bowers v. Hardwick* (106 S. Ct. 2841) to declare the Georgia sodomy statute unconstitutional. Justice Rehnquist would, of course, have drawn the line at *Roe v. Wade,* which did not, according to his dissenting opinion, raise any issue of privacy in the ordinary sense of that word (410 U.S. 172). As John Hart Ely reads the early privacy cases quite differently from Richards, he agrees with Rehnquist that the constitutional right to privacy ought not to have been applied to the abortion decision ("The Wages of Crying Wolf: A Comment on *Roe v. Wade,*" 82 *Yale Law Journal* 929). At the other extreme, Hyman Gross would have aborted *Griswold* and its progeny because in his opinion that case centered on "an issue regarding autonomy and not privacy" (p. 181).

My dictionary defines privacy as the condition of being secluded or isolated from the view of, or from contact with, others. In this ordinary sense, my right to privacy is violated by a dean who bugs my office and listens in on my conversations with students or by a doctor who informs a reporter for our student newspaper that I am afflicted with a venereal disease. It is not obvious, however, that the constitutional right to privacy first explicitly recognized in *Griswold v. Connecticut* can be identified with the right that others not observe one or publish information about one without authorization. Although Justice Douglas, in delivering the opinion of the Court, does seem unwilling to allow the police to search the sacred precincts of marital bedrooms, this concern with the collection and dissemination of sensitive information does not really appear to be central to his judicial reasoning. Subsequent decisions hinging upon the right to privacy center more often upon the concept of ordered liberty from which Justice Harlan derives the right to privacy in his concurring opinion. By the time of *Roe v. Wade,* the right to privacy seems much more like the right to make and act on private decisions. In other cases, this right seems to take on other forms. Indeed, so diverse are the privacy cases that one may well wonder whether there really is any one definition that can plausibly cover them all. All of this should lead us to question the conventional view that U.S. courts, unlike those of Great Britain that admit only a number of specific privacy rights, recognize a generic right to privacy.

One might conclude, as I once did, that the constitutional right to privacy is what Joel Feinberg calls a rights-package consisting of three distinct rights—the right to remain free from unwarranted public observation or publicity, the right to be free from distressing intrusions (such as loud noises or nauseous smells) in private places, and the right to make and act upon private decisions. In this interpretation, autonomy is involved in only the last third of these privacy rights. But this is a desperate expedient. Because the Supreme Court has not drawn these distinctions explicitly, one would prefer an interpretation of its various decisions that presupposes a single generic right to privacy. Accordingly, I shall reconsider my previous conclusion and seek to find a way to reconcile the apparent discrepancies in the judicial reasoning of the privacy cases.

According to my theory of rights, a legal right consists of a core Hohfeldian legal position that defines the content of the right together with a number of associated Hohfeldian positions that confer dominion over this core upon the right-holder in face of one or more second parties in some possible confrontation. To define the constitutional right to privacy, therefore, one must characterize its core. I shall try to identify the core of this right by examining the language of legal sources and the way in which the right bears upon the confrontations to which it applies.

The central issue in *Griswold v. Connecticut,* the case that established the constitutional right to privacy, was whether a statute prohibiting the use of contraceptives was unconstitutional. Subsequent leading cases, such as *Stanley v. Georgia, Eisenstadt v. Baird,* and *Roe v. Wade* similarly declared state statutes unconstitutional on the ground that they violated appellants' rights to privacy. These cases suggest that the core of this right is a constitutional immunity against legislation, or even more broadly, against state legal action that invades the privacy of the individual. But the language of Justice Douglas, delivering the opinion of the court, suggests otherwise: "We deal with a right of privacy older than the Bill of Rights—older than our political parties, older than our school system. Marriage is a coming together for better or worse, hopefully enduring, and intimate to the degree of being sacred" (*Griswold,* 381 U.S. 486). Thus, any constitutional immunity implicit in the penumbras of the Bill of Rights is a recognition of and legal protection for a prior and independent right to privacy. Moreover, to define the constitutional right to privacy as essentially an immunity against state legislation renders unintelligible the way in which it can support actions of a private individual against alleged invasions of privacy by a private corporation (*Nader v. General Motors Corporation,* 292 N.Y.S. 2d 514). Finally, the courts have explicitly rejected the suggestion that this constitutional right runs only against state action (*Galella v. Onassis,* 353 F. Supp. 232). But if the defining core of the constitutional right to privacy is not an immunity, then what is it? The *Galella* decision reads in part as follows:

"The essence of the privacy interest includes a general 'right to be left alone,' and to define one's circle of intimacy; to shield intimate and personal characteristics and activities from public gaze; to have moments of freedom from the unremitted assault of the world . . . " (353 F. Supp. 232). This language reminds us, of course, of the common law right to privacy recognized some decades before *Griswold.* "To date the law of privacy comprises four distinct kinds of invasion of four different interests of the plaintiff, which are tied together by the common name, but otherwise have almost nothing in common except that each represents an interference with the right of the plaintiff 'to be let alone'" (Prosser, *Handbook of the Law of Torts,* p. 804). As the common law right to privacy is a claim-right, or package of claim-rights, perhaps the defining core of the constitutional right to privacy is some sort of claim.

Unfortunately, the precise connection, if any, between the common law right to privacy and the constitutional right to privacy is unclear. Even *Galella v. Onassis,* in which they are characterized so similarly, discusses them separately (353 F. Supp. 227–230 and 231–232). It is also worthy of note that none of the opinions in *Griswold* establishing the constitutional right to privacy appeals to, or even mentions, the previously recognized common law right of the same name. But the fact that they do *use* the same name strongly suggests that they intended to recognize a constitutional right analogous to the common law right to privacy. Moreover, Justice Douglas, speaking for the Court, repeatedly uses language that confirms this interpretation.

> In other words, the First Amendment has a penumbra where privacy is protected from government intrusion (*Griswold,* 381 U.S. 483).
>
> Various guarantees create zones of privacy. The right of association contained in the penumbra of the First Amendment is one, as we have seen. The Third Amendment in its prohibition against the quartering of soldiers "in any house" in time of peace without the consent of the owner is another facet of that privacy. The Fourth Amendment explicitly affirms the "right of the people to be secure in their persons, houses, papers, and effects, against unreasonable searches and seizures." The Fifth Amendment in its Self-Incrimination Clause enables the citizen to create a zone of privacy which government may not force him to surrender to his detriment (*Griswold,* 381 U.S. 484).
>
> The Fourth and Fifth Amendments were described in *Boyd v. United States,* 116 U.S. 616, 630, as protection against all governmental invasions "of the sanctity of a man's home and the privacies of life" (*Griswold,* 381 U.S. 484).
>
> Would we allow the police to search the sacred precincts of marital bedrooms for telltale signs of the use of contraceptives? The very idea is repulsive to the notions of privacy surrounding the marriage relationship (*Griswold,* 381 U.S. 485–486).

The underlying thought is surely that there are certain zones or areas, either literally surrounded as by the walls of one's house or of one's bedroom or more figuratively circumscribed by the privacies of life or of the marriage relationship, that are in some sense the private property of the individual so that any invasion or intrusion by others into those areas is wrongful. Thus conceived, the defining core of the constitutional right to privacy is a legal claim of the individual against others, other individuals and especially the state, that they not invade any zone of privacy.

At first glance, the language of Justice Goldberg, concurring, appears to support this interpretation.

> The Connecticut statutes here involved deal with a particularly important and sensitive area of privacy—that of the marital relation and the marital home. This Court recognized in *Meyer v. Nebraska*, . . . that the right "to marry, establish a home and bring up children" was an essential part of the liberty guaranteed by the Fourteenth Amendment. 262 U.S., at 399. In *Pierce v. Society of Sisters*, 268 U.S. 510, the Court held unconstitutional an Oregon Act which forbade parents from sending their children to private schools because such an act "unreasonably interferes with the liberty of parents and guardians to direct the upbringing and education of children under their control." 268 U.S. at 534–535. As this Court said in *Prince v. Massachusetts*, 321 U.S. 158, at 166, the *Meyer* and *Pierce*, decisions "have respected the private realm of family life which the state cannot enter" (*Griswold v. Connecticut*, 381 U.S. 495).

Justice Goldberg does speak of an "area of privacy—that of the marital relation and the marital home" and again of "the private realm of family life which the state cannot enter." This seems to confirm the view that the defining core of the right to privacy is a claim against any invasion of any area of privacy. But notice that he cites *Meyer*, a decision hinging upon the right "to marry, establish a home and bring up children." These quoted words sound more like the definition of a liberty-right than the formulation of a claim-right. And the ground upon which the Court declared unconstitutional an Oregon act in *Pierce* was that such an act "unreasonably interferes with the liberty of parents and guardians." Perhaps, after all, Justice Goldberg is declaring that the defining core of the constitutional right to privacy is some sort of a legal liberty of the individual.

This possibility admirably fits the reasoning of Justices Harlan and White in their concurring opinions. Justice Harlan: "In my view, the proper constitutional inquiry in this case is whether this Connecticut statute infringes the Due Process Clause of the Fourteenth Amendment because the enactment violates basic values 'implicit in the concept of ordered liberty,'" *Palko v. Connecticut*, 302 U.S. 319, 325. For reasons stated at length in my dissenting opinion in *Poe v. Ullman, supra*, I believe that it does" (381 U.S. 500). And, Justice White: "In my view this Connecticut law as applied to married couples deprives them of 'liberty' without due process of law, as that concept is used in the Fourteenth Amendment" (381 U.S. 502).

The evidence for taking the core of the constitutional right to privacy to be some sort of a legal liberty accumulates as one examines subsequent leading cases. The crucial sentence occurs in *Eisenstadt v. Baird:* "If the right of privacy means anything, it is the right of the *individual*, married or single, to be free from unwarranted governmental intrusion into matters so fundamentally affecting a person as the decision whether to bear or beget a child" (405 U.S. 438). This sentence could well be read as defining the core of the constitutional right to privacy as the liberty of the individual to make and act upon private decisions, that is, decisions that fundamentally affect that individual. This reading would explain the unexpected opinion in *Roe v. Wade.*

> This right of privacy, whether it be founded in the Fourteenth Amendment's concept of personal liberty and restrictions upon state action, as we feel it is, or, as the District Court determined, in the Ninth Amendment's reservation of rights to the people, is broad enough to encompass a woman's decision whether or not to terminate her pregnancy. The detriment that the State would impose upon the pregnant woman by denying this choice altogether is apparent (410 U.S. 153).

The catalog of detriments that follows seems to be intended to show that the abortion decision is a private one because it is one "fundamentally affecting a person." Thus, the right to make and act on private decision, a liberty-right founded in the Fourteenth Amendment's concept of personal liberty, applies to the abortion decision. Much the same conception of the right to privacy is evidenced by *In Re Quinlan:* "Presumably this right is broad enough to encompass a patient's decision to decline medical treatment under certain circumstances, in much the same way as it is broad enough to encompass a woman's decision to terminate pregnancy under certain conditions" (355 A. 2nd 663). Shall we then conclude that the defining core of the constitutional right to privacy is the liberty of the individual to make and act on private decisions, decisions fundamentally affecting that individual?

I think not. As Gross and others have pointed out, this interpretation makes autonomy, and not privacy, the fundamental value protected by this constitutional right. Why, then, has the Court used such a misleading label and, moreover, repeatedly characterized the so-called right to privacy in language so reminiscent of the tort law concerning privacy? Also, why have the courts in *Nader v. General Motors Corporation* (292 N.Y.S. 2nd 514) and *Galella v. Onassis* (353 F. Supp. 232) clearly upheld a claim-right of the individual against invasions of privacy by some second party?

It is possible, of course, that there is no consistent interpretation of the constitutional right to privacy because the opinions of the courts are as confused as they are confusing. But let us try to make sense of the language of these decisions and of their bearing upon the confrontations to which they apply. Working backward, notice that *Quinlan* says that the right to privacy "is broad enough to encompass a patient's decision to decline medical treatment" (355 A. 2nd 663), and *Roe* says that it "is broad enough to encompass a woman's decision whether or not to terminate her pregnancy" (410 U.S. 153). The picture here is that of a constitutional right drawing a circle around private decisions so that they lie within the sort of zone of privacy central to the Douglas opinion in *Griswold.*

Now let us reconsider that pregnant sentence in *Eisenstadt:* "If the right to privacy means anything, it is the right of the *individual,* married or single, to be free from unwarranted governmental intrusion into matters so fundamentally affecting a person as the decision whether to bear or beget a child" (405 U.S. 453). The ambiguity of this sentence is now apparent. Although it could mean to declare a liberty-right to make and act on private decisions, it could equally mean to affirm a claim-right against governmental intrusions into that area of an individual's life where personal decisions lie. I suggest that this second interpretation will enable us to give a coherent account of all the decisions that appeal to the constitutional right to privacy, provided that we recognize that the intrusion of governmental regulation is only one of the several sorts of invasions of privacy against which the right-holder has a claim. The underlying analogy is that between the way in which governmental prohibition of certain actions reaches into the individual's private life in a disturbing manner and the way invading the home of the individual or the bedroom of the couple constitutes a distressing intrusion into a zone of privacy or, in a different manner, the intrusion of blaring music into my private study is also disturbing.

There is, then, a general constitutional right to privacy, not merely a cluster of specific privacy rights. But this is not the right to privacy in general; that is, there is no right to privacy *per se.* Not every sort of privacy is protected by this right. This limitation is hardly surprising, for no constitutional right is unlimited. The right to liberty surely does not include the liberty to abuse one's wife or to acquire wealth by theft or blackmail. The scope of the constitutional right to privacy is best described by Justice White, concurring in *Griswold,* and by Justice Blackmun, dissenting in *Bowers.* Justice White: "An examination of the justification offered, however, cannot be avoided by saying that the Connecticut anti-use statute invades a protected area of privacy and association or that it demeans the marriage relationship" (381 U.S. 503). Justice Blackmun: "I need not reach either the Eighth Amendment or the Equal Protection Clause issues because I believe that Hardwick has stated a cognizable claim that . . . interferes with constitutionally protected interests in privacy and freedom of intimate association" (106 S.Ct. 2849–2850). Accordingly, the defining core of the constitutional right to privacy is the claim of the individual against others, especially the government, that they not invade or intrude into any constitutionally protected area of privacy.

Obviously, the courts can apply this right to particular cases only if there are criteria for determining which areas of privacy are protected by the Constitution. By and large, subsequent courts have adopted the tests first proposed by Douglas, Goldberg, and Harlan in *Griswold:* Justice Douglas: "The foregoing cases suggest that specific guarantees in the Bill of Rights have penumbras, formed by emanations from those guarantees that help give them life and substance. . . . Various guarantees create zones of privacy" (381 U.S. 484). Justice Goldberg: "the Court stated many years ago that the Due Process Clause protects those liberties that are 'so rooted in the traditions and conscience of our people as to be ranked as fundamental'" (381 U.S. 487). And Justice Harlan: "In my view, the proper constitutional inquiry in this case is whether the Connecticut statute infringes the Due Process Clause of the Fourteenth Amendment because the enactment violates basic values 'implicit in the concept of ordered liberty'" (381 U.S. 500).

Although these criteria are quite different, they are all taken to be criteria *for* the same thing—the constitutional recognition of some area of privacy. Species of privacy that lack any such pedigree fall outside the right to privacy.

I would be the first to admit that in the end my attempt to identify a single core of the constitutional right to privacy—the legal claim of the individual against other individuals, private corporations, and the state that they not invade or intrude into any constitutionally recognized area of privacy—may fail. If so, it may turn out that the constitutional right to privacy is really a rights-package, a cluster of distinct rights concerning privacy, each with its own defining core. In that event, the proper conclusion to draw will be like Prosser's conclusion that the common law right to privacy really consists of four distinct claim-rights recognized in the law of torts. Nevertheless, it seems to me that my interpretation fits the various cases well enough to be plausible and that the attempt to find some generic definition of the constitutional right to privacy should be pursued, although with a healthy skepticism, as long as the Supreme Court refuses to recognize any ambiguity in the language of its decisions.

If my definition of the constitutional right to privacy is accurate, or at least approximately correct, just how is this right related to personal autonomy? A tempting hypothesis is that autonomy is located within one portion of this right because one of the constitutionally protected areas of privacy is that of private decisions. Thus, even though the right to privacy is not the liberty-right to make and act on private decisions, it includes the claim-right that others not interfere with these private decisions, for any such interference would be an invasion of a protected area of privacy. I very much doubt, however, that this direct and essential connection between privacy and autonomy has ever been recognized by the courts. For one thing, the expression "a private decision" is conspicuous by its absence from the opinions in the privacy cases, even in *Roe* and *Quinlan* that center on the abortion decision and the decision to refuse medical treatment, respectively. Moreover, this interpretation misrepresents the reasoning of the courts. The argument in *Roe* is not that the abortion decision is constitutionally protected because it is a private decision, but that it is encompassed by the right to privacy because it involves the exercise of one of the fundamental liberties recognized in the U.S. Constitution. Hence the emphasis is upon how fundamental, not how personal and private, the decision is. Again, the argument in *Bowers* is not that homosexual conduct falls outside the right to privacy because the decision to engage in homosexual acts is not a private one, but that this right is inapplicable to that decision because the decision concerns conduct in an area that lacks constitutional recognition. Accordingly, autonomous decisions and actions are protected by the right to privacy only insofar as they are taken within or concern some area of privacy independently defined and legally recognized.

Although indirect, and from a logical point of view accidental, this connection between privacy and autonomy is profoundly important. The constitutional right to privacy *does* protect personal autonomy on many occasions, and typically when autonomy matters most. This is not because the right to privacy is to be defined, as a whole or in part, in terms of autonomy, but because it protects certain zones of privacy—private places, personal relationships, individual liberties—from invasions or intrusions that would hinder or destroy autonomy. One form of intrusion that may be judged impermissible is governmental regulation, including enforcement procedures by the police or in the courts. Obviously, the right to privacy protects autonomy by rendering legal prohibitions applying to decisions and actions within recognized areas of privacy unconstitutional. Another form of intrusion often excluded by this right is the collection and dissemination of information about a person. Alan Westin reminds us that here, too, the right to privacy protects personal autonomy.

> The most serious threat to the individual's autonomy is the possibility that someone may penetrate the inner zone and learn his ultimate secrets, either by physical or psychological means. This deliberate penetration of the individual's protective shell, his psychological armor, would leave him naked to ridicule and shame and would put him under the control of those who knew his secrets (*Privacy and Freedom*, p. 33).

Thus, the right to privacy does not protect autonomy directly and as such. What it does do is to protect constitutionally recognized areas of privacy from invasion and thereby protects personal autonomy indirectly by providing areas within which individual decision and action will be free from intrusions that would damage or destroy autonomy. Moreover, these zones of privacy may well be constitutionally recognized for that very reason. Hence, the personal and social value of autonomy probably figures prominently in the grounds of the right to privacy without defining its content.

We must conclude, therefore, that Professor Richards has failed to demonstrate that homosexual conduct between consenting adults is protected by the constitutional right to privacy, for his reasoning presupposes a mistaken interpretation of that right. The right to privacy cannot be identified with the right to personal autonomy, nor does it include or necessarily imply any right to sexual autonomy. If we are to object, on legal rather than moral grounds, to the decisions in *Doe v. Commonwealth's Attorney* and *Bowers v. Hardwick,* we must show that the decision to engage in homosexual acts with other consenting adults lies within some zone of privacy that has received recognition in the Constitution or in the opinions of the Supreme Court interpreting that text. Whether such an argument can be made remains to be seen. All that I have tried to show in this chapter is the form any such argument must take, given the proper definition of the constitutional right to privacy.

ELEVEN

Procedural Due Process

MICHAEL D. BAYLES

The Fifth Amendment and Section 1 of the Fourteenth Amendment of the U.S. Constitution provide that neither federal nor state governments may deprive persons "of life, liberty, or property, without due process of law." The original intent of this clause is fairly clear, namely, to prohibit the government from executing persons, incarcerating them, or taking their property, as by fines, without a legal proceeding.[1] As with other general constitutional clauses, the Supreme Court has not adhered to the original literal meaning. In recent decades, the Court has separated two questions involved in procedural due process. First, the Court asks whether government action deprives someone of life, liberty, or property so that a due process clause applies. Second, if due process is required, the Court asks what process is due.

This chapter concerns the first question, the so-called trigger for due process. The second question is a separate topic that is not addressed here. Sometimes the Court has failed to keep the two issues distinct. In part, this is due to offering more than one ground for a decision; for example, due process may not be required, but even if it were, the extant procedures would meet the requirement.[2] A second type of argument holds that due process applies, but alternative procedures (such as common law tort actions) exist to protect the claim, so no direct procedures are necessary.[3] Another type of argument can also lead one to confuse the two inquiries. A particular action might meet the conditions for application of due process but there might be no reason to require any specific procedure. This possibility is distinct from the previous one. In the former, there may be good reasons to prefer some procedures, but the alternative provides them. In the latter, there is no reason to prefer any procedure, because the costs outweigh the benefits.

THE SUPREME COURT AND COMMENTATORS

The constitutional question whether due process applies has usually meant: Is a hearing required? Traditionally, both in constitutional law and in common law analysis of natural justice, legislative and adjudicative contexts are distinguished.[4] Legislative contexts address matters of policy, while adjudicative ones primarily concern the application of rules and principles to particular individuals or cases. Of course, policy issues are sometimes significantly raised in adjudicative cases. Moreover, some nonadjudicative processes are close enough to adjudication that the common law classified them as quasi-judicial and imposed the requirements of natural justice. Although difficult issues can arise in distinguishing legislative and adjudicative contexts, they are not pursued here.

The burden of the legislative/adjudicative distinction is that due process applies only to adjudicative decisions. Yet in the past due process was not applied to all adjudicative decisions; in particular, it was not applied to decisions about privileges as opposed to rights. A privilege does not involve a claim to something, whereas a right does. If persons were given or denied something to which they had no preexisting right, then it was a privilege, and due process did not apply. The underlying rationale, which plagues many contemporary analyses, is that if persons do not have a right to something, then they have no claim to something of which they can be deprived; therefore, due process is not applicable. A slightly different rationale is that if the government is merely bestowing a gratuity—a benefit that the government is not required to bestow—then it should have as much discretion as an ordinary citizen does in contributing to a charity. Among the privileges were licenses to run liquor stores,[5] government employment,[6] entry of an alien immigrant into the United States,[7] and government benefits such as pensions.[8]

The distinction between a right and a privilege is not as clear as one might think. Very early, the Supreme Court held that a license to practice law could not be revoked without notice and a hearing.[9] What, one might ask, distinguishes a license to practice law from a license to sell liquor, except that judges possess the former and not the latter? In an industrialized, urban society, what once might have appeared as mere privileges and governmental gratuities, such as licenses to drive automobiles, have become economic necessities.[10]

The right/privilege distinction was laid to rest in *Goldberg v. Kelly.*[11] The issue in the case was not whether the due process clause applied, for the government conceded that it did, but whether due process required a hearing before rather than after termination of welfare benefits. Nonetheless, Justice Brennan went out of his way to note that due process applied and that the right/privilege distinction would not settle the issue before the Court. Of course, the right/privilege distinction would not settle it because that distinction was addressed to whether due process applied, not what it required. However, Brennan suggested what has now become known as the entitlement theory by remarking that welfare benefits are a matter of statutory entitlement for qualified persons.

The entitlement theory has been developed as much by its critics as by its advocates. It has been characterized as follows:[12] If the substantive rules permit the decisionmaker considerable discretion, then a benefit is not an entitlement. If discretion is significantly structured by substantive rules and principles, then an entitlement exists. Generally, if explicit statutory or regulatory standards exist for the decision—termination of employment for cause, specific grounds for suspension from school, or specific conditions for receiving welfare—then due process applies.

But it is not clear why legislated-specific, substantive standards should prevent the operation of the legislated procedures. This problem is the chief difficulty with the entitlement view. One cannot argue on the basis of expectations and reasonable reliance, because one has no reason to rely on receiving more procedural protection than specified in the statute or regulations.[13] As the government need not have made the benefits available at all, why should it not be permitted to specify the procedures for granting and terminating them?

Justice Rehnquist has claimed that substance and procedure cannot be divorced, so the individual's substantive claim is only to a guarantee as protected by the given procedures.[14] Pushed to its extreme, the Rehnquist position involves what has been called the positivist trap.[15] Whether one is deprived of a liberty or property interest, for example, in losing a teaching job, depends on state law. The extent of that interest is also determined by state law, so if the law does not define it as including a right to a hearing, then one has no liberty or property interest to a job with a hearing for termination. Thus, the failure to provide a hearing cannot deprive one of any liberty or property to which one is entitled.

The Rehnquist argument was never endorsed by a majority of the Court. It has recently been explicitly rejected.[16] The Court, with Justice White speaking for everyone but Rehnquist, stated that substance and procedure are separate, that property is not defined by state procedures provided for its deprivation. Procedural requirements are a matter of federal (constitutional) law and thus not restricted by state law. However, this still leaves the problem of determining what conditions invoke due process.

Prompted by agreement or disagreement with the Court's use of entitlement, commentators have staked out many alternative positions. One view largely accepts the entitlement position but restricts, on historical grounds, liberty and property interests to those recognized at the time of the adoption of the amendments.[17] A second view restricts due process to interests in life, liberty, and property recognized in 1925, but allows for more complex ways in which one might be deprived of them.[18] A third approach generally accepts the entitlement view but recognizes certain constitutional rights, such as education and welfare, that are protected only by procedural conditions.[19] A fourth approach accepts the entitlement approach but recognizes an equal protection requirement of minimal rationality for the relation between substance and procedure.[20] A fifth view analyzes the concepts of liberty and property philosophically with a concern to protect individuals from abuse by government monopolies.[21] A sixth approach recognizes the clause as protecting the liberal values of zones of private conduct, political equality, and comprehensibility.[22] A seventh approach recognizes a liberty interest in freedom from arbitrary adjudicative procedures; thus, due process will apply in any adjudicative context.[23] An eighth approach ignores whether the interests of which a plaintiff is allegedly deprived are those of liberty or property and simply focuses on how important they are.[24] A ninth approach construes deprivation "of life, liberty, or property" as basically meaning any adjudication and then looks to administrative law for some limits.[25]

Many of these theories have been developed to avoid the allegedly disastrous consequences of the Court's approach. However, the Court's holdings do not appear to be disastrous. One must distinguish between those cases in which the Court held due process does not apply from those in which it approved existing procedures. There are only about nine such cases, and not all of them are major ones. In *Board of Regents v. Roth*,[26] a teacher on a one-year contract was held not entitled to a hearing or explanation as to why no contract was awarded for the following year. In *Arnett v. Kennedy*,[27] three members of the Court held that due process does not apply to dismissal of a federal employee; however, a majority of the Court held that it did apply, but enough justices agreed that the procedures provided were adequate to deny relief. In *Bishop v. Wood*,[28] due process was held not to apply to a policeman employed at will. In *Meachum v. Fano*,[29] due process was held not to apply to decisions to transfer prisoners from one prison to another; although slightly different, *Olim v. Wakinekona*[30] held essentially the same for transfer of prisoners to out-of-state prisons. *Paul v. Davis*[31] held that due process does not apply to police decisions to include a person on a list of suspected shoplifters circulated to businesses. *Leis v. Flynt*[32] held due process not applicable to court decisions to permit out-of-state lawyers to represent clients in particular cases. In *Martinez v. California*,[33] the Court held that due process does not apply when the state paroles a person who subsequently murders a girl. Nor, according to *O'Bannon v. Town Court Nursing Center*,[34] does due process apply to recipients of medicaid when the government revokes the certificate of the nursing home in which they reside. Finally, *Connecticut Board of Pardons v. Dumschat*[35] held that due process does not apply to decisions to pardon.

AN ALTERNATIVE ANALYSIS

With deference, it is suggested that the Court and commentators have made the issues more complex and difficult than they need be. The due process clauses apply if the state adversely affects certain interests, namely, those to life, liberty, or property. The difficulties raised by the cases are rarely whether property or liberty is involved. Indeed, the cases that commonsensibly might be thought most difficult in this regard—deprivations of education—have not bothered the Court at all.[36] The fundamental question is whether a deprivation of these interests is in question. It is the whole clause—deprivation of life, liberty, or property—that should be the focus of analysis. Neither the Court nor commentators have made this explicit.

Only one commentator has considered the analysis of deprivation, and with the Court's help, he tends to confuse the questions whether a deprivation occurred with who is responsible for it.[37] In *Martinez*,[38] the parents of a girl murdered by a parolee sued the state. The state, however, did not kill the girl; it did not take action to deprive her of life. Similarly, in *O'Bannon*,[39] although the government may have been depriving Town Court of property, it was not acting against the residents. In each case, even if the plaintiff was deprived of life, liberty, or property, the responsibility of the state was blocked by an intervening voluntary act of another—the parolee in *Martinez* and the nursing center or residents who chose to live there in *O'Bannon*. Elementary analysis of causal responsibility, not complex analysis of the due process trigger, is all that is needed for these cases. However, in most of the other cases, an analysis of deprivation will be useful.

Some Distinctions

Before deprivation can be analyzed, distinctions need to be made between burden-imposing, benefit-conferring, benefit-terminating, and burden-relieving decisions. Imposition of a burden makes a person worse off. A typical, uncontroversial burden-imposing decision is one to punish an individual for commission of a crime. Conferral of a benefit makes a person better off. A typical benefit-conferring decision is the award of a grant or promotion. However, some decisions might be viewed as either the refusal to confer a benefit or the imposition of a burden.

Consider a decision to cease providing a person unemployment insurance payments. As something is being taken away, namely, payments, one might view the decision as imposing a burden. Alternatively, as providing unemployment insurance payments is conferring a benefit, one might view the decision as a refusal to confer future benefits. The difference between these two views is what is taken as the baseline. If the baseline is the person receiving payments, then cessation of payments makes the person worse off and imposes a burden. If the baseline is the person's situation before receiving payments, then cessation of payments leaves the person in the baseline condition and is therefore the refusal to provide a benefit. Some of the controversial due process cases concern such debatable situations.

Benefit-terminating decisions are those that cease providing benefits that the decisionmaker or organization the decisionmaker represents previously decided to provide. A decision to cease unemployment insurance payments is a benefit-terminating decision. The agency previously decided to make payments and is now changing its decision. Deprivation of liberty for commission of a crime is not a benefit-terminating decision because the criminal justice system did not previously grant freedom to the particular person. If liberty is granted at all (which is unlikely), it is by the Constitution or an act of the legislature for all citizens and not the result of a determination about the individual in question.

Burden-relieving decisions correspond to benefit-terminating decisions. The former cease imposing a burden that was previously imposed. The decision to impose the burden must have been made by the person making the decision, by an organization that person represents, or by a person or organization with the task of imposing such burdens. The burden-relieving decisionmaker has the task of determining when it should cease. This complicated set of conditions regarding the imposition of the burden is needed to distinguish certain types of cases. For example, if my daughter is being charged interest on her unpaid credit card balance and I pay off her debt so that the interest is no longer charged, my decision or action is a benefit-conferring one, not a burden-relieving one. The credit card company, not I, decided (with her consent) to impose the interest. However, the decision of the president to grant a pardon is an example of a burden-relieving decision. Although a court, not the president, imposed the burden, the task of deciding to relieve the burden by pardon is assigned to the president.

A deprivation constitutes a harm, a setback of a person's interests that makes the person worse off than before.[40] Burden-imposing decisions set back interests. As discussed in more detail below, benefit-terminating decisions also often set back interests; the person is worse off than had the benefits continued. Benefit-conferring decisions advance interests; consequently, denials of benefits do not make a person worse off, they merely fail to advance a person's interests. Similarly, burden-relieving decisions advance interests, and their denial does not make one worse off. Thus, usually, decisions to impose burdens and to terminate benefits make persons worse off; deciding not to do so leaves persons as they were. Decisions to confer benefits and to relieve burdens advance persons' interests; deciding not to do so leaves persons in the state they were in.

Still, one might contend that this distinction is without difference. Whether one is denied a thousand-dollar grant or is fined a thousand dollars, one has a thousand dollars less than had the decision been the reverse. However, there are several differences between them. First, in burden-imposing and benefit-terminating decisions, the government is taking action against one.[41] Second, usually people voluntarily ask for benefit-conferring or burden-relieving decisions, whereas rational persons rarely ask for burden-imposing or benefit-terminating ones. Third, persons do not usually receive the same utility from benefits and burdens of the same dollar amount. Most persons' utility curves decrease more rapidly than they rise from the point representing the person's present situation. One reason is that people count on and allocate to current needs what they have. Future increases are not usually counted on. However, this reliance on current benefits, especially continuing ones such as welfare payments, is not justifiable if one knows that they might be taken away. Nonetheless, in many cases, collateral reliance is necessary to obtain the full value of benefits. For example, an applicant for an original television license has not expended the money in station equipment and a broadcast tower that a renewal applicant, who has operated a station for a number of years, has expended. Consequently, the utility lost when an application is denied is less than when a license is terminated. Similarly, the point of welfare payments is for people to meet current expenses, and this would be partially defeated if persons were encouraged to save significant amounts against payments being discontinued.

These distinctions are illustrated by and help illuminate Supreme Court decisions on whether due process applies. Considering some of these cases also brings in factors that are needed for a sophisticated use of the distinctions. Cases concerning parole and probation primarily concern distinctions between burden-imposing and burden-relieving decisions. The employment cases primarily involve the difference between decisions to confer and to terminate benefits. Finally, licensing, welfare, and social security cases illustrate why some apparently benefit-conferring decisions are similar to benefit terminating or even burden-imposing ones.

Burden-imposing Versus Burden-relieving: Prisoner Cases

The Supreme Court has distinguished granting parole from its revocation. An analysis of liberty will not be of any use here, for clearly liberty is at issue whether the case involves granting or revoking parole. In *Morrissey v. Brewer*[42] the Court held that due process applies to revocation of parole. Revoking parole is a burden-imposing decision and thus involves a deprivation of liberty. One might object that revoking parole or probation is really the termination of a benefit—a release to which one had no claim. However, an important point is involved here. The terms on which parole is granted establish the baseline for analysis whether one's condition can only be worsened or bettered by a decision. Parole is granted conditionally on not performing certain types of actions. It is similar to the liberty nonfelons have, which is conditional on not committing a crime.[43] Although more is involved, many of the conditions for revoking parole and probation are often similar to committing crimes. The parolee, like the ordinary nonfelon, has liberty unless certain specified conditions are violated. Of course, the parolee's liberty is granted whereas that of a nonfelon is not.

In *Morrissey,* Chief Justice Burger suggested that revocation of parole differs from its original grant. The difference is that decisions to grant parole are normally burden-relieving. The normal baseline is that the burden will continue unless certain conditions are met; imprisonment will continue until the end of sentence and the granting of parole relieves that burden. Consequently, parole-granting decisions cannot set back interests, only fail to advance them.

However, in special circumstances, this baseline can be altered. In *Greenholtz v. Inmates of the Nebraska Penal and Correctional Complex,*[44] the Court held that due process applied to decisions to grant parole. That case was perhaps unique, for the statute mandated granting parole unless one of four grounds for denial was found. The statute thus reversed the normal baseline. In effect, the statute converted a burden-relieving decision into a benefit-terminating one. A similar point was involved in *Wolff v. McDonnell.*[45] There, due process applied to the deprivation of automatically earned good time credits as a sanction for misconduct. The baseline was receipt of the credits; their deprivation a burden-imposing decision.

In some of the prisoner cases, the issue concerns whether there is any significant loss not already covered by a procedure. In *Meachum*[46] and *Olim*[47] prisoners were transferred to another prison, and their original trials had already provided due process for imprisonment. In *Vitek v. Jones,*[48] however, due process was held to apply to transfer of a prisoner to a mental institution. The prisoner's trial and sentence did not include confinement in a mental institution. Similarly, in *Hewitt v. Helms,*[49] due process was held to apply to decisions to confine a prisoner in isolation. In both *Vitek* and *Hewitt,* the loss of liberty can be viewed as significantly exceeding that authorized by the original criminal trial. Consequently, a decision to impose a further burden is involved and due process should apply. Although one might disagree with the Court's view that significantly greater loss of liberty is involved in transfer to a mental institution but not in a transfer from a minimum to maximum security prison, the underlying principle is correct. Due process applies when an additional deprivation not authorized by a previous procedure is to be imposed.

Benefit-conferring Versus Benefit-terminating: Employment Cases

Deciding whether a case involves benefit termination or a mere refusal to grant a benefit is not always easy. If benefits are supplied on a periodic basis, then it may be difficult to decide whether the baseline is a person receiving future benefits, making it a benefit-terminating decision, or no future benefits, making it a benefit-conferring decision. Some of the employment cases illustrate this difference. If a person has a job unless certain conditions are violated, then the baseline is continued employment; a decision not to continue the person's employment is a benefit-terminating one. If a teacher has tenure or a person has a position from which he or she can be dismissed only for stated causes, then the decision is a benefit-terminating one that deprives the person of something to which the person has a defeasible claim.[50]

If the baseline is no continued employment, then a decision not to employ is the failure to confer a benefit and thus not a deprivation. In *Board of Regents v. Roth,*[51] Roth was on a one-year appointment; consequently, the baseline was no employment the following year. The decision to employ or not the following year was a benefit-conferring decision. Failure to appoint Roth for another year thus did not deprive him of anything; due process did not apply, and he was not entitled to a hearing or to reasons why he was not offered another appointment. Similarly, in the controversial case of *Bishop v. Wood,*[52] state law had been interpreted to permit firing for no cause. Consequently, the baseline was again no future employment, and the decision was a refusal to confer a future benefit. The objection to the case is not the Supreme Court's decision that under the interpretation of state law due process does not apply, but to the interpretation of the state law.

In *Arnett,*[53] the government employee, Kennedy, did have a permanent position terminable for cause, albeit a general one. Thus, a decision about continued employment was a benefit-terminating one. Thus in his case, due process applied. But whether due process should entitle the employee to a pretermination hearing is a question of what due process requires, not whether it applies. It does seem, however, that due process would prohibit a procedure whereby a supervisor, whom in this case Kennedy had accused of accepting a bribe, makes the initial decision, even if there were an appeal process.

Why then, one might ask, were three members of the Court led astray. The reason: Employment falls under the property part of the due process trigger. Property is commonly analyzed as a bundle of rights, liberties, and powers.[54] In particular, the right to continued possession against the employer is crucial. Kennedy had a right to continued possession of the job (property) that would hold against others; no one other than the government—his employer—could take his job. Nevertheless, his right against the government to continued possession of the job was subject to certain conditions. The government did not provide him with property that had rights to the procedures he requested.

Kennedy's property right in his job has been compared to a holder of a defeasible fee.[55] The holder of a defeasible fee has property against others, but if certain conditions occur, it reverts to the grantor. Thus, if the conditions for terminating Kennedy's employment occur, he has no right against the grantor.

Justice Rehnquist (as he was then) essentially applied this analysis to hold that due process does not apply. However, he went further and held that the government was also entitled to establish the procedures to determine that the conditions defeating Kennedy's right to employment existed. This is not part of a defeasible fee. Although the grantor can state the conditions on which property reverts, in case of dispute as to their existence, the feeholder is entitled to legal process—a civil trial.

The difference between a defeasible fee and custody of personal property is analogous to that between employment subject to termination on conditions and employment at will. A person having custody of goods has physical possession and control of them but no recognized property right; an individual must return them on demand. Persons employed at will are comparable to persons having custody; they can exercise the functions of the job but must surrender it on demand. Consequently, loss of employment at will does not deprive the employee of property. In contrast, persons with a defeasible fee or who are employed subject to certain conditions do have property rights, and termination of their fee or employment deprives them of those rights. Consequently, entitlement to continuing possession as against the government is not crucial to whether there is a deprivation of property,[56] for legal process is required to determine the existence of conditions terminating the property right.

These distinctions thus explain the emphasis in the entitlement approach as to whether a decision is left to discretion or constrained by criteria. However, what counts is not whether decisionmaking criteria are specified, as the entitlement theory suggests, but how those criteria or conditions are structured. If they are specified as "future benefits *B* will be given unless condition *C*," then the baseline is receipt of benefits. If those conditions are specified as "if condition *C* occurs, then benefits *B* will be provided," the decision is a benefit-conferring one. Essentially, this is the difference between a condition subsequent and a condition precedent.[57]

This difference can be illustrated by considering whether failure to pass a vision test triggers due process. Passing such a test is a condition precedent to obtaining an automobile operator's license. Consequently, failure of a test and the denial of a license do not deprive one of anything. However, in termination of employment for cause due to failure of a vision test, the failure operates as a condition subsequent. Consequently, one is being deprived of property and due process applies.[58]

This type of analysis and appeal to state law is not usually necessary for cases involving the deprivation of liberty. As noted above, liberty is not usually granted to anyone. Consequently, there is no one analogous to the reversioner against whom a claim might fail. The exception concerns prisoners. They have been deprived of liberty, so the liberty of possible parole is granted by the state. Usually, the granting of parole is based on conditions precedent; if one meets certain conditions, then parole will be granted. In *Greenholtz*,[59] this was reversed; prisoners were granted parole unless certain events occurred.

Benefit-conferring Versus Benefit-terminating: Government Monopolies

The preceding analysis does not suffice to justify the application of due process to the granting of professional licenses or at least certain welfare benefits. The conditions for obtaining licenses are usually conditions precedent; if one meets certain standards, say, of competence and good character, then one will obtain a license. Yet, the Supreme Court has held that due process applies to the granting of licenses to practice law.[60] Similarly, the social security law places the burden on recipients of disability payments to show a continuing qualification for them.[61] Yet again, essentially without argument, the Court has held that due process applies to termination of disability payments.[62] If, however, a recipient has an obligation to show continuing disability, then surely this is like employment at will, with a condition precedent to continued employment being the continued ability to perform the job well.

Two further factors are needed to explain these decisions. The first—the government monopolization of specific types of benefits—has been significantly developed by several scholars.[63] Normally, one can engage in any lawful employment. Some forms of employment, such as law and medicine, are licensed, and their practice without a license is prohibited. By prohibiting the practice of law unless one is admitted to the bar, the government has deprived all citizens of alternative sources of the benefit of practicing law. The government has a total monopoly, so due process should apply even to benefit-conferring decisions concerning such licenses. The government cannot first deprive one of something (the right to practice law) and then claim that its conferral is a mere gratuity, any more than a slave owner can beat a slave daily and then extol his or her generosity in not beating the slave one day. Denying an applicant a license is the fruit of the tree of previous deprivation, and due process should apply.

The same general analysis applies to many welfare benefit situations, such as Aid to Families with Dependent Children and social security disability. Government entrance into these fields has not completely precluded private charity or disability insurance. However, private organizations have withdrawn or made less favorable arrangements due to government action. For example, private employers probably provide less disability insurance because they rely on government coverage; even if they provide the same total coverage, they contribute less to private insurance than they would were they not also contributing to social security. Consequently, what in the absence of monopoly might be benefit-conferring decisions are benefit-terminating ones and thus require due process.

Essentially the same argument applies to elementary and secondary education. The government has a near monopoly, and anyone who wishes to opt out must still pay taxes to support the public system. Thus, most people have little choice in obtaining these educational benefits except from the state. They must rely on continually receiving the benefits from the government. Consequently, the baseline is shifted to continued receipt of the benefits. Termination of the benefits, even for a brief period, calls for due process protections.[64]

Nevertheless, there is a second condition that must occur before the original granting of a benefit over which the government has a monopoly becomes subject to due process. Consider air traffic controllers. The government has a monopoly on such employment. Yet, a qualified job applicant is not thereby entitled to due process, even the minimum procedure of a statement of reasons for not being hired. One might argue that there is less of a monopoly here, because alternative types of employment exist. However, the same could be said of being a lawyer.

An additional factor is the difference between competitive and noncompetitive or eligibility-based distributions.[65] In competitive situations, only the best are chosen to receive benefits, whereas in noncompetitive situations, everyone who meets the criteria is to receive them. Thus, in competitive situations, meeting the basic criteria does not suffice to shift the baseline to receipt of the benefit. As hiring air traffic controllers is a competitive situation, due process does not apply. The same logic applies to licensing radio and television stations. The licensing of lawyers and granting of social security benefits is a noncompetitive situation, so there the baseline is shifted.

CONCLUSION

The right/privilege and entitlement analyses are groping to understand whether a deprivation occurs. The right/privilege distinction is merely a conclusory and unilluminating way of stating whether a deprivation occurs. The entitlement theory also seeks to determine the baseline for whether a deprivation occurs, but it mistakenly makes it depend simply on whether explicit standards are provided. Explicit standards can be either conditions precedent or conditions subsequent.

In the major cases the issue is rarely whether property or liberty is involved. Money, regardless if it is salary or welfare payments, is a form of property. Likewise, a school spanking is a deprivation of liberty.[66] A license to practice a profession or engage in a business involves both property (income) and liberty. Only cases like school suspension involve difficult problems of whether property or liberty are involved, although even in these cases, it is surprising how little attention is paid to that aspect.

The central feature in most cases is whether a deprivation might occur. To decide that, it is useful to analyze the situation as burden-imposing, benefit-conferring, burden-relieving, or benefit-terminating. Generally, burden-imposing and many benefit-terminating decisions involve deprivations and due process applies; burden-relieving and benefit-conferring decisions do not risk deprivation and due process does not apply. For burden-relieving and benefit-terminating contexts, it is important to determine what the baseline is—continuation of the burden or benefit, or the reverse. Sometimes the baseline is different from the norm. To the extent that the government has a monopoly over an activity, the baseline for benefit conferral is often reversed. If there is government monopoly and the distribution of benefits is noncompetitive, then the baseline is shifted and due process applies even to benefit-conferring decisions.

Finally, a possible objection[67] to this analysis is that it will give due process protection to minimal losses, such as the removal of a prisoner's hobby kit,[68] but not to major losses, such as failure of a nontenured professor to be rehired.[69] The claim is true, but three factors must be noted. First, this inequality of protection results from the textual limitation to deprivations and its analysis. To hold otherwise requires a different analysis of deprivation or ignores the written text. Second, the analysis only determines when due process applies, not what it requires. Small losses need not require elaborate due process protections. Third, the analysis does not preclude nonconstitutional procedural protections of even benefit-conferring decisions. Contrary to what many U.S. citizens think, not all desirable political protections need be found in the Constitution.

NOTES

1. Lino A. Graglia, "Would the Court Get 'Procedural Due Process' Cases Right If It Knew What 'Liberty' Really Means?" *Notre Dame J. of L., Ethics and Public Policy* 1 (1985):818; Charles A. Miller, "The Forest of Due Process of Law: The American Constitutional Tradition," in *Due Process: Nomos XVII*, J. Roland Pennock and John W. Chapman, eds. (New York: New York Univ. Press, 1977), pp. 4–11, 25; Henry Paul Monaghan, "Of 'Liberty' and 'Property,'" *Cornell L. Rev.* 62 (1977):411; Stephen F. Williams, "Liberty and Property: The Problem of Government Benefits," *J. of Legal Studies* 12 (1983):20.

2. See, for example, *Board of Curators v. Horowitz*, 435 U.S. 78 (1978).

3. *Ingraham v. Wright*, 430 U.S. 651 (1977); *Hudson v. Palmer*, 104 S. Ct. 3194 (1984); *Parratt v. Taylor*, 451 U.S. 527 (1981) (section 1983 of U.S. Code claim involving same analysis as due process).

4. *Londoner v. Denver*, 210 U.S. 373 (1908); *Bi-Metallic Investment Co. v. Colorado*, 239 U.S. 441 (1915); R. A. Macdonald, "Judicial Review and Procedural Fairness in Administrative Law: Part I," *McGill L. J.* 25 (1980):532–533.

5. *Smith v. Liquor Control Commission*, 169 N.W. 2d 803 (Iowa 1969).

6. *Bailey v. Richardson*, 182 F.2d 46 (D.C. Cir. 1950), *affirmed* by an equally divided Court, 341 U.S. 918 (1951).

7. *United States ex rel. Knauff v. Shaughnessy*, 338 U.S. 537 (1950).

8. *Lynch v. United States*, 292 U.S. 571 (1934).

9. *Ex parte Robinson*, 86 U.S. 505 (1873).

10. *Bell v. Burson*, 402 U.S. 535 (1971).

11. 397 U.S. 254 (1970).

12. Williams, "Liberty and Property," pp. 4–5; Peter N. Simon, "Economic Analysis of Liberty and Property: A Critique," *U. Colo. L. Rev.* 57 (1986):747;

Thomas C. Grey, "Procedural Fairness and Substantive Rights," in *Due Process: Nomos XVII*, J. Roland Pennock and John W. Chapman, eds. (New York: New York Univ. Press, 1977), pp. 189–190. For an affirmative defense of one version, see Frank H. Easterbrook, "Substance and Due Process," *Sup. Ct. Rev.* (1982):85–125.

13. See Williams, "Liberty and Property," p. 6.

14. *Arnett v. Kennedy*, 416 U.S. 134, 152 (1974). See Karen H. Flax, "Liberty, Property, and the Burger Court: The Entitlement Doctrine in Transition," *Tul. L. Rev.* 60 (1986):918–919.

15. Jerry L. Mashaw, *Due Process in the Administrative State* (New Haven, Conn.: Yale Univ. Press, 1985), pp. 145–151; Jerry L. Mashaw, "Administrative Due Process: The Quest for a Dignitary Theory," *Boston Univ. L. Rev.* 61 (1981):888–891.

16. *Cleveland Bd. of Educ. v. Loudermill*, 105 S. Ct. 1487, 84 L. Ed. 2d 494, 502–503 (1985).

17. Easterbrook, "Substance and Due Process," pp. 85–125.

18. Williams, "Liberty and Property," pp. 30–40.

19. Grey, "Procedural Fairness," pp. 182–205.

20. Rodney A. Smolla, "The Reemergence of the Right-Privilege Distinction in Constitutional Law: The Price of Protesting Too Much," *Stanford L. Rev.* 35 (1982):69–120.

21. Timothy P. Terrell, "'Property,' 'Due Process,' and the Distinction Between Definition and Theory in Legal Analysis," *Georgia L. J.* 70 (1982):861–941; Timothy P. Terrell, "Liberty: The Concept and Its Constitutional Context," *Notre Dame J. of L., Ethics and Public Policy* 1 (1985):545–593.

22. Jerry L. Mashaw, *Due Process in the Administrative State* (New Haven, Conn.: Yale Univ. Press, 1985), especially ch. 5.

23. William Van Alstyne, "Cracks in 'The New Property': Adjudicative Due Process in the Administrative State," *Cornell L. Rev.* 62 (1977):445–493, especially pp. 487–490.

24. Kenneth Culp Davis, *Discretionary Justice* (Urbana: Univ. of Illinois Press, 1971), pp. 176–179, p. 231; see *Bell v. Burson*, 402 U.S. 535, 539 (1971); see also Monaghan, "Of 'Liberty' and 'Property,'" p. 433 (liberty includes decent respect for personal integrity).

25. Edward L. Rubin, "Due Process and the Administrative State," *Calif. L. Rev.* 72 (1984):1044–1179.

26. 408 U.S. 564 (1972).

27. 416 U.S. 134 (1974).

28. 426 U.S. 341 (1976).

29. 427 U.S. 215 (1976).

30. 103 S. Ct. 1741 (1983).

31. 424 U.S. 693 (1976).

32. 439 U.S. 438 (1979).

33. 444 U.S. 277 (1980).

34. 447 U.S. 773 (1980).

35. 452 U.S. 450 (1981).

36. *Goss v. Lopez*, 419 U.S. 565 (1975); *Ingraham v. Wright*, 430 U.S. 651 (1977).

37. Terrell, "'Property,' 'Due Process,'" pp. 918–935.

38. 444 U.S. 277 (1980).

39. 447 U.S. 773 (1980).

40. See Joel Feinberg, *Harm to Others* (New York: Oxford Univ. Press, 1984), pp. 33–34.
41. Henry J. Friendly, "Some Kind of Hearing," *Univ. Penn. L. Rev.* 123 (1975):1295–1296.
42. 408 U.S. 471 (1972); see also *Gagnon v. Scarpelli*, 411 U.S. 778 (1973) (revocation of probation).
43. Flax, "Liberty," p. 904.
44. 442 U.S. 1, 12 (1979).
45. 418 U.S. 539 (1974).
46. 427 U.S. 215 (1976).
47. 103 S. Ct. 1741 (1983).
48. 445 U.S. 480 (1980).
49. 459 U.S. 460 (1983).
50. *See Perry v. Sinderman*, 408 U.S. 593 (1972).
51. 408 U.S. 564 (1972).
52. 426 U.S. 341 (1976).
53. 416 U.S. 134 (1974).
54. A. M. Honore, "Ownership," in *Oxford Essays in Jurisprudence* (first series), A. G. Guest, ed. (Oxford: Clarendon Press, 1961), pp. 107–147; Terrell, "'Property,' 'Due Process,'" pp. 865–874; Monaghan, "Of 'Liberty' and 'Property,'" p. 438.
55. Terrell, "'Property,' 'Due Process,'" pp. 890–891.
56. Monaghan, "Of 'Liberty' and 'Property,'" p. 441.
57. See also Van Alstyne, "Cracks in 'The New Property,'" pp. 459, 467, 469.
58. *Cleveland Bd. Educ. v. Loudermill*, 84 L. Ed. 2d 494 (1985). One cannot avoid this effect by writing the condition as one for reinstatement of benefits by showing absence of C on appeal, for that merely shifts the time and burden of proof of C, not its logical necessity for termination.
59. 442 U.S. 1 (1979).
60. *Willner v. Committee on Character and Fitness*, 373 U.S. 96 (1963).
61. 42 U.S.C. sec. 423(d)(3) (1979).
62. *Mathews v. Eldridge*, 424 U.S. 319 (1976).
63. Terrell, "'Property,' 'Due Process,'" pp. 901–911; Williams, "Liberty and Property," pp. 22–24 ff.; Terrell, "Liberty," p. 579; T. M. Scanlon, "Due Process," in *Due Process: Nomos XVII*, J. Roland Pennock and John W. Chapman, eds. (New York: New York Univ. Press, 1977), pp. 111–112. It is not, as Terrell seems to argue, that government monopoly turns what is not property into property; rather, it changes the baseline from not having the income or license to having it and thus makes a deprivation possible. But see Simon, "Economic Analysis."
64. *Goss v. Lopez*, 419 U.S. 565 (1975).
65. Rubin, "Due Process," p. 1161.
66. *Ingraham v. Wright*, 430 U.S. 651 (1977).
67. See Mashaw, *Due Process in the Administrative State*, p. 155.
68. *Parratt v. Taylor*, 451 U.S. 527.
69. *Board of Regents v. Roth*, 408 U.S. 564 (1972).

SELECTED BIBLIOGRAPHY

Easterbrook, Frank H. 1982. "Substance and Due Process." *Sup. Ct. Rev.*, pp. 85–125.

Flax, Karen H. 1986. "Liberty, Property, and the Burger Court: The Entitlement Doctrine in Transition." *Tulane L. Rev.* 60:889–926.

Friendly, Henry J. 1975. "Some Kind of Hearing." *Univ. Penn. L. Rev.* 123:1267–1317.

Mashaw, Jerry L. 1985. *Due Process in the Administrative State.* New Haven: Yale Univ. Press.

Monaghan, Henry Paul. 1977. "Of 'Liberty' and 'Property.'" *Cornell L. Rev.* 62:405–444.

Pennock, J. Roland, and John W. Chapman, eds. 1977. *Due Process: Nomos XVII.* New York: New York Univ. Press.

Rubin, Edward L. 1984. "Due Process and the Administrative State." *Calif. L. Rev.* 72:1044–1179.

Smolla, Rodney A. 1982. "The Reemergence of the Right-Privilege Distinction in Constitutional Law: The Price of Protesting Too Much." *Stanford L. Rev.* 35:69–120.

Symposium. 1986. "Conference on Procedural Due Process: Liberty and Justice." *Univ. Florida L. Rev.* 39:217–581.

Terrell, Timothy P. 1982. "'Property,' 'Due Process,' and the Distinction Between Definition and Theory in Legal Analysis." *Geo. L. J.* 70:861–941.

———. 1985. "Liberty: The Concept and Its Constitutional Context." *Notre Dame J. of L., Ethics and Public Policy* 1:545–593.

Van Alstyne, William. 1977. "Cracks in 'The New Property': Adjudicative Due Process in the Administrative State." *Cornell L. Rev.* 62:445–493.

Williams, Stephen F. 1983. "Liberty and Property: The Problem of Government Benefits." *J. of Legal Stud.* 12:3–40.

TWELVE

The Exclusionary Rule as Constitutional Renewal: U.S. Integrity and Canadian Repute

CHRISTOPHER B. GRAY

> Where . . . a court concludes that evidence was obtained in a manner that infringed or denied any rights or freedoms guaranteed by this Charter, the evidence shall be excluded if it is established that, having regard to all the circumstances, the admission of it in the proceedings would bring the administration of justice into disrepute.[1]

To exclude evidence obtained in violation of constitutional rights, we must "capture the 'principle' underlying . . . a tortuous and essentially unprincipled life [that is, the history of exclusions] based upon a series of ad hoc determinations."[2] Although avoiding disrepute is more textually accessible to Canadians as their justification for excluding evidence than is maintaining integrity or fidelity to the Constitution, which was long the U.S. rationale, disrepute has had no more determinate an analysis than has integrity missed detractors. This chapter uses earlier U.S. statements on integrity to expand the undeveloped sense of "disrepute," and uses the earliest Canadian jurisprudence on that term in order to help reestablish the U.S. principles and rules.

Deterrence of police misconduct is an alternative rationale. But the unverifiability of negative propositions (if a person does A, B will not occur) is the bugbear to the deterrent argument here as elsewhere. This unverifiability is partly the reason for its failure in U.S. law and in turn the near obliteration of the U.S. exclusionary rule, as well as its dismissal from Canadian caselaw as any more than a minor factor among others, to be discussed later. Deterrence can be put to rest: The exclusionary rule has not been shown to deter, but deterrence is not its sole or best rationale; therefore, it need not be abandoned simply because deterrence fails.

Another red herring is that the public is in jeopardy because the exclusionary rule frees so many guilty and dangerous criminals. But researchers find that the rule is seldom invoked, that few guilty are freed when it is (because its conditions are found not to be present, or because the accused is convicted on other evidence), that these few are clustered in possessory crimes or regulatory offenses rather than in crimes of violence, and that most of those acquitted under it are nonrecidivist offenders.[3] So discussion of the rule cannot be derailed by a lusty disclaimer that, whatever its moral merits, the social contract cannot be honored if we retain it.

A final source of distraction is the claim, usually based on the preceding one, that the public will be disaffected by freeing criminals under the exclusionary rule. Again, when this has been tested instead of only suggested, it has not been found true. The public's support for law, for the exclusionary rule, and for the judicial system that uses it remains high, despite the disaffection of prosecutors and judges.[4]

We can return to integrity and repute as justifications for the exclusionary rule, without deterrence, intolerable costs, or reverse disrepute aborting them. Nor do the differences between our constitutions impede the comparison. The rule applies to both U.S. criminal jurisdictions and to the single Canadian public law, as well as to all of the legal rights under each constitution.

The argument for judicial integrity and the avoidance of disrepute takes its premise from the judges and commentators on the rule, but imposes the encompassing set of four claims that they each put forward only piecemeal or implicitly. (1) The courts, as a branch of *government*, cannot dissociate themselves from the other activities of government. (2) Once associated, the courts' particular roles as one branch of government also demand of them conduct befitting a government. This conduct is judicial *integrity*. (3) Failure to conduct themselves in this way will lead the courts not to be treated in accordance with their role in government. They will be brought into *disrepute*. (4) This attitude toward the courts will change the conduct of society at large; society will no longer act according to the rule of law. This changed conduct will alter the type of *polity* we have into an undesirable form; our political societies will cease to be democracies under the rule of law and enter anarchy or totalitarianism.

This argument is not circular. Its conclusion—that evidence obtained in violation of constitutional rights should be excluded—is not to be found solely in its premise that some modes of obtaining evidence are unconstitutional. For to that premise must be added the considerations of government and polity just outlined, as well as the normative characteristics of unconstitutionality as disreputable and as a loss of integrity. The premise itself, however, does identify some rights as constitutionally protected and some evidence-getting as violations of these, before ever introducing the question of their admissibility. Simply because our conclusion is that constitutionality and admissibility go together, does not mean that they come together; for arguments need to be traversed before we can see that they go together, particularly such arguments that dismiss the competing answers.

Nor should the relative simplicity of the remedy presented here make it suspect. Although others have encouraged exclusionary rules that make much of a complicated balancing, for example, their recommendations are examined and dismissed late in this study. And once they are gone, the absolutist character of the solution offered here becomes not only clear, but distinct as well.

GOVERNMENT

The judiciary shares two roles with other branches of government: (1) it is the moral individual writ large, and (2) it can act only through agents whom it employs. Although the former is one of the most frequently cited explanations, the latter has not been touched at all, even though both are from dissents in the same classic U.S. case. As payer, government is the principal for its agent.

> It is also desirable that the Government should not itself foster and pay for other crimes, when they are the means by which the evidence is to be obtained. If it pays its officers for having got evidence by crime I do not see why it may not as well pay them for getting it in the same way, and I can attach no importance to protestations of disapproval if it knowingly accepts and pays and announces that in the future it will pay for the fruits. We have to choose, and for my part I think it a less evil that some criminals should escape than that Government should play an ignoble part.
>
> For those who agree with me, no distinction can be taken between the Government as prosecutor and the Government as judge. If the existing code does not permit district attorneys to have a hand in such dirty business it does not permit the judge to allow such iniquities to succeed.[5]

Even though this argument suffices to pass on to government a moral responsibility for policing, it leaves untouched a cynical reliance upon information from vigilantes and their private investigators. To also exclude evidence obtained in violation of constitutional rights by these third parties, the second role must be invoked.

> Decency, security and liberty alike demand that government officials shall be subjected to the same rules of conduct that are commands for the ordinary citizen. In a government of laws, existence of the government will be imperilled if it fails to observe the law scrupulously. Our Government is the potent, the omnipresent teacher. For good or ill, it teaches the whole people by its example. Crime is contagious. If the Government becomes a lawbreaker, it breeds contempt for the law; it invites every man to become a law unto himself; it invites anarchy. To declare that in the administration of the criminal law the end justifies the means—to declare that the Government may commit crimes in order to secure the conviction of a private criminal—would bring terrible retribution. Against this pernicious doctrine this Court should resolutely set its face.[6]

The demand is that the court disassociate itself from illegal conduct, and that simple denunciation will not do this. Denunciation may seem to be enough, as in other instances where the court articulates its dislike for enforcement and hopes for reform in provisions that are harsh, outmoded, capricious. However, "when the legislature has failed to intervene, this expresses confidence in judicial ability to find a solution";[7] the same must be said of the executive's failure to intervene in administrative violations. Then, only one disassociation is possible: exclusion. Otherwise, it will appear to be "judicial condonation" if simply ignored or "excused with words of reprobation."[8]

INTEGRITY

In order to determine how the courts must respond to this inseparability from government, their more distinctive roles must be examined. *Judicial integrity* is the name attributed to fulfillment of these roles; but integrity has never been studied as a rubric in its own right apart from the several roles.

Institutional Roles

In general, the courts stand as a buffer between institutions of government and other participants in the social process, especially between the individual and the assembled power of the state visible in its executive branch. Public force can be exercised only in a manner judged proper by the courts. The unconstitutionally obtained evidence is proffered to justify the exercise of public force against the individual to be convicted. To the extent that the evidence is illegally obtained, the individual is not protected from unjustified force. To protect the individual requires that the illegal evidence not be used.

The counter to this, particularly as a deferential Canadian assertion, is that this wariness is itself a distrust, and is not needed in our era when our governments are humane, benevolent, virtuous, or at least are exercised only for the purpose of public well-being.[9] Again, the best replies are from the classic cases. "Experience should teach us to be most on our guard to protect liberty when the Government's purposes are beneficent. Men born to freedom are naturally alert to repel invasions of their liberty by evil-minded rulers. The greatest dangers to liberty lurk in insidious encroachment by men of zeal, well-meaning but without understanding."[10] And, when private papers are only judicially demanded rather than rifled,

> Though the proceeding in question is divested of many of the aggravating incidents of actual search and seizure, yet as before said, it contains their substance and essence, and effects their substantial purpose. It may be that it is the obnoxious thing in its mildest and least repulsive form; but illegal and unconstitutional practices get their first footing in that way, namely, by silent approaches and slight deviations from legal modes of

> procedure. . . . It is the duty of courts to be watchful for the constitutional rights of the citizens, and against any stealthy encroachment thereon. Their motto should be *obsta principiis.* We have no doubt that the legislative body is actuated by the same motives; but the vast accumulation of public business brought before it sometimes prevents it, on a first presentation, from noticing objections which become developed by time and the practical application of the objectionable law.[11]

In reply to the kindred objection, that such illegal action is executed only against public criminals, due process requires that the state not gain an advantage over an accused by its own wrongdoing. The judicial process is not an equal one: Although an accused may have rules of admissibility relaxed in his or her favor, the government cannot claim the same. Not only is the court "charged at all times with the support of the Constitution, and to which people of all conditions have the right to appeal for such fundamental rights,"[12] but it is particularly the most vulnerable, unpopular, and outcast whose protection contributes to the court's moral authority, by reason of its transcending conflicts and not legitimating popular malice. The pressures are greater to relax the protections over vicious offenders; but it is precisely this foreknowledge that imposes the loyalty to guarantees for all. Failing to do so, and victimizing the most vulnerable, would weaken belief in law's legitimacy among all, not just the vulnerable; this would lower the day-to-day legal standards of police work, and threaten the innocent, too.

The structure of the court is designed not only to protect individuals but to serve the public. It has its powers only as an agent of the public. But its agency is perverted when it permits illegality, because what is in the public interest is maintenance of the law. Although this might also have cut against permitting illegalities by a guilty accused who is released, it cuts instead against the use of illegally obtained evidence. This is because, although the court has in hand the power not to stand behind either offence, the protection of the individual under its first role specifies this second role. "Courts have a duty and a responsibility not only to acquit the innocent, but also to protect society itself, by ensuring that the detecting of crime and the prosecution of criminals is done in a manner and according to rules which society holds most dearly."[13]

Next, the common law role of a superior court includes a supervisory power over its own practice as well as that of inferior courts, that is, power to achieve constitutional values beyond the minimum requirements.[14] This is the reason why, within the general common law rule for admissibility of evidence, questions of evidence and its admissibility are primarily matters of common law for the court itself rather than for legislatures. Therefore, the court can arrange for the protection of the judicial system, not only by a stay of proceedings when its own practice is working injustice, but by exclusion of evidence when its own practice is infected by the injustice of others involved in obtaining the evidence. "The Court protects itself."

More than maintaining itself, the court is charged with maintaining the Constitution; it has a role of judicial review. This role is given in regard to all the actions of government, not just to the legislative acts upon which the role is exercised most often, but also to executive actions. As actions taken under a statute later voided or rendered inoperative for unconstitutionality will be open for remedy, so actions taken in violation of constitutional rights must have their outcomes open for reversal, too.

Another manner in which the common law system protects the individual is by establishing an adversarial process before the criminal courts, rather than an inquisitorial one. The truth-telling process is one that the court must have performed for it; the state must shoulder the whole burden of proof for its accusations, which means that the accused is presumed innocent until proven guilty.

This burden lies on the state not because of the unschooled common law juror's inability to sift evidential probabilities; rather, it is again the difference in the parties' powers that explains why, in order to maintain a "fair state–individual balance," government must take the whole burden. It must produce the evidence by its own independent labors, rather than compelling it from the accused by means that violate the citizen's dignity and integrity. Beside the consequentialist data to show that relying on compelled evidence results in more of the guilty being freed, quite apart from any exclusionary rule, this adversarial protection is "philosophically and morally . . . to lay out a standard for the relationship of the state vis-à-vis the individual, . . . not just the criminal in society, but . . . the state and the individual in the large sense."[15]

In sum, the court does not directly seek truth but seeks justice in which truth has some role. If it is unjust to admit illegally obtained evidence, as the reasons of law and equity shall next suggest, then the court may not look behind proof that it may not scrutinize in order to determine what the truth is. The truth may not be proven.

Rules of Law

The most pervasive feature of the courts' distinctive roles in government is to administer the rule of law, both over themselves and other branches. Even without its modern expanded meaning, the Diceyan sense that all citizens great and small have recourse before the same courts under the same rules has many dimensions. Operating under this rule of law, the courts must ensure that, while citizens as natural persons have no prohibitions on their conduct but those explicitly laid down, the government as artificial person has no capabilities nor rights for acting but those explicitly laid down. Because the courts both administer the rule of law and are subject to it, as are other state agents, their duty to do justice is one with their duty to use no injustice from other agents of government. They cannot administer justice and admit evidence obtained while investigators violate constitutional rights.

That the rule of law imposes limits upon government is a different way of saying that government has no capabilities but those given to it. The same conclusion can be drawn by saying that courts cannot take notice of results from actions that government is incapable of performing legitimately, or is limited from doing. To obtain evidence illegally is not a government power; it must be treated as something that cannot be done; it must be excluded.

Again a way to express the rule of law is to speak in terms of fairness. Substantive fairness involves treating likes alike, having the same demands on all the equal parties. The state prosecutes the criminal for acting unjustly in violating the criminal law; the state claims that it is true that an individual has done this, as it would be unjust to punish someone of whom it were not true that he or she had done it, someone innocent. But the state can say this is true only because it has violated the constitutional law. The state is imposing different demands upon itself than upon the accused. This is a source of unfairness that runs contrary to the rule of law.

Another version is the rule of law as procedural fairness. The state cannot impose demands upon its own way of achieving its ends different from those it imposes upon citizens. It forbids citizens to engage in criminal acts as means to various ends—for example, achieving such satisfactions as leisure by embezzlement, as justice by revenge. If the state acknowledges the government's attainment of its own end—achieving justice through truths proven with illegal acts—then the state is acknowledging that this means was successful in accomplishing the legal purpose, and is thereby legitimating the means. "Yet where constitutional guarantees are concerned, the more pertinent consideration is whether those guarantees, as fundamentals of the particular society, should be at the mercy of law enforcement officers and a blind eye turned to their invasion because it is more important to secure a conviction. The contention that it is the duty of the courts to get at the truth has in it too much of the philosophy of the end justifying the means."[16] To reduce the fairness of trials from a strict reliance on procedure to a vague doctrine of fairness, would permit such an injection of individual values that fairness would be largely dissipated.

Rules of Equity

The rule of law is perhaps best served not only through the rules ensuring fair trials but through rules of equity. Of these, the first is the rule of clean hands—that a petitioner not have been involved in creating the wrong whose remedy he or she is seeking. Applying the following version of it as its author intended,

> The door of a court is not barred because the plaintiff has committed a crime. The confirmed criminal is as much entitled to redress as his most virtuous fellow citizen; no record of crime, however long, makes one an

> outlaw. The court's aid is denied only when he who seeks it [the prosecutor] has violated the law [to get evidence of crime] in connection with the very transaction [obtaining evidence]. It is denied in order to maintain respect for law, in order to promote confidence in the administration of justice; in order to preserve the judicial process from contamination. The rule is one, not of action, but of inaction. It is sometimes spoken of as a rule of substantive law. But it extends to matters of procedure as well. A defence may be waived. It is waived when it is not pleaded. But the objection that the plaintiff comes with unclean hands will be taken by the court itself. It will be taken despite the wish to the contrary of all the parties to the litigation. The court protects itself.[17]

The application of clean hands to government is not straightforward: The government is seeking to remedy a wrong (the accused's lawbreaking) by its own wrong (the investigator's lawbreaking)—a different wrong—and so is deprived of help. But the rule's application to the accused is different; the very nature of the criminal law is that not even the criminal is by his or her crime disentitled to protections set up precisely for the benefit of the accused, even those charged with the most heinous offences. "Law triumphs when the natural impulse aroused by a shocking crime yields to the safeguards which our civilization has evolved for an administration of justice at once rational and effective."[18]

A further justification of the exclusionary rule is analogous to the equitable remedy of restitution. The government is considered as having a "benefit" in its acquisition of evidence because it has a political interest in the prosecution of crime, and its personnel have an occupational interest in its success. But because the benefit is acquired with a violation of constitutional rights, the gain is "ill-gotten" and undeserved. No return of this ill-got gain is possible—the analogy fails here. But, then, restitution regards the exploiter as much as it does his or her victim; nevertheless, a principle of restitution would at least require that the ill-gotten gain not be used. Because government is permitted in no way to profit from its illegal activities, the evidence must not only not be used by the courts, but not be used at all in acquiring other admissible evidence. Government must not be permitted to profit from its own wrong.

Another equitable principle—that for any right there must be a remedy—also comes into play. If not a remedy in the sense of an ill-got gain restored, then at least it is the most basic remedy of a restored enjoyment of that right. The use of illegally obtained evidence announces that the right stands only until it is in the interest of government to violate it. Because the focus of these particular rights is precisely to set up a limit to governmental interests, that announcement renders the right illusory, as without a remedy, an "unenforced honor code." The remedy is "logically and constitutionally necessary," an "essential part," an "essential ingredient" of the right.[19]

As well as abusing equity, to make a right illusory that is found in the Constitution also violates the court's principal canon of interpretation—that some meaning must be given to the text. The court owes enough respect for the legislative word not to make it absurd. Although the absurdity in making a right illusory does not go so far as to make it contradictory, it is well beyond making its results undesirable. Without the exclusion, the right "is of no value and . . . might as well be stricken from the Constitution."[20]

DISREPUTE

The court's failure to fulfill these particular roles and maintain its integrity will, in view of its association with the government, lead to its disrepute. As used in cases and commentaries, the term *disrepute* can be brought to greater objectivity by identifying the sort of event it is and the community in whose eyes it occurs. This identification will eliminate the relevance of any "reverse disrepute" to the exclusionary rule, and in turn indicate just what might be the proper sense of the "balancing" often invoked in the caselaw.

Tests: Constitutional Shock

Defining disrepute is not easy in a diversified culture; and even if guidelines were clear, they would be interpreted differently from different cultural viewpoints. In determining what it means, two extremes are available, of which the second is chosen, rather than a midground. One is providing no test at all but simply determining from the facts and their own merits that disrepute is present; this will involve a balancing of "all circumstances," and so seems to have a marked affinity for the Canadian solution. But as it stands, this is the same as saying, you'll recognize it when you see it; it appeals to an intuition that is unsharable and unchallengeable.

The other extreme is the simple test of constitutional violation—that constitutional violation is equivalent to disrepute.[21] This extreme seems again a refusal to define, again an elimination of the term *disrepute* entirely; but it may be filled in so that one can see what there is about a constitutional violation, in any given complex of circumstances, that brings disrepute to the administration of justice. It is also the *terminus ad quem* of the attempts at definition to follow.

A slightly more defined test is to relate disrepute to an emotional complex—the famous "shock test" of U.S. law that has currency as well in Canadian law.[22] The violation of constitutional rights and admission of its evidence must offend, shock, disturb, appall. It must raise a measure of concern, even grave concern. There is an emotive causality: The rights are firmly rooted, their violation causes grave concern; the admission of this evidence also causes grave concern, and disrepute results. Shock must be more than only unfortunate, distasteful, inappropriate, gossamer, not fastidious squeamishness or private sentimentality.[23]

Beside sheer affectivity, the event itself must be offensive, odious. Although no greater specificity is usually attributed to the person whose emotions these are, at times the shock is identified as pertaining to that person's instincts, sensibilities, or conscience; the conscience is further identified as one holding principles or a concept of fairness.[24]

This latter development makes it possible to move from disrepute, which is an emotive state, to disrepute that is not emotion but which is related to emotions. It is not just any shock but only such shock as to bring disrepute. Shock is enough for disrepute, but disrepute may be present even without shock. Shock is a more demanding test than disrepute, for the public may be unaware of actual police powers, as under writs of assistance in Canada. On the other hand, the violation may shock, but the admission of evidence not bring disrepute. Shock may simply show the exceptional nature of those violations that bring the disrepute.[25]

Disrepute is somewhat better defined when it is treated as a cognitive state rather than an emotive state. The admission would "appear" scandalous to the public, appear in their minds as an abuse. Admission would be "seen" to tolerate the violation, as tacit approval, against the spirit and intent of the Charter, as participating in and condoning the violation. This tacit approval would be to send the wrong "message"—that the end justifies the means. It would shatter public confidence in the Charter and the ability of the courts, making the charter be seen as a mockery, a hollow incantation, stripped of meaning. This degradation exacts a feeling—that the administration of justice has been brought into disrepute.[26] Disrepute has become something that is felt, not only something-felt.

What is felt may be the moral resultant: a brutalizing of society, a tainted or contaminated evidence, a loss of the humane and honorable. What is breached is the fabric of society, society's notions of justice, what is just and appropriate in the circumstances, social values, and—"less restrictive than shock"—the public interest in integrity.[27] We have come full circle to suggest the interdefinition this study assumed. The violation of constitutional rights may itself be the immoral resultant, certainly once the violations have been judicially noted, or at least rarely not itself be immoral.[28] Every criminal case is serious by its very nature; that no additional harms to the accused flow from the violation of his or her rights in getting evidence is no argument for admitting the evidence.

Although "a reasonable observer could seldom conclude on the basis of one violation of rights that an entire system was corrupt or otherwise faulty,"[29] shock may arise from a concatenation of otherwise unobjectionably missed niceties, which may become not one failure but a series, an accepted part of law enforcement, a disregard of policy, an invited disregard. Admitting each failure allows similar practices to continue, "sanctions" similar ones as normal, unexceptional, repeated practice.[30]

Excluding the failures is seen less as a matter of deterrence, however, than of denunciation versus approval.

Tests: Constitutional Community

A parallel list confirming this objective definition of disrepute as constitutional violation is found in the catalog of judicial comments on the community in whose estimate that disrepute or shock is found. Initially, the community is just the community at large—most citizens, the picture viewed by society, any community in this land. This definition responds to the need for ensuring that the community is the relevant one (Canadian, lay, possibly national instead of local, traditional instead of momentary; concerned with the generalized issue rather than the particularities of the case)[31] as has often been done, for example, in determining the relevant community for obscenity law. This definition provides an objective test, not the subjective one of what a judge thinks.

But the test has its own limits of applicability. If a poll is not the determinant of who constitutes the community, and few do envisage this, then the average member of the public, the ordinary person, the ordinary citizen confronted with unacceptable practices, must mean more than just anyone.

It may be possible to determine who "the average member" is with greater objectivity, in the sense of what the reaction of the public is, rather than what the judge may think; but the effort would require an act of faith about existing communities, as filled with average citizens who are concerned about the repute of the administration of justice, interested in justice and the protection of Charter rights. Perhaps a law-abiding majority is enough.

The direction of objectivity, however, seems to pursue principle rather than mere fact. The first glimpse of this principle is that the lay community does include the legally informed person—the judge, lawyer, politician, law teacher, policeman, civil liberties activist. The relevant community is "ni le plus libertin ni le plus pudibond," "ni anarchiste impénitent ni justiciaire intransigeant," neither idealists nor pragmatists.[32] It is the community as a whole or at large, not the opinion of anyone, no matter how well-informed, knowledgeable, or expert, as perceived by a judge. This principle is not solely the layperson's test of what constitutes law as reason—surely not when the examples of lay opinion include Plato, Aristotle, and Aquinas![33]

This development brings clarity to the passages that do objectify the community, as right-thinking members of the community, the sensibilities of reasonable persons, the practical and fair-minded members of the community at large, the reasonable person or citizen, and thus objectifies the community's holding the courts in disrepute and the content of integrity. The insights must be "developed" by concerned and thinking citizens. These citizens are those who accept the principles of justice; those who think that when powers are flagrantly and unnecessarily abused, the court should remedy those actions.[34] Although a paucity of consciousness of the rights of citizens may exist among the majority, citizens' rights will be protected anyway.[35]

Disrepute is not a matter of fact, but a question of law in most if not every case. Therefore disrepute can be determined by the court without evidence of actual or even likely effect on anyone or on the administration of justice, just as any other question of evidence. Polls could never manage to include "all the circumstances"; and if they could, it would be an unjust burden of proof upon ordinary litigants.[36]

Disrepute, then, need not be felt by anyone in fact; loss of integrity need not be judged by anyone to have occurred. But if it is right to have felt it, correct to have judged it, then the disrepute and loss of integrity will have occurred. And how does one know what is right and correct to have felt? Short of the directive hand (and we are short of that as this discussion of both constitutional systems remains in the context of democratic societies), we know what is right by what the people have created—their law—by that law that simultaneously creates the people—their constitution. What it is disreputable to do, is to violate constitutional rights; what it is disreputable to admit, is evidence obtained by violation of constitutional rights.

Reverse Disrepute

This conclusion is what makes an irrelevancy of reverse disrepute because the disrepute taken at admitting ill-got evidence is no one's in particular. Reference to disrepute is a morally based metaphor, a personification of what ought to be felt, so that anyone's sharing it is beside the point. For the same reason, someone's sharing of shock at the *exclusion* of evidence, or balancing it against the shock at the admission of evidence, is equally beside the point.

Equally irrelevant is the reverse ploy, to say that disrepute need not be a concern because the reputation of law is so high, that almost any violation can be tolerated without disrepute. That in Canada the police do try to obey the law, that there was no police state before the Charter, that there is no sudden transformation into outrageous behavior and a wilting reputation of the law, no "Poland 1983,"[37] does not allow one to conclude that any violation can be tolerated and that compliance is to be presumed. Once again, the removal of head-counting as the sense of disrepute removes this, too. No room, in turn, remains for the empathetic argument of how-would-you-feel-if, that is, using "the conscience of the community . . . where the crime was committed"; no more than remains for the counterbias of seeking empathy with the parents of the accused, for example, and their urgency to have the evidence excluded.[38]

Balancing: Factors

The core of reverse disrepute, which many suppose to be relevant, is a balancing procedure because proportionality is taken to be a major element in the popular idea of justice. Proportionality in this context is taken to mean that, in determining whether to exclude for disrepute, one consideration among "all the circumstances" is balanced against another. These factors make up a grid for determining whether admitting the way of getting evidence will cause disrepute.

The more muscular use of these factors is to say that their complex is equivalent to disrepute or repute. Either way, however, one must know why each particular factor is relevant to disrepute as defined above, and what one is balancing them toward.

The list of factors, although not intended to be exhaustive, is of judicial and not statutory origin. The ones most heavily used are claimed to be (1) the deliberateness of the violation, (2) its seriousness as compared with that of the accusation, and (3) the deterrence-value for the police.[39] In fact, one hardly ever sees the last in the Canadian cases, but sees instead the disclaimer that this factor should figure at all in the proportionality.

The deliberateness is also problematic: Although malice would almost predetermine exclusion, trickery and deviousness are not excluded but in fact praised. Only if these are flagrant or gross rather than trivial or technical would they suffice to exclude evidence. But the flagrancy and grossness, if judged by anything other than the fact itself of constitutional violation, turn us back toward shock. And the triviality and technicality, as well as a wait-and-see policy as to previously unadjudicated technicalities, run counter to whatever policy led to the insertion of those technicalities into the law. Finally, admitting evidence gained by (4) carelessness or ignorance both put a premium on bad training, and opens to all the other negative policy implications associated with the new U.S. "good faith" exception.

The seriousness of the accusation has the same problem as (5) the urgency for preserving the evidence and (6) the importance of this evidence to the prosecution's case. The problem is that it is difficult to set up each of these factors in any other way than as the end justifying the means.[40] The only different reading suggested for them is that they refer to the attitude of the public toward these factors; but the circularity is apparent, in using that as a criterion for factors that are themselves the determinants used in weighing disrepute, still taken as shock.

The seriousness of the violation of rights, understood as the extent of the offence to human dignity and social values, and other elements, such as (7) whether the admission would be unfair to the accused and (8) the harm caused to the accused and to other third parties, are the only other factors admissible into a balance of proportionality. Each of these seems to require the weighing of offence against offence, harm against harm, even before balancing them against previous factors. But no such double jeopardy in the balancing is needed. For the weighing of the seriousness in the offence has already been carried out by insertion of the offended rights as constitutional ones; no more serious violation of law than this is possible. Rather than it being disreputable not to weigh them, it would then be disreputable to balance them against anything else.

Balancing: Normative Counters

Another suggested way of carrying out the balance of proportionality in determining disrepute is to provide not merely a factual characterization to the quanta for balancing, one of which may predominate in particular circumstances, but rather a moral characterization in terms of such deontic types as needs, rights, interests, policies, and values. Thus, the *need* for fair and effective law enforcement can be weighed against the *right* of citizens to be reasonably free from illegal and unreasonable police conduct; or the interests of society, against the competing interests of the individual; or the social need that crime be repressed, against the social need that laws not be flaunted; or the interest of the state to secure evidence, against the interest of the citizen in protection from illegal invasion of his or her liberties. One can balance the interests of society *and* of the individual on the one hand, against the regard in which the search for truth is held, on the other. The rights of society and the undoubted rights of the accused balance; but if violations are gossamer, the first predominate; if substantial, the second. Neither can be insisted upon absolutely, so as to make the other disappear.[41]

The weighting, even if a compromise, need not be at a midpoint. The very reason for setting up the proportionality now as a balance among moral qualifiers is because the balance is already tilted, requiring more of one to outweigh the other. In the view of those who see the scales weighted toward admissibility, truth outweighs the rights of the accused and their violations and is outweighed only by strong reasons of public policy; public safety as protection of the public right outweighs those who endanger it because the individual right is not meant for wrongdoers; public benefits and interest outweigh the dismal social costs of an illusory remedy. Because "little equity" would lie in the opposite balance, the error by the officer is more tolerable than a windfall for the guilty party.[42] To this catalog of judicial weightings, one can add the search for equilibrium *within* the public interest: between the public interest in evidence, in upholding law and in protecting innocent persons. There are two paramount interests: the right to convict those who commit crimes, and the right of the accused not to be convicted other than by due process of law. In a minor case, disrepute follows from admitting into evidence any violations of the great and fundamental right of the individual to privacy, but in a serious case the interests of society would not bring disrepute from admitting violations.[43]

Despite the twistings in this sampler of deontic weighting, its means-end morality has been remarked upon earlier. Of the previous examples, none succeed in replacing what the given society has already clearly done by constitutionalizing its rights, as in the preceding section, by the idiosyncratic estimates of what is the more important in society.

Balancing: Values

Besides community values and the protection of society, among all the circumstances that require balancing are the very values infringed by constitutional violations. These have variable weight among themselves, say the cases. Charter rights to security from search and seizure on persons themselves are the more serious, fundamental, and important, because these rights are cherished and traditional. So also are the Charter rights to security of the home from search and seizure, which, although less important than the person, are more so than that of one's car, for example, however "illogical" the distinction may be. The social values in sanctity and privacy of the home warrant more scrupulous and critical care by the court, as rights of a more fundamental and cherished importance, than do such lesser ones as the right to information of the charge without delay. Such weighting of Charter rights by a "purposive approach," by determining what they are meant to do, has recently become popular.[44]

But while rights to security from search and seizure would succumb to the value of truth-getting, the right to counsel does not. *Prima facie,* disrepute would accompany the admission of evidence obtained by its violation. Similarly, the right to be informed of thc right to counsel outweighs community values; this is so because this right has been newly inserted into the Charter. At least here, the rights of the accused have primacy over the Crown's right to use an evidentiary presumption; and perhaps they always do.[45]

These two sets of arguments—that rights are weightier if traditional (and so not do not need to be written) and that rights are weightier if newly written (thereby evidencing a vigorous public intent)—can be harmonized. Their incorporation into a constitutional charter in Canada, or their derivation from a constitutional bill in the United States, is the sign if not the source of their overriding importance. The source of the importance may be the timeless tradition or the emergent insight; but its overriding importance from either source is strongly presumed from its presence in the respective constitutions. Moral qualia need not be weighed, any more than factual circumstances, for the single factor of constitutional violation is made the determining moral consideration.

That is, beyond the alternatives of all rights being equal—and so equally negotiable or equally absolute—is this other alternative: that constitutional rights are absolute, and not to be weighed or balanced.

> We are not unmindful that hypothetical situations can be conjured up, shading imperceptibly from the circumstances of this case and by gradations producing practical differences despite seemingly logical extensions. But

> the Constitution is intended to preserve practical and substantial rights, not to maintain theories.[46]
>
> Mais je ne crois pas que le citoyen moyen serait prêt à admettre qu'il y a de grands et de petits droits pouvant faire l'objet de grands ou de petits violations. Je ne suis pas disposé à reduire la Charte à la dimension d'un paillason sur lequel il serait defendu de poser le pied mais qu'on pourrait salir impuniment à la condition de n'y faire que de petites taches.[47] [I do not think the ordinary citizen would readily agree there are little rights and big rights, that make for little violations and big ones. I have no inclination to make the Charter into a mere doormat, that you are forbidden to tread upon, but that you can soil as long as you only make little spots.]

The "rational perception," balancing constitutional violation against social utility, as though the official violator's wrong could somehow be recycled into a public benefit, is the perverted version of natural law seeing any present markets as the best of all possible markets, or as manipulable as any other, which Marx dubbed "horsepiss."[48]

POLITY

If the attitude of disrepute is not only a psychological event or the flotsam of public opinion, but also a moral demand that inspires action, then the citizens' conduct and the shape of their actions together—the state—cannot be unaffected. The demand for "principles which will command the respect and hence the support of the public for the system of criminal justice" without which "the system cannot survive"[49] has the advantage over a purely empirical verification, in that jurists are able to explain a "too lenient" image and thus recover lost support, but cannot explain away an "unjust" image. This set of circumstances is fortunate, because this conclusion about polity is only mildly verifiable by observation and testing. Even such an example as the following formulation of a hypothesis requires that the researcher first identify illegalities, and then preserve and manipulate them: *"Judicial acceptance of deception in the investigative process enhances moral acceptance of deception by detectives in the interrogatory and testimonial stages of criminal investigation, and this increases the probability of its occurrence."*[50] Evidence is available for some legal domains, such as taxation law; its self-assessment system depends on the public's belief that all are doing their fair share. Elsewhere, something more in the line of historical evidence is all that may be available. "Any student of modern history knows well the lesson that totalitarian power over the citizenry has only been accomplished in countries where the State has been able to persuade its judges to turn a blind eye to the erosion of the rights of the individual in the name of the alleged welfare of the society."[51]

Besides the contrary historical postulate, that "it is a truism of political philosophy rooted in history that societies perish from excess of their basic principles,"[52] the counterargument could be made that the action to which citizens may be moved is reform of the legal institution rather than its marginalization. However, the caselaw suggests confirmation of the hoary principle that one cannot be a good (public) person in a polity that is (perceived to be) bad. For example, what begins as a suggestion that the admission of ill-got evidence "discredits and thereby brutalizes the temper of a society" develops into its own evidence: The brutal search accorded the suspected dealer in a bar leaves others in the bar "apparently unconcerned over it."[53]

DIFFICULTIES

The bite of this advocacy for an absolute exclusionary rule, whether it is so called in both Canada and the United States, may be softened by bringing out further the implications for polity.

Public-Private Classification

There is no set-off between the private individual's interest, need, right, or value on the exclusionary side, and the public's collective claim on the inclusionary side. There is a public interest in each, as there is a private; and when legitimated, both a collective and an individual right in each. The fallacy is to take a classification as either public or private to settle the question without further examination.

An exemplary exercise in penetrating this fallacy details how the cynical emasculation of the U.S. exclusionary rule has either followed from or used as its tool such a classificatory gambit. Constitutional rights to privacy are set out as no more than an exclusively private right, so that the standing to seek exclusion of evidence for their violation is unavailable to any but the most narrowly defined group. At the same time, the remedy for such violations is classified as exclusively a collective remedy, namely deterrence, so that no remedy by exclusion can be granted where deterrence is unlikely, which is nearly everywhere, as previously described.

Doernberg suggested relaxing the standing rules, for that would supply a collective dimension to the right; this dimension fits the collective dimension of the remedy identified in the preceding paragraph.[54] To his solution, the present study can be read as a counterpart solution. As far as our U.S. business is concerned, this study seeks to re-engender the individual dimension of the remedy and accommodate the individual dimension of the right by reviving judicial integrity as the avoidance of disrepute, through the protection of individual constitutional rights.

Legal-Constitutional Rights

If it is the violation of rights in acquiring evidence that brings disrepute or loses integrity, why isn't this true of all illegally obtained evidence, rather than only of evidence obtained in violation of constitutional rights?

Why isn't evidence excludable when obtained in violation also of rights under law without constitutional entrenchment?

A ready answer lies on the U.S. side, in that although violations of police disciplinary codes or ordinary criminal statutes may not frankly violate concrete protections of the first ten amendments, they do violate the due process provisions of the Fifth or Fourteenth. This violation permits exclusion even for ordinary illegalities as constitutional violations at the time of judicial hearing even if not at the time of their initial commission.

But for both constitutional cultures a more global answer is possible. If the only reason why disrepute is "objective"—that is, grounded in sheer violation rather than in the public's grief—is because constitutional protection enhances a right's moral stature, then disrepute in this strong sense would not follow from violations of extraconstitutional legalities, at least not by definition, even if the public is mightily aggrieved. That, however, may be yet a further and different reason for the exclusion of such illegalities.

Subsection 24(2)

One problem is peculiarly Canadian, because it arises on the words of the Subsection. As the price for an explicit exclusionary rule, one should expect to have to shoulder some problems. The Subsection limits the exclusions to those that violate constitutional rights, even though there are other rights that Canadians hold. But this pool of rights appears to need more than its violation in order for exclusion to ensue. For evidence from constitutional violations is excluded only upon a condition being fulfilled, namely, if admitting it brings disrepute, all things considered. This conditional exclusion seems to imply that there are some violations that do not meet that condition; or, more pointedly, that disrepute depends not only on the fact of constitutional violation, but on *ceteris paribus*. If not, what are the conditional words for? They must be given some sense, some work to do, not just to say that violations are excluded *if* they are violations.

If only some violations bring disrepute, how can we say that all do? One would not want to escape by distinguishing the administration of justice from police behavior, nor by distinguishing the disrepute for violation from the disrepute for admission, nor certainly by distinguishing circumstances in which constitutional violations bring disrepute from circumstances in which they do not. All of these ploys run counter to the argument of this chapter.

As a first reply, the legal rights are not the only constitutional rights. There are also fundamental freedoms, democratic rights, mobility rights, official language rights, minority language educational rights, multicultural and aboriginal rights. But not all of these are guaranteed the same unexceptionality of protection, for a legislature may declare that its enactments operate notwithstanding the constitutional protections for some of these rights. Those rights that cannot be so overridden, however, include the fundamental freedoms, legal rights, and equality rights, implying that these rights take a higher and more demanding priority.[55]

This prioritization is made by the Canadian constitution itself. So it can answer which constitutional rights there may be whose violation when admitted into evidence would not be disreputable. Thus, the problematic Subsection has sense and does not foreclose the solution recommended here; for the prioritization has the same source as the disrepute, namely, the constitutional provision itself. It also leaves the present solution fully applicable to the legal rights, which have been assumed to be the main matters of concern throughout.

The alternative response is that judicial integrity demands the solution put forward here.[56] It has been evidenced that the legal ethos of both constitutional systems requires on its best interpretation, albeit of many dissents and dicta, that evidence obtained in a manner that violates constitutional rights be excluded. Even if the statute is discordant with that, and the preceding paragraph has shown that this discordance need not be affirmed, then it is the constitutional act that is disreputable and in need of amendment. Blame not the exclusionary rule, but the amendment, says one who is no friend of the rule.[57] It is "not alone on syllogism, metaphysics, or some ill-defined notions of natural justice," not "mere logical symmetry and abstract reasoning," nor "nice ethical conduct" that alone conclude the issue, but the best interpretation of the resources in our particular legal systems. "The sense of decency and fairness of English-speaking peoples"[58] in their law has become morally relevant, fortifying and specifying the norms in the moral world at large.[59]

NOTES

1. Constitution Act, 1982, Canada, s.24(2).
2. J. R. Weisberger, "The Exclusionary Rule: Nine Authors in Search of a Principle," 34 *So. Carolina L. Rev.* 253 at 269 (1982).
3. Thomas Y. Davies, "A Hard Look at What We Know (and Still Need to Learn) About the 'Costs' of the Exclusionary Rule: the N.I.J. [National Institute of Justice] Study and Other Studies of 'Lost' Arrests," *American Bar Found. Res. J.* 610 (1983); Peter Nardulli, *The Societal Cost of the Exclusionary Rule; an Empirical Assessment, ib.* 585.
4. Dale Gibson and Janet K. Baldwin, eds., *Law in a Cynical Society?* (Calgary: Carswell, 1985), first several studies; Liva Baker, *Miranda: Crime, Law and Politics* (New York: Athenaeum Press, 1983), *passim.*
5. *Olmstead v. U.S.*, 277 U.S. 438 at 470 (1927), per Justice Holmes, dissenting.
6. *Olmstead* at 485 per Justice Brandeis, dissenting.
7. Bernard Downey, "Judicial Discretion and the Fruit of the Poisoned Tree," 8 *Hong Kong L. J.* 43 at 52 (1978).
8. *Hogan v. The Queen,* 18 C.C.C. (2d) 65 at 81 (S.C.C.) (1975).
9. Baker, p. 305, citing Burger and Blackmun cases to this effect.

10. *Olmstead* at 479 per Brandeis.

11. *Boyd v. U.S.*, 116 U.S. 616 at 635 (1886), per Justice Bradley.

12. *Silverthorne Lumber Co. v. U.S.*, 251 U.S. 385 (1920), quoted in Donald L. Doernberg, "The 'Right of the People': Reconciling Collective and Individual Interest Under the Fourth Amendment," 58 *N.Y.U. L. Rev.* 259 at 275 (1983).

13. *R. v. Tyrell*, Ont. Pr. Ct. at 7 (November 17, 1982).

14. Doernberg, p. 291.

15. Justice Fortas, to counsel in *Miranda v. Arizona*, 384 U.S. 436 (1966), in Baker, p. 143.

16. *Hogan v. The Queen*, 26 C.R.N.S. 207 at 224 (1975), per Justice Laskin, dissenting.

17. *Olmstead*, at 484, per Brandeis, dissenting.

18. *R. v. Samson (no. 7)*, 37 O.R. (2d) 237 at 240 (1982), per Borins, Pr. Ct. J.; rev. 44 O.R. (2d) 205, 9 C.C.C. (3d) 194 (1982) (Ont. C.A.).

19. *U.S. v. Leon*, 104 S. Ct. 3412 (1984), per Justice Stevens, dissenting; *Mapp v. Ohio*, 367 U.S. 643 (1961), quoted in Doernberg, p. 279, although it is applied there only to the deterrent remedy.

20. *Mapp*, quoting *Weeks v. U.S.*, 232 U.S. 383 (1914), in William R. Baldiga, "Excluding Evidence to Protect Rights; *Principles Underlying the Exclusionary Rule in England and the U.S.*" 6 Boston College Int. and Comp. L. Rev. 133 at 166 (1983).

21. *R. v. Simmons*, 11 C.C.C. (3d) 193 at 229 (1984), per Justice Tarnopolsky, dissenting (Ont. C.A.).

22. *Mapp* at 277, quoting test's origin in *Burdeau v. McDowell* 256 U.S. 465 (1921), per Justices Holmes and Brandeis, dissenting; *Rothman v. The Queen* 25 C.R. (3d) 97 at 153 (1981), per Justice Lamer.

23. *R. v. Hartley*, B.C. Co. Ct. at 22 (October 27, 1983); *R. v. MacIntyre, Stoyles and Lamb*, 69 C.C.C. (2d) 162 at 167 (1982); *Rochin v. California*, 342 U.S. 165 at 172 (1952).

24. *Rochin* at 172; *R. v. Sozg*, 16 M.V.R. 59 (B.C.S.C.) (1982), at 62.

25. *R. v. Chapin*, 7 C.C.C. (3d) 538 at 542 (1983); *R. v. Collins*, 3 C.R.R. 79 at 82 (1982), per Justice Wong (B.C. Co. Ct.); rev. (1983), 5 C.C.C. (3d) 141 (B.C.C.A.); *R. v. Stevens*, 35 C.R. (3d) 1 at 29 (N.S.C.A.) (1983); *R. v. Simmons*, 11 C.C.C. (3d) 193 at 218 (Ont. C.A.) (1984); *R. v. Duguay, Murphy and Sevigny*, 50 O.R. (2d) 375 at 393 (Ont. C.A.) (1985); *R. v. Therens*, 59 N.R. 122 at 140 (S.C.C.) (1984).

26. *R. v. Dyment*, 9 D.L.R. (4th) 614 at 620 (P.E.I.S.C.) [1984]; *R. v. Unrau*, 24 Man. R. (2d) 5 at 8 (Man. Co. Ct.) (1983); *R. v. Cohen*, 33 C.R. (3d) 151 at 190 (B.C.C.A.) (1983), *R. v. Charlton*, 21 M.V.R. 107 at 124 (1983), per Justice Anderson, dissenting (B.C. Pr. Ct.); *Therens* at 125, per Justice Estey.

27. *Cohen* at 189–190; *Duguay* at 391; *R. v. Lerke*, 41 C.R. (3d) 173 at 180 (Alta Q.B.) (1984); *Rothman* 59 C.C.C. (2d) 30 at 49 (1981), per Justices Estey and Laskin, dissenting; *Simmons* at 218.

28. *Therens* at 141, per Estey; Chief Justice Dickson at 141, Justice Lamer dissenting at 142; and Justice LeDain, dissenting at 140 as only *prima facie* so; *Simmons* per Justice Tarnopolsky dissenting at 229; *R. v. Eatman*, 45 N.B.R. (2d) 163 at 166 (1983); *R. v. O'Connor*, Ont. Pr. Ct. at 3 (December 1, 1982).

29. Dale Gibson, "Determining Disrepute: Opinion Polls and the Canadian Charter of Rights and Freedoms," 61 *C.B.R.* 377 at 389 (1983); "Enforcement of the Canadian Charter of Rights and Freedoms (Section 24)," in *The Canadian*

Charter of Rights and Freedoms: Commentary, edited by Walter S. Tarnopolsky and Gérald-A. Beaudoin (Toronto: Carswell, 1982), pp. 489–528 at 517.

30. *Charlton* at 121; *Therens* at 292, per Justice Estey; *R. v. Dzadic,* 1 C.T.C. 346 (Ont. H.C.) (1985); *R. v. Gibson,* 37 C.R. (3d) 175 (Ont. C.A.) at 188 (1983).

31. Gibson in *C.B.R.* at 378, 387–389; *Collins* at 151; *MacIntyre* at 116.

32. *R. v. Bezille,* C.S. Québec) 100-01-00573-820 at 11 (February 14, 1983); *R. v. Nelson,* 32 C.R. (3d) 256 at 263 (Man. Q. B.) (1982); *Collins* at 151 per Justice Seaton.

33. *R. v. McDonald,* 20 M.V.R. 255 at 261–263 (1983) per Justice Meldrun (N.B.Q.B.).

34. *R. v. Caron,* 31 C.R. (3d) 255 at 260 (1982); *R. v. Rex,* 8 C.R.R. 170 (B.C. Co. Ct.) (1983); *Gibson* at 187; *Collins* at 83 per Justice Wong; *Collins* at 145 per Justice Seaton; *Nelson* at 263.

35. *R. v. Heisler,* Alta Pr. Ct. at 23 (March 17, 1983); rev. 11 C.C.C. (3d) 475 (Alta C.A.) (1984).

36. *Cohen* at 167, *Therens* at 140 per LeDain.

37. *Gibson* at 189, *MacIntyre* at 167, *Duguay* at 391.

38. Everett Dirksen in changing to oppose *Miranda* judges, in Baker, p. 253; *Duguay* at 38.

39. Dale Gibson, "'Shocking the Public': Early Indications of the Meaning of 'Disrepute' in Section 24(2) of the Charter," 13 *Man. L. J.* 495 (1983).

40. *Charlton* at 123.

41. *R. v. Davidson,* 40 N.B.R. (2d) 702 at 710 (1982); *Cohen* at 188; *Collins* at 149; *MacIntyre* at 168.

42. *Duguay* at 390; *Collins* at 150, 153; *R. v. Myers,* 14 C.C.C. (3d) 82 at 92 (PEI. C.A.) (1984).

43. *R. v. Wai Ti Ling (No. 2),* 6 W.W.R. 146 at 157 (1976); *Stevens* at 29 per Justice J. A. MacDonald.

44. *Rex* at 15; *Therens* at 134; *R. v. Glowa,* 7 C.R. Dec. 425.60-01 (1985); *R. v. Carriere,* 32 C.R. (3d) 117 at 132 (1983).

45. *Therens* at 140; *Unrau* at 11; *R. v. David,* Ont. Pr. Ct. at 15 (August 15, 1983).

46. *Rochin* at 174, quoting *Davis v. Mills,* 194 U.S. 451 (1903).

47. *Bezille* at 13.

48. *Grundrisse* at 273, in Maureen Cain and Alan Hunt, *Marx on Law* (London: Academic Press, 1979), p. 140.

49. *Rothman* at 51 per Estey, quoting *DeClerq v. The Queen,* S.C.R. 902 (S.C.C.) at 911 [1968].

50. Jerome H. Skolnick, "Deception by Police," in *Moral Issues in Police Work,* Frederick A. Ellison and Michael Feldberg, eds. (Totowa: Rowman and Allenheld, 1985), pp. 75–98 at 83.

51. *David* at 17.

52. Chief Justice Burger, dissenting *Miranda* decision, reported in Baker, p. 195.

53. *Rochin* at 174; *R. v. McLean,* B.C. Pr. Ct. at 3 (November 4, 1983).

54. Doernberg, pp. 294–295.

55. Subsection 33(1), as in many international rights documents.

56. The sense is now that of Ronald Dworkin in *Law's Empire* (Cambridge, Mass.: Harvard Univ. Press, 1986), p. 225.

57. Potter Stewart, "The Road to *Mapp v. Ohio* and Beyond: The Origins, Development and Future of the Exclusionary Rule in Search-and-Seizure Cases," 83 *Columbia L. Rev.* 1365 (1983).

58. *Rochin* at 169. See G. Grant, *English-Speaking Justice* (Sackville, New Brunswick: Mt. Allison Univ., 1974).

59. After this chapter was completed, the Supreme Court of Canada decided a cluster of five recently reported cases, whose lower court judgments are discussed above along with *Therens,* its only significant decision on point until now. This cluster does not alter the law significantly nor the conclusions I drew about it at all. The central case of *R. v. Collins* (1987) 1 S.C.R. 265 does, on the one hand, take up my general discourse of "avoiding judicial condonation" and of the court's "dissociating itself" from flagrant violations of Charter rights; as well, it confirms our "reasonable man" as the standard for disrepute, a lower threshold and a more objective test than community shock. On the other hand, the court continues to envisage some balancing of the several factors, and to set them off against what was called "reverse disrepute" above. Thus, the three cases favoring those accused by excluding the evidence all do so because of a relative seriousness in the violation of constitutional rights; each is sent for retrial, however; *Collins; R. v. Manninen,* Ibid., 1233; *R. v. Pohoretsky,* Ibid. 945. The two that uphold convictions do so because, despite violations of rights that again are serious (indeed, the very same: choke-holds), writs of assistance had not yet been found unconstitutional at the time the searches under them were made, as writs had been by the time of trial: *R. v. Sieben,* Ibid. 295; *R. v. Hamill,* Ibid. 301.

SELECTED BIBLIOGRAPHY

Doctrine: Monographs

Baker, Liva. 1983. *Miranda: Crime, Law and Politics.* New York: Atheneum Publishers.

Gibson, Dale, and Janet K. Baldwin, eds. 1985. *Law in a Cynical Society?* Calgary: Carswell.

Grant, George. 1974. *English-Speaking Justice.* Sackville, New Brunswick: Mt. Allison Univ.

Doctrine: Articles

Baldiga, R. 1983. "Excluding Evidence to Protect Rights; Principles Underlying the Exclusionary Rule in England and the U.S." 6 *Boston College Int. and Comp. L. Rev.* 133.

Doernberg, Donald L. 1983. "The 'Right of the People': Reconciling Collective and Individual Interest Under the Fourth Amendment." 58 *N.Y.U. L. Rev.* 259.

Proulx, Michel. 1986. "Redéfinir les rapports de force au procès criminel: l'effet de la règle d'exclusion de l'article 24(2) de la Charte canadienne des droits et libertés." 20 *Rev. jur. Themis* 109.

Canadian Jurisprudence

Regina v. Collins, 5 C.C.C. (3d) 141 (B.C.C.A., leave to S.C.C.) (1983).
Regina v. Therens, 59 N.R. 122 (S.C.C.) (1984).

U.S. Jurisprudence

Olmstead v. United States, 277 U.S. 438 (U.S.S.C.) (1927).
United States v. Leon, 104 S. Ct. 3412 (U.S.S.C.) (1984).

About the Contributors

Michael D. Bayles is professor of Philosophy at Florida State University. He is the author of *Principles of Law, Principles of Legislation,* three other books, and more than 75 articles on political and legal philosophy and ethics. He has also edited or coedited six books. He has been a fellow at the Harvard Law School, the Hastings Center, and the National Humanities Center. Currently, Professor Bayles is preparing second editions of two books and working on a book on administrative justice.

Richard T. De George, a past president of AMINTAPHIL, is university distinguished professor of philosophy at the University of Kansas. He is the author or editor of fifteen books, including *The Nature and Limits of Authority* and *Business Ethics.* He is currently working on issues of international ethics, both in business and in politics.

Emily R. Gill is a professor of political science at Bradley University in Peoria, Illinois. Her recent publications include "Walzer's Complex Equality: Constraints and the Right to be Wrong," in *Polity* and "Goods, Virtues, and the Constitution of the Self," in *Liberals on Liberalism,* edited by Alfonso J. Damico. Her research interests include liberal theory and its critics, democratic theory, theories of citizenship, and theories of virtue and/or the virtues.

Christopher B. Gray teaches philosophy at Concordia University in Montreal, Québec. He received his Ph.D. in philosophy from the Catholic University of America and degrees in law at McGill University. He has published a monograph and a translation of the French jurist Maurice Hauriou as well as published articles in journals of philosophy and of law on legal hermeneutics, patrimony, personhood, and punishment. He is currently working on a monograph concerning legal entity. He is the current president of the Canadian section of the International Association for Philosophy of Law and Social Philosophy and a joint member of the U.S. section.

Stephen M. Griffin is research instructor in law, New York University School of Law. His article "Reconstructing Rawls' Theory of Justice" is forthcoming in the *New York University Law Review.* He is currently at work on an article concerning the nature of constitutional theory.

Virginia Held is a professor of philosophy at the City University of New York (Graduate School and Hunter College). She has been a visiting professor at UCLA and Dartmouth, and has also taught at Yale and Barnard. She directed an NEH summer seminar for teachers of law and has been a visiting scholar at Harvard Law School. Her most recent book is *Rights and Goods: Justifying Social Action;* she has edited *Property, Profits, and Economic Justice* and other collections. She is on the editorial boards of *Ethics, Hypatia, Political Theory* and *Social Theory and Practice.*

Kenneth Henley is associate professor in the Department of Philosophy and Religion at Florida International University. He previously taught at the University of Kentucky, after receiving his Ph.D. from the University of Virginia in 1972. He has published articles on ethics in several philosophical journals. With Michael Bayles, he edited *Right Conduct: Theories and Applications.* He is currently working on the topic of the rule of law as a distinct political ideal.

H. Hamner Hill is an assistant professor of philosophy at Southeast Missouri State University. His current research interests include legal philosophy and applied ethics. He received his Ph.D. from Washington University in St. Louis and his J.D. from William and Mary.

Kenneth Kipnis is professor of philosophy at the University of Hawaii at Manoa. He is the author of *Legal Ethics,* coeditor (with Diana T. Meyers) of *Economic Justice: Private Rights and Public Responsibilities* and *Political Realism and International Morality: Ethics in the Nuclear Age* (Westview, 1987), coeditor (with Lawrence C. Becker) of *Property: Cases, Concepts, Critiques,* and editor of *Philosophical Issues in Law: Cases and Materials.* He is currently working on ethical issues involving AIDS and problems of professional responsibility in early childhood education.

Lester J. Mazor teaches at Hampshire College at Amherst, Massachusetts. Although his title is professor of law, he holds with Gramsci that we are all called upon to be philosophers. Having published in the fields of constitutional law, criminal law, and the legal profession, he celebrated "The Crisis of Legal Liberalism" in the *Yale Law Journal* (1972) and came out of the closet with "Disrespect for Law" in *Nomos XIX: Anarchism* (1978). Appropriately for the post-everything era, and for his age, time has become the central preoccupation of his research and writing. His "Law in the Eye of Time," appeared in *Rechtstheorie* (1986). He is now considering the implications of the collapse of time through the new information technology.

Michael Mc Donald teaches philosophy at the University of Waterloo, Ontario, Canada. He was the first president of the Canadian section of the International Association for Philosophy of Law and Social Philosophy and currently is the English-language editor of the bilingual philosophical journal *Dialogue,* which is sponsored by the Canadian Philosophical Association. Most of his research has been in political, moral, and legal philosophy with a special emphasis on Canadian issues.

Diana T. Meyers is associate professor of philosophy at the University of Connecticut. She is the author of *Inalienable Rights: A Defense* and of *Self, Society, and Personal Choice.* With Kenneth Kipnis, she edited *Economic Justice: Private Rights and Public Responsibilities* and *Political Realism and International Morality: Ethics in the Nuclear Age* (Westview, 1987); with Eva Kittay, she edited *Women and Moral Theory.*

Cornelius F. Murphy, Jr., is professor of law, Duquesne University School of Law, and formerly visiting scholar, Harvard Law School (1973–1974). He is the author of *The Search for World Order; Modern Legal Philosophy;* and *Introduction to Law, Legal Process, and Procedure.* His work has been included in *Best New Poets.* His current research concerns the relationship between moral idealism and jurisprudence.

William Nelson is a professor of philosophy at the University of Houston. He is the author of *On Justifying Democracy* as well as a number of articles on topics in political philosophy. He is currently conducting research on the philosophical foundations of liberalism.

Carl Wellman is professor of philosophy at Washington University in St. Louis. He is also a member of the Executive Committee of the International Association for Philosophy of Law and Social Philosophy and the chair of the Committee on Philosophy and Law of the American Philosophical Association. His books include *The Language of Ethics, Challenge and Response, Welfare Rights,* and *A Theory of Rights.* His current research deals with those areas in which moral philosophy and the philosophy of law intersect, especially with the theory of legal and moral rights.

Index

Abortion, 110, 156. *See also Roe v. Wade*
Academic freedom, 164, 172
Access, 159, 166, 167–168, 170–172, 173, 175(n5)
Adjudicative decisions, 207
Advertising, 159, 160–161, 163, 173
Affirmative action, 84
Aid to Families with Dependent Children, 216
Air traffic controllers, 217
Alberta (Canada), 185
"Alternative Views" (television program), 171
American Association of University Professors, 164
American Revolution, 27, 64
American Society of Newspaper Editors, 161
Amish, 194(n37)
Anti-Federalists, 36, 41
Apportionment of representatives, 2, 95, 139–140, 142–143. *See also* Fourteenth Amendment
Aristocracy, 21, 26, 29, 30, 32
Aristotle, 24, 38, 70
Arnett v. Kennedy (1974), 209, 214
Articles of Confederation, 27
Artistic expression, 48
Assembly, freedom of, 122
Association, freedom of, 122
Austin (Texas), 171
Authority, 65, 66, 69, 77, 78, 86
  abuse of, 83
Authorization, doctrine of, 98
Autonomy, 196, 198, 201, 203, 204–205

Baker v. Carr (1962), 139, 140, 141
Balanced budget amendment, 60
Basic rights, 57, 126
Bayles, Michael D., 155, 157
Benefit-conferring decisions, 157, 210, 211, 212, 213, 214, 215, 216, 217, 218
Benefit-terminating decisions, 157, 210–211, 212, 213, 214, 216, 217, 218
Bentham, Jeremy, 98–99, 100
Berger, Raoul, 96
Bicameralism, 142, 143
Bickel, Alexander, 97, 112, 128
Bill of Rights, 2, 3, 7, 11, 41, 59, 65, 67, 68, 70, 77, 78, 88(n3), 111, 113, 141, 198, 203, 239
Bios politikos, 64
Bishop v. Wood (1976), 209, 214
Blackmun, Harry A., 202
BNA Act. *See* British North America Act
Board of Regents v. Roth (1972), 209, 214
Bork, Robert, 78, 94, 96
Boston (Mass.), 41
Bowers v. Hardwick, 197, 202, 204, 205
Boyd v. United States (1886), 199
Brennan, William, 96, 144, 181, 182, 187, 207
British Columbia (Canada), 185
British North America (BNA) Act (1867), 184, 192(n19)
Brown v. Board of Education (1954), 94, 101, 102, 109, 110, 114, 187
Buchanan, Allen, 166
Buchanan, James, 8
Burden-imposing decisions, 157, 210, 211, 212, 213, 217
Burden of proof, 227, 233
Burden-relieving decisions, 157, 210, 211, 212, 213, 217, 218
Burger, Warren, 69, 158, 167, 213
Burke, Edmund, 63, 97, 112, 113

Calvinism, 37
Canada, 156, 157, 180, 181, 182, 184–186, 189, 190, 223, 230, 234, 238
  Confederation (1867), 184, 185
  Constitution. *See* Canada Act
  writs of assistance, 231
Canada Act (1982), 184, 185, 239, 240
Canadian Charter of Rights and Freedoms, 185, 231, 232, 233, 236

Capitalism, 9. *See also* Free enterprise
Carnegie Commission report (1979), 161, 172
Censorship, 171
Centralization, 41, 70
Checks and balances, 7, 17, 61
Chisholm v. Georgia (1793), 111
Choper, Jesse, 128
Cicero, 65
Citizen participation, 21, 24, 25, 26, 35, 58, 69, 94, 127
Citizenship, 24, 35, 37, 64, 134, 189
Civic republican tradition, 20, 21, 22–26, 27, 28, 30, 31, 32, 36, 37
Civil disobedience, 45
Civil rights, 3, 8
 movement, 49
Civil War (1861–1865), 3, 6
Collective rights, 156, 182, 183–184, 185, 187, 188–190
 defined, 183
Colonial constitutions, 2
Commerce, 23
Commerce Clause, 50
Commercial interests, 162, 163, 164, 165, 172
Common good, 5, 12, 20, 21, 22, 23, 30, 31–32, 38
Common law, 146, 189, 199, 203, 206, 207, 226, 227
Common Market, 6
Community Education Program, 187
Competition, 9, 58, 163, 217
Compromise, 95, 134–135, 136, 137, 139, 141, 148
Concentration camps, 46
Condition on argument, 121
Confessional schools. *See* Religious schools
Conflict resolution, 143
Connecticut, 200, 202, 203
Connecticut Board of Pardons v. Dumschat (1981), 209
Conscience, liberty of, 122
Consensus, 110, 111, 112–113, 114
Constitution
 amendments, 2, 3, 4, 5, 7, 8, 60, 66, 105, 111. *See also specific amendments*
 Article I, 41
 Article I (section 2), 143
 Article I (section 4), 139
 Article I (sections 9 and 10), 113
 Article IV (section 2), 143
 Article V, 140
 and balance of power, 4, 5, 6, 7, 41, 70, 80, 155
 Commission on the Bicentennial, 69
 and contemporary values and beliefs, 3, 4, 5, 8, 10, 13, 52, 94, 101, 102, 106, 114
 drafted (1787), vii, 3, 61, 64
 and economy, 6–7, 50
 flexibility of, 2, 14, 40
 and framers' intentions, 100–101. *See also subentry* and interpretation
 framers' values and beliefs, 46, 63, 70, 94, 101. *See also Federalist, The,* papers; Publius; Sovereignty
 and interpretation, 65–66, 134, 135–136, 138–139, 142, 143, 144, 146, 147. *See also* Compromise; Nonpositivist noninterpretivists; Positivist interpretivists; Positive noninterpretivism; Supreme Court
 as nonphilosophical document, 1, 2, 14
 philosophical roots of, 3–14, 17
 as political document, 1, 2, 13
 preamble, 9, 12, 18, 40–51
 ratified (1789), vii, 1, 3, 61
 revisions. *See* Constitutional conventions; *subentry* amendments
 and slavery, 2, 7, 14, 46, 48, 137, 141–142, 143–144
Constitution, The, the Courts, and Human Rights (Perry), 102
Constitution Act (1867) (Canada), 184
Constitutional Convention (1787), 142
Constitutional conventions, 59, 60, 63, 64, 65, 67, 68
Constitutional rights (Rawls), 122–123, 124, 126, 128. *See also* Public values
Contract, rights of, 76
Contractualism, 77, 78
Contradiction, tolerance of, 45, 76
Conventionalist concept, 136, 138, 139
Corporation for Public Broadcasting, 171
Corruption, 23, 24, 27, 29
Court ideology, 32
Cox, Archibald, 158, 167, 168
Creditors, 44
Criminal law, 229
Crosskey, William W., 101
Cruel and unusual punishment, 97, 144–145, 146, 147
Culture, 160, 162–163, 164, 165, 166, 167

Death penalty, 144–146
Declaration of Independence, 1–2, 182
Defeasible fee, 214, 215
Defense, 18, 43–44

Defense, secretary of, 43
Democracy, 18, 51–52, 57, 69–70, 76, 77, 79–81, 88–89(n9), 96, 112, 119
  elitist view, 58
  and morality, 77–78, 79
  See also Direct democracy; Participatory democracy; Radical democracy; Representative democracy
Democracy and Distrust (Ely), 80
Democratic relativism, 94, 119, 128, 131
  defined, 129
Demonstrations, 168, 169
Deontologists, 13, 235
Difference principle (Rawls), 167
Diggins, John Patrick, 20, 21, 25, 26, 27, 31, 32, 33, 35, 37
Direct democracy, 35, 52
Dissenters, 164–165
Doernberg, Donald L., 238
Doe v. Commonwealth's Attorney for the City of Richmond, 197, 205
Douglas, William O., 197, 198, 199, 201, 203
Dred Scott decision. *See Scott v. Sanford*
Due process, 97, 106, 122, 145, 146, 155, 157, 206, 207, 208–210, 212–218, 226, 239
  deprivation of, 157
Due Process Clause (XIVth Amendment), 141, 147, 200, 203
Dworkin, Ronald, 94, 135–136, 137, 138, 139, 141, 142, 143, 144, 145, 180, 181, 182, 185, 186

Economic Bill of Rights (Roosevelt), 73–74(n22)
Education, 7, 10, 172–174, 186–187, 200, 208, 216
  linguistic organization of, 188
  See also Religious schools
Eighth Amendment, 202. *See also* Cruel and unusual punishment
Eisenstadt v. Baird, 198, 201, 202
Elections, 62
Eleventh Amendment (1795), 111
Ely, John Hart, 78, 80, 81, 96, 128, 197
Emerson, Thomas, 170
Employment, 9–10, 11, 157, 208, 209, 212, 213–215, 218
Enabling rights, 156, 159, 166, 174
English Revolution (1688), 62
Entitlement
  programs, 157
  theory, 207–208, 215, 217
Equality, 5, 7–9, 47, 57, 58, 59, 68, 94, 125
Equality of opportunity, 8, 125
Equal pay, 5
Equal protection, 78, 83–87, 108, 208
Equal Protection Clause (XVth Amendment), 80, 81, 84, 95, 97, 98, 110, 134, 140, 202
Equal rights, 155
  for women, 5, 7, 8
Equal Rights Amendment proposal, 8
Equity, rules of, 228–230
Evidence. *See* Exclusionary rule
Exclusionary rule, 155, 157, 222–224, 226, 228, 229–230, 233, 234, 237–240
Executive branch, 4, 41, 70
Expression, freedom of, 78, 79–81, 82–83, 87
Externalities, 75
Extraconstitutional values. *See* Positivist noninterpretivism

Fairness, 228
Fairness Doctrine (FCC), 169–170
FCC. *See* Federal Communications Commission
Federal Communications Commission (FCC), 163–164, 169, 170, 171
Federalism, 5, 6–7
Federalist, The, papers (Publius), 6, 17, 18, 20, 21, 22, 28, 29, 30, 31, 34–35, 64, 143
  No. 10 (Madison), 27
  No. 62 (Madison), 142
  No. 78 (Hamilton), 62, 66
Federalists, 30, 36
Feinberg, Joel, 198
Feyerabend, Paul, 112
Fifteenth Amendment (1870), 3, 8
Fifth Amendment. *See* Due process; Grand jury; Self-Discrimination Clause
First Amendment, 199. *See also* Press, freedom of the; Religion, freedom of
First through Tenth Amendments. *See* Bill of Rights
Fiscal policy, 9
Fiss, Owen, 96
Fourteenth Amendment (1868), 3, 6, 8, 11, 97, 106, 108, 111, 114, 141, 144, 145, 147, 157, 200, 201, 206, 239. *See also* Due Process Clause; Equal Protection Clause
Fourth Amendment, 199
France, 41, 43
Frankfurter, Felix, 128
Free enterprise, 5, 6–7, 9–10

Free expression. *See* Speech, freedom of
French Revolution (1789), 62
Fundamental rights, 174
Furman v. Georgia (1972), 144, 145

Galella v. Onassis, 198, 199, 201
Gay rights, 48. *See also* Homosexual rights
General welfare, 12, 18, 19, 50–51
Georgia, 197
Germany, 41
Gill, Emily R., 17, 18
Global solidarity, 42
Goldberg, Arthur J., 200, 203
Goldberg v. Kelly (1970), 207
Grand jury, 145, 146
Grand Rapids v. Ball (1985), 181, 182, 187
Gray, Christopher B., 155, 157
Great Britain, 2, 27, 41, 43, 63, 197
Great Depression (1930s), 10
Greeks, 64–65
Greenholtz v. Inmates of the Nebraska Penal and Correctional Complex (1979), 213, 215
Gregg v. Georgia (1976), 145
Grey, Thomas, 96
Griffin, Stephen M., 94
Griswold v. Connecticut (1965), 101, 113, 196, 197, 198, 199, 202, 203
Gross, Hyman, 156, 196, 197, 201
Grundnorm (Kelsen), 99
Gutmann, Amy, 78

Hacker, Andrew, 160
Hamilton, Alexander, 17, 20, 29, 34, 41, 61, 62, 66, 67
Hand, Learned, 113
Hanging, 46
"Hard Cases" (Dworkin), 180
Harlan, John, 128, 197, 200, 203
Held, Virginia, 155, 156
Henley, Kenneth, 94, 95
Heraclitus, 45
Hewitt v. Helms (1983), 213
Hill, H. Hamner, 94
Hobbes, Thomas, 36, 67, 68
Hohfeldian position, 198
Holmes, Oliver Wendell, 101, 111, 112, 163
Homosexual rights, 156, 197, 204, 205
House of Representatives, 95
Human rights, 3, 10, 11, 102, 103
Hume, David, 2, 21, 22, 32, 33–34, 35, 36–37, 38
Humphrey-Hawkins Act, 11
Hutchinson, Anne, 48

Illegal immigrants, 49
Income distribution, 76, 167
Independence, 22, 23, 24, 25, 26, 27
Indian tribes, 43
Individual liberty, 5, 7, 8, 11–12, 19, 48, 155, 182, 201
Individual rights, 5, 6, 11–12, 17, 28, 46, 67–68, 75, 77, 122, 156, 157, 165–166, 182, 185, 187–188, 189, 190. *See also* Autonomy
Individual welfare, 10
Insurance, 216
Integrity
  limited, 139, 144, 147–148
  See also Judicial integrity; *under* Law
Intentionalist fallacy, 100–101
Interdependence, 23, 25, 37
Interest-group pluralism, 22, 119
Internal rebellion, 44
International Covenant on Economic, Social and Cultural Rights (1966), 11
Italy, 41

Jackson, Andrew, 118(n46)
Jay, John, 17, 20
Jefferson, Thomas, 45, 62, 63, 64, 182
Jones, Harry W., 105–106
Judicial branch, 4, 61, 62, 66–67, 99, 106, 224
  and lawmaking, 98, 127
Judicial disrepute, doctrine of, 157, 222, 223, 230–237, 239
  reverse, 233
Judicial integrity, doctrine of, 157, 222, 223, 225–230, 238, 240
Judicial review, 78, 82, 83, 84, 85, 86–87, 97, 100, 108, 119, 129, 130, 227
  according to Rawls, 126–128
  See also Positivist noninterpretivism; Social change; Supreme Court
Justice, 7, 8, 9, 18, 21, 23, 33, 45–47, 57, 120, 227, 232
  natural, 207
  See also Public values

Kant, Immanuel, 46, 182
Kellner, Douglas, 171
Kelsen, Hans, 98, 99
Korematsu v. U.S., 109
Kuhn, Thomas, 112

Laissez-faire, 111
Landholders, 7, 46
Law, 98, 99, 105, 106, 108, 232
  as integrity, 136, 137, 138, 143
  lacunae in, 109, 117(n41)

rules of, 227–228
See also Natural law
Law enforcement agencies, 7, 235, 239
Legal positivism, 106
Legislative branch, 4, 41, 43, 61–62, 65, 70, 105, 127, 155
See also Judicial review
Leis v. Flynt (1979), 209
Leviathan (Hobbes), 67
Lex supra legis, 67
Liberalism, 19, 126, 155
Liberation, 49, 50
Libertà, 25
Libertarian rights, 77, 81
Liberty, 18, 24, 27, 47–50, 57, 68, 69, 70, 82, 120, 200, 202, 203
basic, 122
equal, 122
fair value of, 125, 130
principles of, 124, 125
restrictions on, 80, 86, 88, 123, 202
and security, 48–49
worth of, 124, 125
See also Due process
Licenses, 207, 212, 216, 217
Lochner v. New York (1905), 101, 110, 114
Locke, John, 2, 17, 20, 37, 48, 67, 68, 155

Mc Donald, Michael, 155, 156
Madison, James, 17, 20, 27, 29, 30, 35, 63, 64, 142, 143, 182
Magazines, 160, 161
Magna Carta (1215), 47, 146
Majority rights, 50
Majority rule, 77, 78, 79, 80, 83, 85, 108, 112, 113, 126, 129
Mapp v. Ohio (1961), 101
Marbury v. Madison (1803), 96, 101
Marshall, John, 96, 118(n46)
Marshall, Thurgood, 144, 145
Martin, Rex, 122
Martinez v. California (1980), 209, 210
Mary II (queen of England), 63
Massachusetts, 41
Mass media, 156, 159, 160–161, 164, 165, 167, 168, 169–170, 171, 172, 173, 176(n11)
Materialism, 51
Mazor, Lester J., 18
Meachum v. Fano (1976), 209, 213
Medical care, 11, 209
Medical treatment, refusal of. *See Quinlan* decision
Meyer v. Nebraska, 200
Militias, 44
Mill, John Stuart, 36, 48
Minimal state, 75, 76, 77
Minority rights, 50, 76, 79, 83, 84, 85, 87, 108, 113
Mixed government, 24, 25, 28
Mohammed (prophet), 48
Monetary policy, 9
Monopoly, 163, 164, 216, 217, 218
Montesquieu, Charles, 2, 17
Moral decisionmaking, 103, 104
Morality, 3, 21, 32, 33, 59, 77–78, 87, 235
and law, 98
Morrissey v. Brewer (1972), 212, 213
Movies, 160, 163
Multiple voting, 140
Murphy, Cornelius F., Jr., 58, 59

Nader v. General Motors Corporation, 198, 201
National Endowment for the Arts, 171
Nationalism, 41, 42
National Road, 50
National unity, 18, 41, 42
Natural law, 102, 108, 181, 237
Natural rights, 2, 46, 155
Negative rights, 155, 186
Nelson, William, 59, 113
Neo-Harringtonian interpretation, 23, 27
Neorepublican philosophy, 94, 119. *See also* Public values
New Brunswick (Canada), 185
New Deal (1930s), 10, 50
Newfoundland (Canada), 185
Newspapers, 159, 160, 161, 170
Nineteenth Amendment (1920), 8
Ninth Amendment, 201
Noncommercial broadcasting, 164
Nonpositivist noninterpretivists, 94, 96, 97, 102–104, 108
Nonrecidivist offenders, 223
Nova Scotia (Canada), 185

O'Bannon v. Town Court Nursing Center (1980), 209, 210
Olim v. Wakinekona (1983), 209, 213
Ontario (Canada), 184, 185, 187
Order, 18, 44–45, 47
Oregon, 200
Oregon v. Mitchell (1970), 111
Original position concept, 120–121, 122, 124–125

Pacifists, 43
Paine, Thomas, 63, 64
Palko v. Connecticut, 200

Pangle, Thomas L., 21, 22, 25, 26, 31, 33, 35, 37
Pardon, 209, 211
Parental rights, 187
Parmenidean culture, 45
Parole, 157, 209, 210, 212–213, 215
Participatory democracy, 52, 57
Paul v. Davis (1976), 209
Pentagon, 43
People, sovereignty of the, 61, 62, 63, 64, 67, 68–69, 71, 78, 105, 106, 107, 112
Perry, Michael J., 94, 96, 102–104, 108
Philosopher-king, 64–65
Pierce v. Society of Sisters, 200
Plato, 64
Plessy v. Ferguson (1896), 94, 134
Pluralistic society, 12, 13, 182, 190
Pocock, J.G.A., 23, 24, 26, 31, 32, 37
Poe v. Ullman, 200
Politeia, 26, 31, 65
Political parties, 58
Politics, 21, 24, 25, 26, 29
Polity, 237–238
Pollock v. Farmer's Loan and Trust Co. (1895), 111
Poll taxes abolished. *See* Twenty-fourth Amendment
Polyarkhia, 64
Polybius, 24
Populists, 58
Positivist interpretivists, 94, 96, 97–102, 104, 105, 106
Positivist noninterpretivism, 94, 97, 104–114
Power, 14, 36, 41, 63, 65, 69, 75
Pragmatists, 13, 136
Preservation, 75, 76
President, 2, 43, 65
  two-term limit, 7
  See also Executive branch
Press, freedom of the, 45, 117(n35), 122, 159
Price, Richard, 62
Prince Edward Island (Canada), 185
Prince v. Massachusetts, 200
Privacy, 11, 86, 87, 155, 156, 196, 197–205, 236, 238
Private decision, 203–204
Private preferences, 119, 120
Privilege/right distinction, 207, 208, 217
Probation, 212
Professional standards, 164, 165
Property, 23, 27, 28, 32, 36, 44, 45, 76, 122, 125, 208, 209, 210, 214, 217
  English law of, 47–48
Proportionality, 233–234, 235
Public forum, 169
Public good, 18, 19, 20, 21, 23, 24, 25, 27, 28, 29, 31, 33, 37
Public office, 122
Public values, 94, 119–121, 125–126, 127, 128, 129, 130–131
  defined, 120
Publius (pseudonym), 17, 18, 20, 21, 22, 27, 32, 33, 34–35, 37, 38

Quakers, 43
Québec (Canada), 184, 185, 188
Quinlan decision, 201, 204

Racial equality, 110
Radical democracy, 113
Radio, 160, 161
Rawls, John, 8, 57, 94, 112, 120, 121–128, 129, 130, 131, 167, 182
Raz, Joseph, 98
Recordings, 160
Red Lion Broadcasting v. Federal Communications Commission (1969), 169, 170
Reference Re an Act to Amend the Education Act (1986) (Canada), 184
Reflections On the French Revolution (Burke), 63
Rehnquist, William, 94, 96, 128, 197, 208, 214–215
Religion, 3, 44
Religion, freedom of, 87–88, 122, 155, 156, 180, 181, 187
Religious schools, 156, 180, 181, 182, 183, 184–186, 187
Representative democracy, 5, 59, 86, 87, 96, 143
Representatives, 28, 29, 30–31, 32, 57, 62, 64, 81
Republicanism, 28, 52
Res publica, 25, 26
Restitution, 229
Reynolds v. Sims (1964), 140–141, 142
Richards, David A.J., 156, 196, 197, 205
Richmond Newspapers, Inc. v. Virginia (1980), 167
Rights of Man (France), 62
"Rights of Man, The" (Paine), 63, 64
Right to counsel, 236
Roberts, Owen J., 97
Roe v. Wade (1973), 11, 101, 110–111, 197, 201, 202, 204
Romans, 65
Roosevelt, Franklin D., 73–74(n22)
Rousseau, Jean-Jacques, 2
Russell, Bertrand, 112
Russia, 43

Sager, Lawrence, 127
Salvation Army, 185
San Antonio School District v. Rodriguez (1973), 134
Sanctuary, 47
Saskatchewan (Canada), 185
Scanlon, Thomas M., 82, 166, 167
Scarcity, 50
Schmidt, Benno C., Jr., 158
Scottish moral philosophy, 20, 21, 32. *See also* Hume, David
Scott v. Sanford (1857), 111, 144
Search and seizure, 236
Search warrant, 157
Segregation, 134
Self-Discrimination Clause (Vth Amendment), 199
Self-evidence, 2
Self-government. *See* People, sovereignty of the
Self-interest, 19, 20, 21, 22, 26, 27, 29, 32, 33, 37, 75, 76, 94. *See also* Private preferences
Senate, 95, 140, 141, 142–143, 146
Senators, 7
Separability thesis, 98, 108
Separation of church and state, 187, 191(n5)
Seventeenth Amendment (1913), 7
Shays, Daniel, 44
Sherman, Gary, 100
Sinopoli, Richard, 35
Sit-in, 45
Sixteenth Amendment (1913), 8–9, 111
Skepticism, 103–104, 137, 138
Slaughterhouse Cases, 141
Slavery, 8, 24, 45, 122. *See also* Thirteenth Amendment; *under* Constitution
Social change, 101, 102, 105, 109–111
Social contract theory, 120, 121
Social preferences, 75, 76
Social primary goods, 122
Social security, 49, 212, 216
Social solidarity, 47
Sodomy statute (Ga.), 197
Sources thesis, 98, 107, 109–110
Sovereignty, 5, 42, 61, 63, 98, 99, 100, 104, 105–107. *See also* People, sovereignty of the; States' rights
Spain, 43
Specialization, 23
Speech, freedom of, 59, 122, 155, 156, 158–161, 164, 166, 167–174
Stanley v. Georgia, 198
State senates, 28, 140
States' rights, 2, 5, 6, 7, 52, 70, 140, 141, 142, 143, 146, 147
Stevens, John Paul, 167
Stewart, Potter, 113
Subsidiarity principle, 6
Supreme Court, 2, 4, 11, 65–66, 67, 69, 70, 93–95, 96, 101, 102, 108, 110–111, 123, 128, 134, 135, 167, 169, 170, 171, 181, 187, 208, 209, 212, 214, 216
  reversals, 111
  See also Constitution, and interpretation
Switzerland, 6
System of Freedom of Expression, The (Emerson), 170

Taxes, 2, 50, 87, 216. *See also* Sixteenth Amendment
Tax-resisters, 46–47
Television, 159, 160, 161, 163, 171
Ten Commandments, 3
Tenth Amendment, 7
Theory of Justice, A (Rawls), 124
Third Amendment, 199
Thirteenth Amendment (1865), 3, 111
Torts, 203, 206
Tribe, Laurence H., 167
Truman, Harry, 111
Truth, 227, 235
Twenty-fourth Amendment (1964), 8
Twenty-second Amendment (1951), 7
Twenty-sixth Amendment (1971), 8, 111

Ultra vires, 106, 109, 184
Umori, 25
Unemployment, 9
United Nations Universal Declaration of Human Rights, 10, 11, 70
United States of Europe, 6
U.S. v. Butler (1936), 97
Utilitarian maximization of preference satisfaction, 57
Utilitarians, 13, 50, 51

Vermont, 52
Vigilantes, 224
Virginia, 142
Virtù, 25, 26
Virtue, 21–22, 23–24, 25, 26, 29, 31, 32, 33, 37, 38, 50, 51
Vitek v. Jones (1980), 213
Voting rights, 57–58, 79, 122. *See also* Fifteenth Amendment; Nineteenth Amendment; Twenty-sixth Amendment

Walzer, Michael, 76, 78, 189, 190
Warren, Earl, 140, 142
Wealth
  and access, 167, 168, 173, 174
  distribution of, 125, 167
  redistribution of, 8
Welfare benefits, 216
Welfare rights, 5, 10, 11, 73–74(n22), 208, 212
Wellman, Carl, 155
Westin, Alan, 204
Whig ideology, 32
White, Byron R., 200, 202, 208
Williams, Raymond, 161
William III of Orange (king of England), 63
Wills, Gary, 30
Wisconsin v. Yoder (1972), 194(n37)
Wolff v. McDonnell (1974), 213
Women, 49. *See also* Nineteenth Amendment; *under* Equal rights

Yugoslavia, 6

www.ingramcontent.com/pod-product-compliance
Lightning Source LLC
LaVergne TN
LVHW011122300926
849160LV00008B/479

* 9 7 8 0 3 6 7 2 9 8 2 9 6 *